COUNTDOWN TO ETERNITY

*A CONCISE ACCOUNT OF REVELATION'S EVENTS
LEADING UP TO THE SECOND COMING*

Jay Zinn, Ph.D.

www.iZeeBooks.com

Countdown to Eternity—A Concise Account of Revelation's Events Leading up to the Second Coming

Contents

Foreword

Dr. Jay Zinn's commentary on "Revelation" should find its place on the library shelf of any serious student of the Bible. It's a good read and the chapters with fiction are particularly well written. I was saved all over again reading some of Jay's frightening pages on the end times!

Depending on a person's eschatological background, not everyone will agree with everything written in the apostle John's fascinating and inexhaustible book of Revelation. Over the years of personal study, I've had to learn and relearn many things about this magnificent book and have often said to people, "Only history proves prophecy." Even the prophet Daniel and the apostle John didn't fully understand the things they wrote as some were reserved for this "end-of-the-age" generation.

Dr. Zinn has been ruthlessly honest about his journey of learning and relearning over the years and so I encourage you to read this book, ponder it, and put it on your library shelf to read again at a future date. It just may prove itself right!

Again, "only history proves prophecy." We may all be surprised when things work out. God has everything under HIS control and He will work all things according to HIS plans!

—Kevin J. Conner

Melbourne, Australia

2015

BELOW EVERY PREACHER is a floor held up by their mentors. Jesus mentored the twelve disciples and told them to teach other disciples what he had taught them. He became their floor. Paul exhorted Timothy to entrust to reliable men what he had been taught. Paul was Timothy's floor. Timothy would become the floor of those he would teach, and then he would equip others to teach—and so it goes on.

Mentoring has always been part of God's plan for continuity. It involves teaching, training, and equipping the next generation in order to advance God's kingdom purposes.

Today my floor is the ceiling of those who have mentored me one-on-one, along with those book authors and classroom teachers who I have found particularly helpful. The most prominent among them has been theologian, Bible teacher and best-selling author of many Biblical textbooks, Kevin J. Conner, from Australia. To him I owe much of what I've learned and have come to understand about the book of Revelation. More importantly, Kevin challenged me to test his teachings through the principle of using Scripture to interpret Scripture. The Bereans in Thessalonica did this when they examined the Scriptures to see if Paul's teachings were true. This pleased Paul and he exhorted his spiritual son, Timothy, to do the same by examining and *accurately* dividing the Word of truth.

When others teach us God's Word, we have a personal responsibility to explore their teachings until their insights become our own through the process of purposeful examination. To examine and test creates in us our own voice rather than a recording playing someone else's song. Especially when it comes to the end times.

Learning from other teachers and scholars of eschatology gets the ball rolling and provides us with the necessary tools to unlock the Scriptures. As for my own journey in this, I've been studying and testing the teachings of others for more than four decades, and continue to do so. It is my hope that you'll give serious consideration to examining my thoughts on the subject presented in this book.

—The Author

Introduction

ALL THE EVENTS we see happening on the world stage today are accumulating signs of the coming rule of the Antichrist. A global, crumbling economy; the decline of America's influence; the acceleration of Islamic terrorism; the progressive Arab Spring; Russia's advance to reclaim Crimea and the Ukraine; Net neutrality; China's growing economic power; the cancerous spread of the three *isms*—socialism, communism, and Islamism; the tolerance movement of political correctness; the rising trend of pestilence and diseases; and the blatant hostility of nations toward Christians who are being martyred. These are all events that will grow exponentially as they precede the imminent rise of a new world order.

Each day's news brings us a step closer to when the pieces come together to complete the end-time picture of the book of Revelation. The journey you are about to embark on is a glimpse into what that picture could look like. We will walk through the pages of Revelation in a concise and linear way to grasp the symbolism and order of its events.

Many Christians avoid this subject and understandably so—first, because it's scary, but more likely because of the immeasurable hours of study required to make sense of it. Both reasons are intimidating, as they were for me when I first began reading Revelation. I quickly discovered the endless tributaries and quagmires of symbols to interpret.

For these reasons, it's easier for most to go with the flow and rely on what's popular. Just leave the interpretation for the end-time scholars to unpack. But there are two problems with this approach. The first is that degreed eschatology "scholars" disagree when it comes to interpreting the book of Revelation. The second is that too many echo the seminary professors or commentaries without putting their teachings to the test. Paul admonishes us to "test all things [first], and *then* hold on to what's good."[1]

In 1973 an older Christian deceived me by teaching me false doctrine concerning Revelation. He claimed he was the *manchild* of Revelation 12:5 and that I would be one of the two Revelation 11 witnesses who would be called to testify about the manchild's arrival. Still young in my faith, my ignorance and ego made me vulnerable to his ideas. After several months of this, the man felt "led by God" to move out of the state. His departure gave me the time and freedom I needed to wake up from my deception.

Once I realized just how easily I had been led astray, I promised myself I would closely examine the Scriptures taught by others and not accept their interpretations at face value. I began and continue to approach the study of Revelation with both passion *and* caution. I have learned that what I believe about *any* doctrine can affect my faith and God holds me accountable for what I might teach others.[2] That man's teaching harmed me, but God used it to show me how to accurately handle his Word through serious examination.

Today we live in a pop culture driven by rhetorical "sound bites" and ideologies that are rarely challenged by reason and logic. Our lives are so fast paced it limits our time to examine what's taught from our pulpits and lecterns. This makes us candidates for deception.

---

[1] 1 Thessalonians 5:21
[2] James 3:1

Our educational system, too, has changed. Students are required to agree with their teachers and never question or challenge the process of how they reach their conclusions. Instead, students are required to be quiet, download the information into their brains, and spit out the same rhetoric. Another cause for deception.

This practice has subtly crept into churches and seminaries as well; not all of them, but it's making inroads to our pulpits. How is that? When preachers or teachers respond to thoughtful, inquisitive minds with condescending remarks, they intimidate their listeners into *accepting* rather than *thinking* about the tenets and doctrines of faith being offered. They request submission, but submission without freedom to think is legalism disguised. To impart information in this way to God's people is very unhealthy and also grounds for deception.

When secular or religious institutes require students to memorize and pass their exams with only textbook answers to graduate, the students become parroting missionaries of the same propaganda, same ideologies, and same teachings. The world and political correction increasingly demand we get in line or else. This is serious because it is in this type of culture that the Antichrist will thrive.

Jesus said, "If you seek the truth, you will find it." The operative word in that sentence is "if." In the culture of his day, Jesus understood that seeking truth required *effort*. At twelve his parents found him listening and talking to the rabbinical teachers at the temple in Jerusalem; teachers who were amazed by his understanding and answers to their questions.[3] Today, many assume that Jesus entered the world filled with knowledge of the Scriptures, like computers that come already loaded with a Bible software program. The truth is, Jesus dug out and possessed the hidden treasures of

---

[3] Luke 2:46-47

God's Word by his own effort.

My mentor, Kevin Conner, once said at a conference that revelation is 10 percent inspiration and 90 percent perspiration. By this he meant that seeking truth takes thought, time, and serious examination—something the rabbis and teachers of Christ's day encouraged and instilled in their disciples. They understood that to know truth was to know its counterfeit. That truth needs no defense, if it is truth. They understood that truth can hold up under scrutiny; and if you present your case through multiple layers and angles of Scripture—not just a single passage—then you had a strong, solid foundation for that truth.

Truth *always* prevails because it covers all bases. False doctrine does not. The holes in its framework are so monumental the house will collapse. To understand the book of Revelation requires a consistent interpretation to keep the order of events from colliding into each other. Revelation, therefore, must be approached with great thought, great questions, and great respect for its contents. In the pages of this book, I hope to offer such an experience.

Textbooks on Revelation abound, sharing details and multiple layers of information on every verse. This is a good thing, but verse-by-verse studies are seldom fast and easy reads. Such books are called *expositions*. My goal, however, is to give you an overview of Revelation without jeopardizing the foundation and framework of its amazing prophecy.

Please know that, as you proceed, you'll read some things you've never heard before. If you stay with it, you'll return to your Bible to review passages in which you once thought you had locked down. I know how that feels when you face new thoughts that contradict your belief system of eschatology. I've been there, too, but I'm glad I made the effort to reconsider, rethink, review, and restudy the things I believed before I began my own journey.

As you begin to read this book, remember that it isn't my goal to make your views align with mine. At best, I only hope to challenge your thinking about what you believe to be true and, if so, accomplish one of two things: to solidify your beliefs or be drawn into a new territory of study and thought that could turn out to be quite an adventure. Enjoy the journey.

Jay Zinn

Chapter 1

Why Should I Care?

A NONFICTION BOOK is a compilation of thoughts on a subject, ending with a conclusion. But a case must be made for why it merits our attention. If a writer doesn't make that case early, the reader yawns, throws the book aside and grabs the TV remote. So let me address a few "Why should I care?" questions before we dive into the meat of this book.

Whenever indisputable facts or truths are presented to an audience, a response is required. For example, the cornerstone of the Christian faith is that Jesus Christ is God come in the flesh.[4] When confronted with this truth in the gospels or the book of Acts, people ignore it, fight it, or embrace it. What they can't do, however, is alter it; and no matter how they respond to the fact of his divineness, Jesus made one thing very clear; their response to his claims will have eternal consequences—good or bad.

We live in a time where the world seems to be coming apart. Journalists have said in the social media, "The world is going to hell in a hand basket." This generates a rising trend of claims by prominent evangelicals that we're witnessing the end times unfolding before our very eyes. But few understand what that means, how it all fits together, or how it will impact our lives.

---

[4] 1 Timothy 3:16; John 1:1-2, 14

Based on what I understand in the Scriptures, and our current events, it's imperative to know where it's all heading and how it affects our behavior—especially if we're around long enough to live through Revelation's events leading up to Christ's return.

Jesus said to the Pharisees:

> When evening comes, you say, "It will be fair weather, for the sky is red," and in the morning, "Today it will be stormy, for the sky is red and overcast." You know how to interpret the appearance of the sky, but you cannot interpret the signs of the times.[5]

The Pharisees had a rich knowledge of the Scriptures and could quote them verbatim. However, they couldn't interpret the *signs of the times* when their Messiah actually came and looked them in the eyes. What caused their misdirection? I'll tell you what caused it. Jesus didn't match their profile of what they imagined him to be—so they rejected and crucified him.

Everything Jesus did fulfilled what the Scriptures predicted the Messiah would do. But the Pharisees couldn't see it. They were blinded by their own prejudice and self-preservation. It will be the same for us regarding the events leading up to the return of Christ, if we aren't adequately equipped to discern them. We will either recognize what's coming or not—depending on how we interpret the Scriptures.

You and I are invited by God to read and be blessed in our understanding of end times.[6] We've also been given free will to ignore it. But to ignore it is to believe it's not important.

---

[5] Matthew 16:2-4
[6] Revelation 1:3

I've often heard people say, "I am not *pre*-trib, *mid*-trib, or *post*-trib in my beliefs,[7] I am *pan*-trib which means—it will all *pan out* in the end." That's another way of saying, "I prefer to ignore the subject." But to ignore it is a belief system that any knowledge of end times is irrelevant to a person's life today. Their attitude is, "All that end-time stuff will happen in the sweet by and by, but, today, I'm just trying to deal with the nasty now and now." Such thinking, however, can limit our ability to make the hard choices we'll need to make, even though they might derail the plans we have for our future.

So why not do both? Why don't we dream and plan for a future that also includes a backup plan? We can explore the subject of end times to acquire understanding to help us interpret the signs of the times, while living in today's world.

No matter what we choose to do about the truth of the end times—that is, explore it or ignore it—we still can't escape the fact that either position will determine a belief system that can set a course toward an eternal state of being *after* the return of Christ. I will address that further in the sequel to this book.

Here's how it works

Beliefs always determine *action*, and action determines *destiny*—for good or for bad. Should we live long enough to experience the biblical proportions of the last-day events, my question is, "How will we live through it and come out on the other side by the measure of our current understanding or lack thereof?"

For example, if we believe the pre-trib teaching that all Christians are raptured to heaven *before* all hell breaks

[7] The three different views of interpretation on how and when the events of the last days unfold. "Trib" is an abbreviation for "tribulation." Pre, mid, and post refer to before, in the middle, and after the last days of the tribulation period.

loose, then we might ignore the following questions: What happens if we're not raptured? If we're alive during the time of Great Tribulation, will we be ready to deal with that?

Or, if we believe it's possible that Christians will go *into* the Great Tribulation period and are martyred for their faith, perhaps we would feel more inclined to prepare and equip ourselves for that particular outcome (and I'm not referring to storing up a cache of food, guns, and ammunition).

If we believe Christians will be raptured *before* the Antichrist comes into full authority and power, then we might ignore equipping ourselves with the knowledge to discern his ability to deceive—if possible—the very elect.[8]

On the other hand, if we believe it's possible that Christians will be around *during* the global regime of the Antichrist, we might pay more attention to building an intimate relationship with Jesus now, so we can discern the *phony* Jesus then.

Jesus warned his disciples to beware of false christs and false prophets.[9] The apostle Paul predicted a great falling away of saints *before* the man of lawlessness, the son of perdition, would be revealed.[10] So choosing a complacent attitude about knowing this subject can have a significant impact on our future behavior and choices. Ignorance of what's coming might make us prime candidates for *falling away from the faith* because we will then believe the lie and take the mark of the beast.[11]

The dangers of complacency and ignorance

> Woe to you who are complacent in Zion. —*Amos 6:1*

---

[8] Matthew 24:24
[9] Matthew 24:23-24
[10] 2 Thessalonians 2:3
[11] 2 Thessalonians 2:9-11; Revelation 13:16-17

If political correctness and social media can persuade active church members to vote for politicians whose ideologies are *anti*-Jesus, *anti*-God, *anti*-life, *anti*-freedom and *anti*-moral, then how can they possibly resist the most powerful, charismatic leader ever to rise in the last days—a leader who will become all of the "anti's" above a hundredfold?[12] The Antichrist will be a global tyrant with political correctness as his scepter, and the social media as his throne.

The complacency of Christians who bow to political correctness is the result of interpreting Scriptures through the secular lens of humanism[13] and universalism.[14] These doctrines have already crept into the church over the last hundred years, and will continue to spread as a cancer until a world federation of churches emerges under the umbrella of a polytheistic,[15] world religion. In Revelation this one-world religion is called Babylon, which means *confusion*. This is a false church, *intolerant* of any Christian or orthodox Jew who refuses to dine at the table of heretical delicacies and political correctness.

When it comes to knowing the Bible, understanding the times, or recognizing false teachers and political messiahs, many saints will be ill-equipped to discern the true nature of the Antichrist. He will have their attention because their hearts have been captured *today*. He will have their attention because they thirst for a powerful, charismatic leader *today*. He will have their attention because Hollywood consistently fuels the appetite for superheroes who will save

---

[12] 2 Thessalonians 4:4, 9

[13] **Humanism**—*n*, the denial of any power or moral value superior to that of humanity; the rejection of religion in favor of a belief in the advancement of humanity by its own effort.

[14] **Universalism**—*n*, a system of religious beliefs maintaining that all people are predestined for salvation no matter what nature of their character.

[15] **Polytheism**: poly ("many"), theoi ("gods"). The doctrine of or belief in more than one god or in many gods.

the world from doom and destruction with their superpowers.

We all hunger to see justice prevail over injustice. We all hunger for a strong leader to emerge and actually *do* something with the mess we're in. The world clamors for a hero who will put things right, and there's nothing wrong with that. But this is why it's important to know the Bible's portrayal of the Antichrist. We need to know how he'll come into power and what he will do to deceive us. We must be equipped to spot this false savior who will appear on the world stage like an alien from another planet. A false savior promising peace, joy and harmony through a demonstration of counterfeit signs and wonders.[16] In the last days, ignorance can be the downfall of the complacent Christian, and ignorance will be no excuse.

The overwhelming testimony of the Bible

In my first three years as a Christian I read through the Bible four times. During that time it became evident that a repeated thread of Scripture surrounded the subject of events in the last days.

The Old Testament contains eleven books[17] with Scripture references on the end times, and the New Testament has nineteen (two-thirds of the books in the New Testament).[18] Combine these numbers from both testaments and you have thirty out of sixty-six books of the Bible speaking directly to this subject. If the Bible addresses this

---

[16] 2 Thessalonians 2:9
[17] They are found in Job, Psalms, Isaiah, Ezekiel, Daniel, Joel, Amos, Micah, Zephaniah, Zechariah and Malachi.
[18] They are found in the New Testament in Matthew, Mark, Luke, John, Acts, Romans, 1 Corinthians, 2 Corinthians, Ephesians, Philippians, 1 Thessalonians, 2 Thessalonians, 1 Timothy, 2 Timothy, Hebrews, James, 2 Peter, 1 John, Jude and Revelation.

with so much attention, isn't it reasonable to assume having *some* knowledge about end times is important?

These Scriptures come to us as signposts about the future. Our future. They equip us to discern the times today when we hear talk of a new world order, or of a one-world currency, or the necessity of a global economic policy, or the call for a one-world government led by a one-world leader.

The testimony of these Scriptures will help us make sense of why things are unfolding so fast on the social and geopolitical landscape. The Scriptures will help us answer questions in people's minds about these days and, even more, what to say when these supernatural events erupt from the heavens.

End-time Scriptures will challenge us to arm and equip ourselves with enough knowledge to discern the ruse of the Antichrist and the spirit of the antichrist pervading the world *today*.[19] They will also provoke us to live a more circumspect life, and a more intimate life with Jesus.

The last recorded words of Peter

Of the twelve chosen by Jesus, Peter was the most outspoken apostle. His first recorded words, as a spirit-filled believer, came on the day of Pentecost when he spoke to the crowds about the resurrected Christ. He warned them in that day to save themselves from a corrupt generation, and he still does so today.[20]

Peter received the keys of the kingdom[21] to unlock the door to the Gentiles and became the first man to share Jesus with them.[22] The role Peter played, when the church was

---

[19] 1 John 4:1-3
[20] Acts 2:14-41
[21] Matthew 16:18-19
[22] Acts 10—Peter at the house of Cornelius.

born, cast him into a position of authority to speak as an ambassador on Christ's behalf.

If Peter's words about the *first* coming of Christ brought the first Jew and Gentile converts into the church in the first century, how much more should we pay attention to his last recorded words about the *second* coming of Christ?

Peter answered the "Why should I care?" question shouted from the crowd on the day of Pentecost. And again, in 2 Peter 3, he makes his case for *why* we should know about the last days. Please read this carefully:

> Dear friends, this is now my second letter to you. I have written both of them as reminders to **stimulate you** to wholesome thinking. I want you to recall the words spoken in the past by the holy prophets [in the Old Testament] and the command given by our Lord and Savior through your apostles [in the New Testament].
>
> First of all, **you must understand** that in the last days scoffers will come, scoffing and following their own evil desires. They will say, "Where is this 'coming' he promised? Ever since our fathers died, everything goes on as it has since the beginning of creation." But they deliberately forget that long ago by God's word the heavens existed and the earth was formed out of water and by water. By these waters also the world of that time was deluged and destroyed. By the same word the present heavens and earth are reserved for fire, being kept for the Day of Judgment and destruction of ungodly men.
>
> But *do not forget* this one thing, dear friends: With the Lord a day is like a thousand years, and a thousand years are like a day. The Lord is not slow in keeping his promise, as some understand slowness. He is patient with you, not wanting anyone to perish, but everyone to come to repentance.
>
> But the day of the Lord will come like a thief. The heavens will disappear with a roar; the elements will be

destroyed by fire, and the earth and everything in it will be laid bare.

Since everything will be destroyed in this way, ***what kind of people ought you to be?*** You ought to live holy and godly lives as you look forward to the day of God and speed its coming. That day will bring about the destruction of the heavens by fire, and the elements will melt in the heat. But in keeping with his promise ***we are looking forward*** to a new heaven and a new earth, the home of righteousness.

So then, dear friends, since you are looking forward to this, ***make every effort*** to be found spotless, blameless and at peace with him ... ***be on your guard*** so that you may not be carried away by the error of lawless men and fall from your secure position. But grow in the grace and knowledge of our Lord and Savior Jesus Christ. To him be glory both now and forever! Amen.

—2 Peter 3:1-14, 17-18

In this one single discourse, Peter makes a similar case to what I shared with you in this chapter. So let's all be on our guard for what's ahead.

Chapter 2

My Journey into End-Time Studies

I WANT TO SHARE with you how I started this journey and arrived at the theories presented in this book. This can be helpful since most of you will read through the lens of your own journey, filtering what I show you through what you may or may not have already accepted as the *only* view. Of course we should process new ideas in keeping with Paul's admonition to test all things and hold on to what's good.[23]

The study of end times is no easy task. Not only is it composed of a vast collection of Scriptures, but it's also a moving target on the tides of the past, present, and future. Nearly half the books in the Bible address this subject. That's a lot of verses to decipher and assemble into a chronological order. Many attempt to do so in varying degrees within three prominent views—one of which you likely hold whether you know it or not. These views are: *pre*-tribulation, *mid*-tribulation, and *post*-tribulation. Let me define them briefly, as I understand them.

Pre-tribulation view

This teaches that seven years *before* the visible return of Christ, living Christians are caught up (or raptured) to meet Christ in the air *before* the days of the Antichrist. The dead in Christ will resurrect, also, to meet him in the air first.

---

[23] 1 Thessalonians 5:21

Those living who reject Christ are left behind to experience worldwide hardships of famine, war, pain, and suffering, brought on by the seven seals, seven trumpets, and seven bowls of wrath in the book of Revelation. They can still be saved, but are left behind to go through the tribulation period. After seven years are complete, Jesus returns with his saints and sets up a millennial kingdom on Earth.

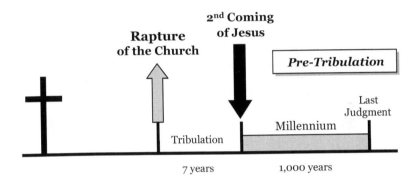

This teaching originated in the early 1800s through four principle parties: 1) a Jesuit priest from Chile named Manuel de Lacunza. He wrote a book in 1812 called, *The Coming of the Messiah in Glory and Majesty,* 2) a Scottish preacher named Edward Irving who had Lacunza's book translated into English, 3) a 15 year old Scottish girl named Margaret MacDonald from Port Glasgow, and 4) an English preacher named John Nelson Darby from the Plymouth Brethren movement.

In 1831, Margaret MacDonald believed God showed her a new revelation of a "split coming" of Christ, and that all Christians would be raptured up before the Antichrist came into full power. Both Edward Irving and John Darby visited Margaret MacDonald at her home and were impacted by the vision she had written down and shared with others. They embraced it and propagated it.

Darby introduced the pre-tribulation views at prophetic conferences on a number of trips to America where it was embraced and popularized in the *Scofield Reference Bible*. Today, it is the most widely held view on end times in America, probably due to the promotion of pre-tribulation doctrine in literature, novels, seminaries, movies, and prominent preachers on radio, television and cable.

Mid-tribulation view

This teaches that the rapture of the church will occur in the *middle* of the seven years of the tribulation period. Instead of a rapture happening at the beginning of the seven years, Christians will go three-and-one-half years into the seven years of tribulation before the rapture takes place, and before the severest outpouring of God's wrath upon the Earth. It is the least-embraced theory of the three. It also happens before the millennial reign of Christ.

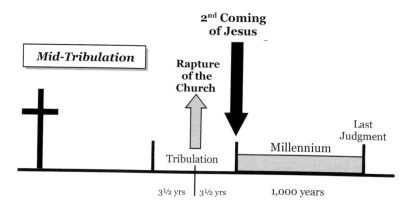

Post-tribulation view

This is the third and longest-held view in church history, and teaches that the rapture takes place at the *end* of the Great Tribulation. Believers will go through the Great

Tribulation period, many will be martyred by the Antichrist, and those who are alive and remain will be raptured following the resurrection of the dead in Christ at the second coming. Jesus then sets up his millennial reign.

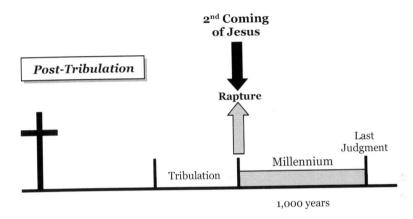

In a nutshell: Pre-trib's rapture takes place *seven* years before the second coming of Christ, mid-trib's rapture takes place *three-and-one-half years* before his second coming, and post-trib's rapture takes place simultaneously *at* the second coming. These are the three most-prominent theories.

Jesus is coming back

I was an airman at Eglin Air Force Base in Fort Walton Beach, Florida, when I was saved on January 9, 1972. My recently converted friends had dedicated their lives to Jesus at a church off base and invited me to attend their next Sunday meeting. Before the main service we sat outside in a circle with other young adults for a Sunday school class taught by the pastor. I was intrigued that not only were these young guys and girls *in* church, but they were carrying their own Bibles and eager to learn. The pastor had them open to the gospel of Matthew, chapter 24. Not having a Bible, I followed along with the guy beside me and noticed his verses were underlined and blocked in a rainbow of colors.

At an early point in the teaching, the pastor paused and scanned our faces. Then he said something I had never heard before, "Jesus is coming back and it could be any moment— possibly today. Are you ready for him?"

That statement shocked and scared me. So much so, I made a decision later in the main service to do what my two friends had done weeks before and follow Jesus. Because of those alarming words from the pastor that day, I've been an avid student of end times.

My journey begins

Fascinated by the idea of Christ's return, I collected many cassette teachings and books on end times. In the process of my studies, I discovered differences among the teachers when it came to *how* the events fit together before Christ returns. These teachers all fell into one of the three views I mentioned earlier: *pre*-tribulation, *mid*-tribulation, or *post*-tribulation.

After I was saved I came into contact with many Christians at the Air Force hospital where I worked. I found that most of their churches embraced the *pre*-tribulation view. They each held strong points in their beliefs, but I wanted to know which one was right. Since the church I attended believed in the "any moment" rapture, and most of the other churches did, too, I picked the first of the three views. I studied this view for a couple of years until I felt I had a fair understanding of how things might play out. I loved to talk about it with others who shared the same interest. My confidence in that theory was challenged, however, when I received orders for my next assignment at Elmendorf AFB in Anchorage, Alaska.

Shaken to the core

After I arrived I joined an exciting and fast-growing church during the height of the Jesus movement in the early 1970s. I became a firmly established member and loved the solid biblical teaching. One day I discovered they believed in the *post*-tribulation theory. I resisted the teaching at first, but rather unsuccessfully, because they were able to unravel my *pre*-tribulation beliefs so effectively through Scripture— in love, of course.

They took me to the same verses I used, and compared their interpretation to mine. Over time, it began to make more sense, but in one final effort I set out to prove my beliefs were more accurate. Not only for pride, but I preferred being raptured out *before* everything collapsed. I just couldn't bring myself to understand how anyone could believe we would go through such a horrible time. God wouldn't let that happen to us ... would he? Doesn't the Bible say:

> How awful that day will be! None will be like it. It will be a time of trouble for Jacob, *but he will be saved out of it.*   *—Jeremiah 30:7*

> For God *did not appoint us to suffer wrath* but to receive salvation through our Lord Jesus Christ.   *—1 Thessalonians 5:9*

I love those Scriptures. They were a comforting promise to me that I would be saved out of it all and not experience any of the wrath of the Great Tribulation period. I would be raptured out. But I didn't know or have the complete picture, yet. I didn't understand the context surrounding those verses, which I had been taught applied to the rapture. I'm afraid there's a much larger landscape. I discovered in Scripture that we do not have the assurance of escaping tribulation or martyrdom.

Chapter 3

Martyrdom

YEARS AGO I READ a fascinating story about a man named Jim Elliot. He and four other missionaries traveled to Ecuador to share the gospel with an unreached tribe called the Huaorani. Jim and his pilot, Nate Saint, had made contact with the tribe from their airplane by using a loudspeaker and lowering a basket down to offer them gifts.

After many months of providing gifts in this way, the five missionaries decided to set up camp a short distance from the Indian village, along the Curaray River. Flying in one by one, they only had to wait four days before being approached by a small group of Huaorani. The connection was significant enough that they gave an airplane ride to one of the Indians. They called him, "George."

Because the Huaorani were so friendly during this encounter, the missionaries decided it would be safe enough to visit their village. However, they did not know that George had lied to his tribe about the missionaries' intentions. Two days later, just as they started for the village, a band of Huaorani warriors arrived and killed Jim Elliot and his four companions on January 8, 1956. All of the men's bodies were found along the bank of the river.

In Jim's journal entry for October 28, 1949, he expressed that the work he dedicated to Jesus was more important to him than his own life. In his now famous quote, he wrote:

He is no fool who gives what he cannot keep to gain that which he cannot lose.

The death of Jim Elliott and his friends did not end the mission to reach the Huaorani. Within two years, Jim's wife, Elisabeth Elliott, their daughter, and other relatives of the slain missionaries moved into the village and many of the Huaorani converted to Christianity.

What an early Christian apologist, Tertullian, said is an appropriate summation for such an outcome:

The blood of the martyrs is the seed of the church.

Last days' martyrdom

According to Jesus, martyrdom is part of the end-time experience, something we have to come to grips with if we're going to be serious students of end times. I'm not excited about that possibility, but it's a reality and, if necessary, will serve as a redemptive purpose, like the deaths of the missionaries, which eventually won the Huaorani to Christ. Jesus predicted this when he said:

> Then you will be handed over **to be persecuted and put to death**, and you will be hated by all nations because of me. At that time *many will turn away from the faith* and will betray and hate each other, and many false prophets will appear and deceive many people. Because of the increase of wickedness, the love of most will grow cold, but he who stands firm to the end will be saved. And this gospel of the kingdom will be preached in the whole world as a testimony to all nations, and then the end will come.[24]

---

[24] Matthew 24:9-14

The thought that God would allow his saints to suffer persecution to the extent of possible martyrdom—for the sake of Christ—is hard for people to accept.

So let's consider this with these questions: Did God spare John the Baptist from being beheaded for his message and call to the Jews to repent?

Did the Father spare his only begotten Son from the whipping post and the brutality of the cross?

Did God spare Stephen in Acts from being stoned to death for his message to the Jews?

Did God spare the early apostles from cruel deaths, with the exception of John, who died a natural death exiled on the island of Patmos?[25] Here's what they faced:

- James, the son of Zebedee—beheaded with the sword
- Philip—scourged and crucified
- Matthew—slain with the sword
- Mark—severely beaten, bled to death, and body burned
- James, the brother of John—beaten and stoned to death
- Matthias (replaced Judas)—stoned and beheaded
- Andrew—hung on a cross with cords three days and died
- Peter—scourged and then crucified, head down
- Jude, the brother of James—crucified
- Bartholomew—slain by a sword or beaten to death with clubs
- Thomas—thrust through with a spear
- Simon, the zealot—crucified

Did God spare the early church Christians from suffering persecution at the hands of Saul of Tarsus?

---

[25] John Foxe, *Foxe's Christian Martyrs of the World* (Chicago, IL: Moody Press, public domain), 27-35.

Did God spare Paul (who was Saul converted in Acts) from being whipped, stoned, imprisoned and beaten for his message, and ultimately beheaded by Nero for his faith?

Have you ever read *Foxe's Christian Martyrs of the World*,[26] which contains gruesome, detailed accounts of the torturous persecution of the apostles and early church saints under the emperors, kings, and governors of their time?

Have you ever read stories from "The Voice of the Martyrs,"[27] an organization about Christians who have been martyred in other lands for their faith—today?

Have you ever read *Hebrews 11:35-40* with its report of God's people who were commended for their faith because they endured incredibly serious trials and tortuous deaths?

Since the answer to all these accounts is obvious, why should we believe we're immune to such a fate? All of the church saints above believed in the second coming of Christ, but were not saved from the flames of persecution and death. When I began to read about these accounts, those passages I used to quote from Jeremiah 30:7 and 1 Thessalonians 5:9 about being saved from trouble and not suffering were not as promising for my way out of this world.

A rapture rescue

Many end-time teachers believe we'll escape impending trouble because the rapture will rescue us before the world begins to collapse. They believe God will spare us. I sincerely hope they're right. Who wouldn't prefer to bypass all that hardship and be raptured *before* persecution arrives? But what if they're wrong? Then I must consider the possibility that Christians will face martyrdom in the last days; a scenario that aligns with reports of saints who have

---

[26] Ibid.

[27] Watch *Liena's Prayer* (www.persecution.idop/), The Voice of the Martyrs, P.O. Box 443, Bartlesville, OK (www.persecution.com).

experienced this throughout the ages and with those saints who are in the news now. For me, mounting evidence from the book of Revelation strongly indicates martyrdom will occur in the last days. Review these verses to see what they tell us:

Revelation 6:9-11

When he opened the fifth seal, I saw under the altar the **souls of those who had been slain** because of the word of God and the testimony they had maintained. They called out in a loud voice, "How long, Sovereign Lord, holy and true, until you judge the inhabitants of the earth and **avenge our blood**?" Then each of them was given a white robe, and they were told to wait a little longer, until the number of their fellow servants and brothers *who were to be killed as they had been was completed*.

Revelation 7:13-14

Then one of the elders asked me, "These [dead] in white robes — who are they, and where did they come from?"

I answered, "Sir, you know."

And he said, "These are they who have **come out of the great tribulation**; they have washed their robes and made them white in the blood of the Lamb."

Revelation 12:11

They [the saints] overcame him [Satan] by the blood of the Lamb and by the word of their testimony; they did not love their lives so much as **to shrink from death**.

Revelation 13:5-7

The beast [Antichrist] was given a mouth to utter proud words and blasphemies and to exercise his authority for forty-two months. He opened his mouth to blaspheme God, and to slander his name and his dwelling place and those who live in heaven. He was given power to **make war against the saints and to conquer them**.

Revelation 13:15-17

He [the False Prophet] was given power to give breath to the image of the first beast [Antichrist], so that it could speak and cause all who refused to worship the image **to be killed**.

Revelation 14:12-13

This calls for patient endurance on the part of the saints who obey God's commandments and remain faithful to Jesus. Then I heard a voice from heaven say, "Write: Blessed are the dead **who die in the Lord from now on**."

Revelation 15:2-3

I saw what looked like a sea of glass mixed with fire and, standing beside the sea, those **who had been victorious over the beast and his image and over the number of his name**. They held harps given them by God and sang the song of Moses the servant of God and the song of the Lamb.

Revelation 16:5-6

Then I heard the angel in charge of the waters say: "You are just in these judgments, you who are and who were, the Holy One, because you have so judged; for **they have shed the blood of your saints and prophets**."

Revelation 17:3, 6; 18:24

I saw a woman [the harlot church] sitting on a scarlet beast that was covered with blasphemous names ... the woman **was drunk with the blood of the saints**, the blood of those who bore testimony to Jesus .... In her was found **the blood of prophets and of the saints**, and of all who have been killed on the earth.

Revelation 19:1-2

Hallelujah!

Salvation and glory and power belong to our God, for true and just are his judgments.

He has condemned the great prostitute [harlot] who corrupted the earth by her adulteries.

He has avenged on her **the blood of his servants**.

Revelation 20:4

I saw thrones on which were seated those who had been given authority to judge. And I saw the souls of those **who had been beheaded** because of their testimony for Jesus and because of the word of God. They had not worshiped the beast or his image and had not received his mark on their foreheads or their hands.

During the forty years I served as a pastor, I've had the privilege of visiting many countries and nations on mission trips where I ministered to church leaders and congregations. In those travels I discovered that mostly American churches taught *pre*-tribulation. Rarely, if at all, was it taught in churches of other countries, especially those suffering at the hands of oppressors within Communist or Islamic-dominated territories. So my earliest belief that I would escape the Great Tribulation and be raptured out began to dissipate over time with Scripture, history, and reality.

Do I like the idea of suffering or martyrdom? No. Is it possible it could happen to me someday? Yes ... and if so, then I would want to have a relationship with Jesus that is so real and intimate, I would never denounce him at my execution as a Christian. That's why the apostles and other devoted saints in church history were able to endure suffering and pain. They followed the example of Jesus who had died for them, and they for him, not merely for a cause, but for their love and devotion to the *person* of Jesus Christ, their Lord.

To die for Jesus is the highest honor any man or woman could have. It is the ultimate statement of one's unquestionable love and devotion to Christ. It isn't something to be feared, but to embrace if it's our lot to experience and give witness to those who execute us.

The apostle Andrew, brother of Peter, was threatened with death by the governor of Greece for preaching against the idols at Patras. Because he refused, he was sentenced to crucifixion on a cross of two equal length pieces of wood anchored into the ground. Instead of nails, they fastened him with cords so that his death would be slower. He hung there for three whole days, continuing to tell the people around him about the love of Jesus. They listened and believed his words, pleading for the governor to take him down. The governor yielded to their request, but when they cut him down, Andrew had already departed to heaven.

In John Foxe's account, he quotes an ancient writer telling of the apostle's courage and fearlessness at his crucifixion:

> When Andrew saw the cross prepared, he neither changed countenance nor color, as the weakness of mortal man is inclined to do; neither did his blood shrink; neither did he fail in his speech; his body fainted not; neither was his mind molested; his understanding did not fail him; but out of the abundance of his heart his mouth did speak, and fervent love did appear in his words. He said, "O cross, most welcome and often looked for; with a willing mind, joyfully and desirously, I come to you, being the scholar of Him who did hang on you; because I have been always your lover, and longed to embrace you!"[28]

---

[28] John Foxe, *Foxe's Christian Martyrs of the World* (Chicago, IL: Moody Press, public domain), 30. *Note:* a few of the King James words were edited out and replaced with today's language.

Chapter 4

My Best Understanding

SINCE MY CONVERSION in 1972 I've been an ardent student of end times. I've developed and taught classes on the books of Revelation and Daniel at Bible colleges and the three churches I planted. Preparing for those classes required every necessary tool to present "my best understanding." I endeavored to teach my students as a faithful steward—rightly handling the word of truth,[29] and laying aside my own preferences.

Because the Bible is alive, each time I presented "my best understanding" on end times, I received more insight in my studies. I still grow in that way today, and my theories are subject to change upon further enlightenment given by the Holy Spirit. By keeping this mindset, I remain pliable concerning such a complex subject.

Our disadvantage

When it comes to understanding end-time prophecy, we truly are at a disadvantage in a number of ways. We are limited in our knowledge and use of the two original languages of the Bible (Hebrew and Greek), including the idioms of those languages, the symbols of the Bible, and the culture and customs of the times in which these prophecies were written.

---

[29] 2 Timothy 2:15

We are also influenced by commentaries of end-time scholars who vary in their interpretation of the order in which the events occur, leading up to the second coming.

We've been influenced by our mentors and teachers, too, just as they have by theirs.

But if we take what we've been taught, embracing and examining it in light of other end-time scholars, and use the proper tools of interpretation to arrive at our own conclusions, we'll be able to offer our own *best understanding*—hopefully with an open mind *and* an open hand.

Some of my colleagues once called me an "expert" on this subject. I was flattered, but disagreed and still do. Though I've studied this subject thoroughly, perhaps more than most, I'm really a student for life. In the case of end times, there is still much to discover and the future we see in prophecy hasn't happened, yet. We can theorize about what could happen, but the outcome is not finalized.

Saying, "my best understanding," may not sound scholarly or boost your confidence in what I believe and teach—but that's okay. I do feel confident, however, that I can offer you "seed thoughts" that will sprout and lift you up to a higher plane of revelation in your own studies.

Saying, "my best understanding," permits you to challenge my theories and put your powers of reason to use. If I would ever say, "This is how it *will be*," I am being dogmatic, which can restrain or suppress genuine study and interpretation. I want to encourage everyone to explore beyond my own discoveries, as my teachers have done so with me.

Conviction versus preference

It is within reason that you might rant, grunt, or groan about what I share in this book. Hopefully, there will be a lot of "aha" moments, too. But when the questions come, I encourage you to mark in the margins of these pages. Underline everything that flies in the face of what you've been taught or perceived as *your* take on the subject. As you read each chapter, ask the Holy Spirit to show you what's possible. Ask yourself, at each challenge to your beliefs, "Is it possible for God to do something like this?" If you think, "No, it isn't possible," then take a sheet of paper and write down the reasons *why*. Then find Scripture references to support your objections. If you are unable to find them, then consider the possibility that what you object to might be founded on *preference* rather than *conviction* grounded in Scriptures.

Conviction goes to the quarries to mine for gold through arduous study. Preference goes to the echoes of hearsay, or what's desirable, and what's easier to embrace. Preference is like political correctness, which is just another way of saying, "Don't rock the boat in the face of popular opinion."

Truth, however, offends and Jesus was very good at doing that. So was Paul. If we ever feel our blood boiling when our beliefs are challenged on a subject we've locked down, we might possess a *preference* rather than a *conviction*. To possess a conviction requires purposeful study until the questions and objections of others are incapable of sounding more reasonable than what your studies produced. The results will be a calm and peaceful spirit within us when challenged about our beliefs because the truth we hold through trial and sacrifice can't be shaken. Truth stands as a rock in the face of opposition. What is true will always stand while the teachings or opinions of what is not true will fall in the test of time.

When it comes to the subject of end times, I ponder all new thoughts that come my way and filter them through the Scriptures, in context, to look for inconsistencies. If there are none, then I add the new revelation to my foundation, like adding the next piece that fits into the puzzle on the table.

If you're able to say, "Yes, it's possible it could happen that way," then you're on the road to a humbler state. When future events unfold, our crowbarred theories may fall apart. Even my mentor and teacher, Kevin Conner, the most well-versed theologian I know on this subject, would listen to my theories and say, "That's possible—we'll know someday, won't we?"

The first and second coming of Christ

The theological term for "studying end times" is *eschatology* (es-ka-tol'-a-je). It actually comes from two Greek words, *eschatos*—meaning "last, farthest" and *ology*—meaning "the study of." As a noun, it refers to *a branch of theology concerned with the final events in the history of the world and of humankind.*

Another Greek word to introduce is *protos*—meaning "first." So we have *protos*—"first," and *eschatos*—"last." Jesus referred to himself in the book of Revelation as "the first [*protos*] and the last [*eschatos*]."[30] So, there are two comings of Christ we see in the Bible: the *first* coming happened when he came to Earth, preached the good news, ministered to the lost, trained twelve disciples, died, and rose again. The *second* coming will occur when he returns to set up his glorious kingdom on Earth at the beginning of a thousand-year reign called "the millennium."

The religious and biblical scholars in Christ's day had their own theories of whom and what the Messiah would be at his *first* coming. In his book, *More Than a Carpenter*, Josh McDowell writes:

---

[30] Revelation 1:17

The Old Testament contains sixty major messianic prophecies and approximately 270 ramifications that were fulfilled in one person, Jesus Christ.[31]

Wow! That's incredible! And if that's the case, how could the priests, scribes, and Pharisees miss the very "One" who fulfilled every single prophecy written about him? They were Bible scholars and knew about the prophecies describing the events leading up to their Messiah's "first" coming. But they got it wrong. They missed the mark and they missed the window for redemption and salvation (though it is still in play). Their long-awaited Messiah came to them and they nailed him to the cross. Why? Because he didn't measure up to their *preference*. They crucified the *real* Messiah and continued to believe in a *false* one—the Messiah *they* wanted, not the One the Father had sent.

I believe this mistake will be a repeated at the *eschatos*, the *last* coming of Christ. Many Bible professors and scholars in the last days will cast off the *real* Christ and embrace the *false* one: the Antichrist. Just like the Pharisees at Christ's first coming, many last-day teachers, who are married to their dogmatic preferences, will lead others astray by *their* image of the Messiah when he returns.

For this reason I add this book to the pile of other theories in order to nudge, challenge, and stir up a new interest in the ancient landmarks of eschatology. I do this because I am concerned that many could risk their chance to embrace the Bridegroom when he comes. As in the parable of the ten virgins, those who are less discerning will lack the knowledge just when they need it the most.[32]

The priests, scribes, and Pharisees all had their *protos* theories, but refused to acknowledge the possibility of being

---

[31] Josh McDowell and Sean McDowell, *More Than a Carpenter* (Carol Stream, IL: Tyndale House Publishers, Inc., 2005), 142.
[32] Matthew 25:1-10

wrong about Jesus of Nazareth, and wrong about the events leading up to his first coming. Of all the Pharisees, only Nicodemus opened his heart and mind to Jesus. He was saved because he opened his eyes to truth while the rest remained blind, leading the blind.

I don't want to be a blind guide. I want to stand with conviction and boldness, but also receptive to the idea that our times in the last days might not be as rosy as we would prefer. We could be wrong about what Jesus might look like as the Bridegroom when he comes. We could be wrong about what the church might look like, or be like, when the Bridegroom comes. We could be as wrong about the events leading up to the *second* coming of Christ as the scholars were about his *first* coming. Had they been more open to reading the Scriptures through a different lens, they might have been able to join Nicodemus in his quest for truth.

Had they approached the *first* coming as their "best understanding" rather than their *only* understanding, they might have been prepared to receive new revelation and insight about Jesus of Nazareth, just as Peter did when he declared:

You are the Christ, the Son of the Living God![33]

Overview not exposition

In the pages of this book, you *won't* be reading a "no-stone-left-unturned" exposition with hundreds of qualifiers to back and support every theory and opinion. I'll leave that for another day if the Lord allows me to present a more detailed exposition of the book of Revelation. In the meantime, I highly recommend Kevin Conner's exposition

---

[33] Matthew 16:16

on the book of Revelation.[34] He has the best book out there for that.

For now, I'll declare my beliefs as a journalist/theologian describing what I think we might see in the future. If there is truth in what I share, your spirit will bear witness to the context of the whole, and the Holy Spirit will confirm it to you in later studies.

As you read, I ask that you refrain from trying to pin me down into just *one* of the three major views of eschatology. All three views hold some measures of truth that I agree with—just not all in the same areas of Scripture or in the same order.

So I share my best understanding with you until the Holy Spirit moves another piece on the chess board to tweak my beliefs.

Let's begin the countdown with a future prediction from an Old Testament prophet named, Ezekiel.

---

[34] Kevin J. Conner, *The Book of Revelation: An Exposition* (Vermont, Victoria: K.J.C. Publications, 2001).

Chapter 5

War in the Middle East

The word of the Lord came to me: "Son of man, set your face against Gog, of the land of Magog, the chief prince of Meshech and Tubal (Russia); prophesy against him and say: 'This is what the Sovereign Lord says: I am against you, O Gog, chief prince of Meshech and Tubal (Russia). I will turn you around, put hooks in your jaws and bring you out with your whole army—your horses, your horsemen fully armed, and a great horde with large and small shields, all of them brandishing their swords. Persia (Iran), Cush (Ethiopia) and Put (Libya) will be with them, all with shields and helmets, also Gomer (Ukraine) with all its troops, and Beth Togarmah (northeast Turkey) from the far north with all its troop —the many nations with you.

"'Get ready; be prepared, you and all the hordes gathered about you, and take command of them. After many days you will be called to arms. In future years you will invade a land that has recovered from war, whose people were gathered from many nations to the mountains of Israel, which had long been desolate. They had been brought out from the nations, and now all of them live in safety. You and all your troops and the many nations with you will go up, advancing like a storm; you will be like a cloud covering the land.'"

—Ezekiel 38:1-9

IF ANYONE WANTS TO TRY to make sense of what's happened in the last two decades in the United States, Israel, Europe, Russia and the Middle East, a reliable source would be biblical prophecy. Once we understand what prophets like Ezekiel were told concerning the last days, some of the confusion and questions clear up as the puzzle is pieced together.

We begin our journey toward the second coming with this intriguing prophecy about an impending invasion against Israel in Ezekiel chapters 38 and 39. The predictions are remarkably detailed and have held the attention of biblical scholars for centuries. Some scholars believe this prophecy will be fulfilled at the end of the thousand-year period in the book of Revelation 20:7-8; others place it somewhere *before* the appearance of the Antichrist. I'm of the latter opinion.

If an event like this were to happen, then its potential for fulfillment in the next thirty years is highly plausible as we witness the growing struggle for power in Russia and in the Middle East. This event would also fit in with other biblical predictions of a last-days' buildup toward a one-world government. Let's consider some thoughts as to how this could play out in today's geopolitical landscape.

The invasion of Israel

The potential for what Ezekiel wrote in chapters 38 and 39 appears to be developing swiftly in today's news. The prophet predicts a sweeping invasion against Israel within its borders. Clearly the upheaval in the Middle East is positioning the nations Ezekiel predicts will be the major players in this war—i.e., Russia, Iran, Libya, Ethiopia, Turkey, and the Ukraine.[35] With Ezekiel's prophecy as the outline, let's create a possible scenario of how current events could fulfill his predictions.

---

[35] Ezekiel 38:1-6—Meschech and Tubal (Russia), Persia (Iran), Cush (Ethiopia), Put (Libya), Gomer (Ukraine), Beth Togarmah (Turkey), and many unnamed nations allied with Russia.

Ezekiel indicates that Russia will carry the dominant role in this invasion. This means Russia will make every attempt politically, strategically, economically, and tactically to first reclaim strategic territories that were lost in the 1991 dissolution of the USSR—especially the region of Ukraine, which is in the process of happening now. Crimea has already been acquired. As this continues to develop, the United States and western Europe will stand on the sidelines like a pack of Chihuahuas yipping at a Rottweiler. Both America and western Europe's inability to intervene for Israel will stem from four things: 1) a weak resolve to engage in a third world war, 2) economies grown too weak and encumbered by debt to fund such a war, 3) the inequitable downsizing of the United States and European militaries and nuclear arms in contrast to Russia and, 4) the succumbing of Europe and the U.S. to socialist policies and political correctness that have pressured lawmakers into passing entitlements and regulations that chip away at the economic stability and military might of Israel's closest allies.

Since the Arab Spring of 2010, extreme Islamist militant groups have advanced undeterred by the diminished presence of U.S. embassies and military bases on strategic fronts in the Middle East. The United States pulling out of Middle East territories has and will continue to leave a vacuum for Islamist groups, like ISIS,[36] to claim strategic battlefronts.

Why Russia and Islam?

By collaborating with Iran and certain Islamist factions in the Middle East, Russia seeks the opportunity to gain

---

[36] ISIS now calls itself IS (Islamic State). IS has evolved through a number of name changes to reflect its growth. It began with **al-Qaida** in Iraq, changed to **ISIL** (Islamic State of Iraq and the Levant), from **ISIL** to **ISIS** (Islamic State of Iraq and Syria), and now to **IS** (Islamic State) because its goal is to combine both Syria and Iraq into one Islamic state.

access to strategic ports and shipping routes in the Persian Gulf and Mediterranean Sea. Ezekiel implies that Israel's natural resources, agriculture, oil, and billions of dollars—found in the Dead Sea's natural chemicals, salt and minerals—will be a huge attraction to the intruders.[37] Such a treasure trove of spoils can add trillions toward funding the wars of two behemoth ideologues bent on world conquest.

Ezekiel prophesies that Russia will devise an evil scheme saying:

> I will invade a land of unwalled villages; I will attack a peaceful and unsuspecting people—all of them living without walls and without gates and bars. I will plunder and loot and turn my hand against the resettled ruins and the people [Jews] gathered from the nations, rich in livestock and goods, living at the center of the land.[38]

In this scheme, Russia will be allied with extreme Islamic terrorists, each carrying their own brand of Islamism and deeply religious in their beliefs toward a supreme deity (Allah). Can a nation of atheist ideologues work together with multiple factions of religious fanatics? The answer is, yes, because they're all on the world stage to serve their own objectives and will do whatever it takes. The geopolitical landscape of Russia and the Middle East is morphing before our very eyes—and there's a reason for that on God's prophetic clock.

---

[37] Ezekiel 38:12-14
[38] Ezekiel 38:10-12

Chapter 6

Islam and the Middle East

THOUGH ISLAM ISN'T mentioned in chapters 38 and 39 of Ezekiel, his prophecy does refer to Russian allies in Islamic-dominated regions.[39] This means Muslims will play a key role in the development of Ezekiel's prophecy. So before I present my case, I'm going to lay some groundwork about Islam to clarify what's going on in the Middle East, and why I believe it will impact us in the last days.

The two sects of Islam

The Prophet Muhammad founded Islam in A.D. 610. The word, "Islam," means "surrender to Allah's will," and its adherents to the faith are called Muslims. This religion has two major sects—the Sunni and Shiite.

The Sunnis are Islam's largest sect, approximately 80-90% of the Muslim global population. They dominate countries like Egypt, Saudi Arabia, and Pakistan. Their name is derived from *Sunnah,* which refers to "the trodden path" or "tradition." The Sunnis follow the core beliefs and traditions of Islam, though they differ from the Shiites in their rituals and interpretation of Islamic law.

---

[39] Ezekiel 38:1-6—Meschech and Tubal (Russia-14% Islam), Persia (Iran-98% Islam), Cush (Ethiopia-45% Islam), Put (Libya-97% Islam), Gomer (Ukraine), Beth Togarmah (Turkey-99% Islam), and many unnamed nations allied with Russia.

The Shiites make up 10-20% of the global Muslim population and dominate countries like Iran, Lebanon, Sudan, and other parts of Africa. Shiites broke off early from the main body of Muslims after a dispute over the succession of leadership following Muhammad's death. They believe that successors (imams) should come through Muhammad's bloodline. The Sunnis, however, believe Islamic leaders (caliphs) should be *elected*. This schism between the two sects has been churning for fourteen centuries.

Fast forward to today and you can see this struggle between two prominent Shiite and Sunni players fighting for control over the same land in the Middle East. This particular struggle has been going on since the late '70s, and has accelerated since the toppling of Saddam Hussein. The players are Iran (Shiite) and Saudi Arabia (Sunni) and are behind the agitation of civil wars in Iraq and Syria. They each see Iraq and Syria, not as two countries, but as one region needed to obtain their opposing objectives.

What the common outsider sees is a civil war in Syria that they don't understand, with radical Sunni insurgents called ISIS (now IS[40]) taking ground in Syria and Iraq to create one Islamic State. What they don't see is the chess game between Sunnis and Shiites (the Saudis and Iranians) covertly backing their own insurgents to take control of strategic military, economic, and political regions.

If Iran wins by backing Shiite factions and regimes to manage and control Syria and Iraq as one state, then the Shiites can advance their brand of Islamic theocracy and Sharia law through an imam, and in particular, the Twelfth Imam, who they believe has been hidden and will return.

---

[40] ISIS now calls itself IS (Islamic State). IS has evolved through a number of name changes to reflect its growth. It began with **al-Qaida** in Iraq, changed to **ISIL** (Islamic State of Iraq and the Levant), from **ISIL** to **ISIS** (Islamic State of Iraq and Syria), and now to **IS** (Islamic State) because its goal is to combine both Syria and Iraq into one Islamic state, erasing its borders.

This, of course, is unacceptable to the Saudi Sunnis and threatens the future of the Saudi Kingdom and their interpretation of practicing Islamic law.

If the Saudi Kingdom wins the struggle, by covertly empowering and backing Sunni factions and regimes to manage and control Syria and Iraq as their one state, then the Sunnis continue to rule and control their own traditional brand of Islam and the caliphs they choose to lead it. This will also maintain a necessary buffer between themselves and Iran.

When it comes to the struggle (called jihad, which means holy war) between Sunnis and Shiites, there is no middle ground and no resolution—ever. So they must induce and fund organized militant sects of Islam reflecting their own agendas—which puts Christians, liberal-Muslims, non-Muslims, and lesser branches of Islam in harm's way of the Sunni-Shiite war.

Islam or Islam*ism*

American historian, writer, and political commentator, Daniel Pipes is the president of a think tank called *The Middle East Forum*.[41] In June 30, 1998, he wrote an article for CSIS[42] to show the difference between Islam and Islamism.[43] Here is an excerpt from that article:

> Islam*ism* is an ideology that demands man's complete adherence to the sacred law of Islam and rejects as much as possible outside influence, with some exceptions (such as access to military and medical technology). ... The word "Islamism" is highly appropriate, for this is an "-ism" like

---

[41] http://www.meforum.org/
[42] Center for Strategic and International Studies
[43] Daniel Pipes, "Distinguishing between Islam and Islamism," Middle East Forum, June 30, 1998, http://www.danielpipes.org/954/distinguishing-between-islam-and-islamism.

other "-isms" such as *fascism* and *nationalism.* Islamism turns the bits and pieces within Islam that deal with politics, economics, and military affairs into a sustained and systematic program. ... Like Marxism-Leninism or fascism, it offers a way to control the state, run society, and remake the human being. It is an Islamic-flavored version of totalitarianism.

Upon reading Pipes' definition of Islam*ism*, it reveals that not all Muslims are Islam*ists.* Nonviolent, moderate Muslims embrace the core beliefs of Islam, but not the fascist ideology of Islam*ism.* They do derive, however, different interpretations from the same writings of the Prophet Muhammad, which puts them at odds with the extremism of Islamists.

Islamism comes from a strict adherence to Islamic law and counts any and all Muslims who don't adhere to the same interpretation of that law as "liberals." When hardline extremists don't see liberal Muslims as true believers, they kill them, justifying their actions as a duty to cleanse and purify Islam of these infidels.

A nuclear Iran

As the Sunni-Shiite war (jihad) continues over Syria-Iraqi lands, the Islamic Republic of Iran (a Shiite state) proceeds to build centrifuges towards a nuclear armament capacity and ability. Obviously the Saudis oppose this because it would become the chess piece that corners the king with a "checkmate." The leverage would then swing to Iran to control the Middle East with its theocratic rule and Sharia law. In light of this threat, the Saudis are allies of the United States—both with vested interests—allowing U.S. military presence as a deterrent to Iran's progress toward becoming a nuclear state.

Ezekiel predicts that Iran will be a major player in this invasion of Israel and casts them as an ally with Russia. This alliance is readily observed today in their proxy support of the wars in Syria and Iraq. Russia and Iran have another thing in common, too—they hate the West. So when they unite to invade the land of Israel in the future with their other Islamic allies—Ezekiel predicts the Saudi's and western nations will be no more than sideline onlookers voicing their opposition to the invasion. Here's what he says:

> **Sheba, Dedan**, the merchants of **Tarshish**, and all their **young lions** will say to you, "Have you come to take plunder? Have you gathered your army to take booty, to carry away silver and gold, to take away livestock and goods, to take great plunder?"
>
> —*Ezekiel 38:13* NKJV

Ezekiel provides a significant clue here about the sideline objections of the United States, western Europe, and the Saudis. Most scholars agree that "Sheba and Dedan" is an ancient reference to the current region of Saudi Arabia. The western onlookers are interpreted from the phrase, "the merchants of Tarshish, and all their young lions."

Tarshish goes back to the ancient maritime merchants who carried their trades between Palestine and Europe, as far north as the British Isles (possibly the western kings of "distant shores" described in Psalm 72:10). Tarshish was the predecessor to the colonial empires that had emerged in Europe and especially Great Britain. So the "young lions" of the "merchants" of Tarshish are believed to represent Great Britain's colonial offspring of the United States, Canada, Australia, New Zealand, South Africa and the commonwealth of fifty-three countries. All of which are *pro*-Israel.

Ancestral scholars believe that David's lineage (of the tribe of Judah) actually traces its way up through Europe, as far north as the British Isles. It is from this belief that the interpretation is derived, and that the "young lions" are the colonial nations of Britain. So with Saudi Arabia, western Europe and the United States as allies, this would certainly fit into Ezekiel's prophecy of them objecting to the invasion from the sidelines, but doing nothing to stop it.

If the United States and western Europe continue to concede to Russia and Iran's ability to come out on top in negotiations over nuclear arms proliferation, it's highly possible that Iran will possess nuclear arms and threaten to use them if we interfere with Iran and Russia's future invasion of Israel. With Russia and Iran both threatening to use nuclear arms—in that time—who then will be able to intervene on Israel's behalf without inciting a global nuclear war? Israel will be on her own unless she acts unilaterally to take out Iran's nuclear power plant through a stealth mission. Israel is certainly equipped, prepared, and highly motivated to do so. "Never Again!" is very much alive in the hearts of her people.

Chapter 7

Setting the Stage

WITH THE RISE OF ISLAMIC terrorism in the last two decades, the world is waking up to the tenets and objectives of Islam. Setting aside all the confusion of the sects, branches, and territorial wars, it's important to learn about the core religious duty of Muslims—whether Shiite or Sunni. That duty is to ultimately gain political control over the collective affairs of *all* societies, and run them in accordance with the principles of Sharia law. *Sharia* means "the path to a watering hole." It is a religious code for living according to the Islamic system of law and the total Islamic way of life.

In the future world of a devout Muslim—whether they live to see it or not—non-Muslims will either convert to Islam or accept the limited role of *dhimmitude*, the established Muslim system used to control non-Muslim populations that have been conquered. One method is through taxation. Any rogue Muslims or non-Muslims who resist the established Islamic state, whether they are Shiite or Sunni, will be captured and executed.

Islam's eschatology

Muslims understand well the seriousness of this undertaking toward world dominance. It isn't a "one-generation" effort; it's a perpetual war for succeeding Muslim generations committed to their part in the struggle.

Islam's goal encompasses their eschatology—to establish a global Islamic state under Sharia law, led by a messianic figure called the *Mahdi* (or "Guided One"). Depending on which branch of Islam is the most dominant at that time, the Mahdi will either be a Sunni caliph[44] or a Shiite imam. Representatives elect Sunni caliphs, whereas a Shiite imam is directly descended from Muhammad, and chosen by Allah.

To the Sunnis, the Mahdi is the successor of Muhammad by election democratically and expected to emerge to rule the world and reestablish righteousness. The Shiite's Mahdi, however, follows the bloodline of Islam's founder, Muhammad, through his cousin and son by marriage, Ali.

Ali was appointed the first imam, succeeded by eleven others in his bloodline. The Twelfth Imam[45] from Ali was Muhammad al-Mahdi who disappeared in A.D. 878 and, according to Shiite tradition, remains hidden to this day until he returns to unite the Muslims and conquer the world.

The Sunni's Mahdi will emerge from a *future* generation, elected to power by the representing body of the Sunni branch. The Shiite's Mahdi—the Twelfth Imam—will return from a *past* generation (A.D. 878), somehow preserved in *occultation* (Arabic: *Ghaybah*—"absence")[46] until that time arrives. The Shiite's Mahdi comes *back*; the Sunni's Mahdi comes *forth*. For obvious reasons, both branches of Islam would like to claim that spot for their messiah.

Despite the differences in how Sunnis and Shiites view the Mahdi, they are in agreement with the core, fundamental doctrines and practices of Islam. The differences that seriously divide them lie in their modes of operation in leadership and piety. Thus the factions.

---

[44] Chief ruler of the Islamic community. Sunnis do not have imams.
[45] The Twelfth Imam who, in succession to the prophet, has the right to the absolute command of the Muslims in all religious and secular affairs.
[46] A term used by the Shiites to refer to the occultation of the hidden imam.

Jihad and the caliphate

The effort to accomplish Islam's end-time goal of world conquest for their Mahdi comes through the vehicle of *jihad*. Jihad is a noun that translates into "struggle," which means *to strive, to exert,* and *to fight.* The word appears in many verses of the Quran.

Muslims adhere to five religious pillars or creeds as their religious duty. An added sixth *duty* is the jihad or "holy war." They have two types of jihad. The "greater" jihad is the internal spiritual struggle one wages against sin to stay on the straight path and strive for Allah's cause. The "lesser" jihad is the traditional holy war launched in the name of Allah against infidels (unbelievers) and the enemies of Allah and Islam. They believe that anyone who dies in a holy war is guaranteed eternal life in heaven (Muhammad 47:5 in the Quran).

It is the height of naiveté for politicians to believe that Islamist extremists can be appeased diplomatically through tolerance and kindness. The very opposite is true. To believe this deception assists the tactics of jihadists to infiltrate and/or invade non-Muslim societies. Diplomacy with Islamist extremists fails at every turn because *jihad* is Islam's holy war—the spiritual struggle and crusade against infidels. Jihad is not only their religious duty but it is also the most effective tool for promulgating their objective for global dominance.

As referred to earlier, two branches make up Islam today: the Sunni and Shiite. Offshoots of tribal and ethnic factions (from liberal to conservative) exist within both sects. As the Islamic minority (10-20 percent), Shiites are aggressive jihadists and the agenda of the Shiite imam in each faction determines the type of jihad used. Sunnis are equally aggressive in jihad, which varies in methods by their agenda and the territories they need to protect.

The most visible and aggressive jihadists in the Middle East are found among the current, various factions of the Taliban (Sunni), al-Qaeda to ISIL to ISIS and now IS (Sunni), the Muslim Brotherhood (Sunni), Hezbollah (Shiite), and Hamas (Sunni).

Jihad takes place through a variety of tactics to advance the ultimate goal of a *caliphate*, which is a global, theocratic, sovereign polity. The relentless, long-term commitment of jihadists in achieving a global caliphate is due to the fact that it may not occur in their lifetime. They sacrifice their lives to fight for the succeeding generations of Muslims who might live to witness it, which is why they can patiently wait for a foreign occupation to grow weary of war and leave.

As for those nations waging long, arduous fights against these extreme factions, the political will of the populous wanes and battle fatigue sets in. The occupying nations lose interest in completing their plans because the financial pressures mount back home and politicians are pressured by their constituents to pull out. Military forces finally leave, and the Islamists take back (or acquire) the ground that was lost.

The many faces of jihad

Muslims enact jihad in a variety of ways. Migrating across borders into strategic cities of different societies to colonize is one way—like they've been doing in France, Great Britain and Germany. They move in, push out the culture and values of the locals, intimidate the local and regional governments toward tolerance of their increasing demands, and then hijack neighborhoods surrounding their mosques. They create "no go zones" in areas of cities where the police and non-Muslims will not enter for fear of assaults. Within these isolated zones from the "host" countries, Sharia law is established. The Muslim demographics increase drastically, as well, through having many children and eventually overtake the resident population.

While they exist initially as the minority of a host country, they'll submit to civil laws and government, but maintain their religious practices with the goal of building a mosque as a stake in the ground. They'll then infiltrate strategic positions in local, regional, and national politics with visitor-friendly, socialist leanings, acquire government positions on local, regional, and national levels, join branches of the military, become military officers, and invade all levels of education to help reshape the minds of children and youth toward religious tolerance and the acceptance of Islam. These *passive-aggressive* forms of jihad are taking place all over the world—even in America.

Here is a recorded sample of this from the *Middle East Quarterly*, written by David Littman in the September 1999 issue. Its title: "Islam Grows Stronger at the United Nations."

> In recent years, representatives of some Muslim states have demanded, and often received, special treatment at the United Nations mostly via the Commission on Human Rights (UNCHR). As a result, nondiplomatic terms such as "blasphemy" and "defamation of Islam" have seeped into the United Nations system, leading to a situation in which non-Muslim governments accept certain rules of conduct in conformity with Islamic law (the *Sharia*) and acquiesce to a self-imposed silence regarding topics touching on Islam.[47]

---

[47] David Littman, "Islam Grows Stronger at the United Nations," *Middle East Quarterly* 6, no. 3, (September 1999): 59-64. David Littman, a historian, was a representative to the United Nations (Geneva) of the Association for World Education, http://www.meforum.org/477/islamism-grows-stronger-at-the-united-nations.

Not a surprise. But there's still much more.

Jihad also advances through the economic tactics of infiltrating the states and nations of weakened economies. Muslims gain the upper hand through marketplace enterprises (backed by oligarchs) and purchase prime real estate to dot the landscape with mosques. Again, passive-aggressive forms of jihad requiring a little more patience and dedication, but every bit as effective.

Devout Muslims are born into jihad and die in jihad because they constantly live in the state of an offensive posture to dominate the world with Islam. There is no negotiating that objective. Only a relentless commitment to perpetual jihad is kept alive until a global caliphate is achieved. That's why jihad doesn't stop at passive-aggressive efforts deemed "peaceful" in the eyes of the naïve.

The most visible and violent forms of jihad are the *aggressive* acts of terrorism by Islamic extremists meant to destabilize regions, demoralize infidels through televised propaganda, and weaken the economies of stronger nations (as the U.S. experienced after 9/11). They disrupt and topple governments through violent protests and revolutions, making every attempt to rid Islamic-controlled states and nations of foreign embassies. Instability is their goal, so they routinely incite powder-keg factions into violent demonstrations against any critics who oppose or mock Muhammad and Allah. And to fuel this fire of terrorism, don't forget that Sunni and Shiite oligarchies[48] fund these jihadist wars with their wealth to serve their regional interests and advance the spread of Islam abroad. Passive-aggressive and aggressive jihads are both sides of the coin. The one opens up doors for the other and vice versa.

---

[48] Oligarchy—a small group of people having control of a country, organization, or institution.

Jihad also advances through media propaganda and cyber attacks. Iran has developed this capability every bit as much as China and Russia to advance their agenda to gain a strategic advantage over the United States and western Europe. On these fronts, Iran, Russia, and China are the greatest threats to the liberties of the free world today. China and Russia specifically have outpaced and taken the lead on many unconventional warfare developments such as space conquest, military buildup, the increasingly technological warfare through cyberspace attacks, ecological warfare, international law warfare, nuclear arms development, financial warfare, and territorial expansion—all of which diminishes and erodes the superpower status of the United States.

How has this happened and why?

I believe this all sets the stage of a prophecy God gave Ezekiel ahead of his time. The diminishing of the influence and strength of the United States and European allies must happen, before this invasion can occur. And in light of all that's been transpiring over the last two decades, there's no question we're moving toward the potential of such a scenario.

One more thing: jihad isn't limited to Muslims and the tactics of Islamists; the many faces of jihad also extend to alliances with ideologues who share the same hatred for Israel, the United States, and the rest of the free world.

Islam and Russia

To understand further how Ezekiel's prophecy about Russia could happen with Muslims in the equation, we must return to the fact that jihad, in all its forms, will never go away until the Mahdi (or Guided One) appears to save the world. For Muslims, jihad is their vehicle, their religious duty, their purpose and cause, driving them to do everything they can to achieve it—even if it means getting in bed with communist Russia. *Deceit* and *alliance* with the enemy is considered a legitimate tactic of jihad, as long as the end game is achieved—whether for short-term purposes or long-range goals.

To occupy and control the land of Israel is at the top of the list for Islamists in the Middle East, though not immediately. Procuring the land of their most hated enemy would be a great step for Islam toward dominating the *entire* Middle East and ousting "Little Satan" (the United States is the "Great Satan").

Muslims have the Mosque of Omar as their stake in the ground in Israel on the historical site of Solomon's temple, plus they also dominate the northeast quarter of the city of Jerusalem, adjacent to the temple site.

For Muslims, Jerusalem is the third holiest city, after Mecca and Medina, but they don't own the city or the land. Therefore, to align with Russia and utilize her socialist agenda will be a necessary, tactical form of jihad to accomplish the conquest of Israel and the annihilation of the Jews. So when Russia pulls the trigger to invade Israel, Islamists will join the crusade to maintain their presence and objective towards furthering their global dominance.

Ironically this plays into Russia's goals as well since it will acquire a strategic corridor through Israel to the Mediterranean Sea, the Gulf of Suez, and the Gulf of Aqaba.

For Russia, as with all socialist/communist regimes, the political, economic, and military *jihads* of Islam serve a useful purpose for advancing communist territories, too. Each will scratch the back of the other; and each will be holding a knife with the other hand—behind their backs, of course.

Given the Bible's predictions of a new world order in the end times, the advancement of Islamism and Communism will inadvertently establish a tactical, global advantage for the Antichrist to come and establish his own new world order on the backs of their achievements. And more ironic than that, the invasion of Israel will provide God with the opportunity to display his glory to the world—that he is sovereign over the nations.[49]

> And so I [God] will show my greatness and my holiness, and I will make myself known in the sight of many nations. Then they will know that I am the Lord.
> —*Ezekiel 38:23*

> All the peoples of the earth are regarded as nothing. He [God] does as he pleases with the powers of heaven and the peoples of the earth. No one can hold back his hand or say to him: "What have you done?"
> —*Daniel 4:35*

---

[49] See Ezekiel 39:1-8, 21

Chapter 8

Divine Intervention and Revival

This is what will happen in that day: When Gog [Russia] attacks the land of Israel, my hot anger will be aroused, declares the Sovereign Lord. In my zeal and fiery wrath I declare that at that time there shall be **a great earthquake** in the land of Israel. The fish of the sea, the birds of the air, the beasts of the field, every creature that moves along the ground, and all the people on the face of the earth will tremble at my presence. The mountains will be overturned, the cliffs will crumble and every wall will fall to the ground. I will summon a sword against Gog [Russia] on all my mountains, declares the Sovereign Lord. Every man's sword will be against his brother. I will execute judgment upon him with plague and bloodshed; I will pour down **torrents of rain, hailstones and burning sulfur on him** and on his troops and on the many nations with him. And so I will show my greatness and my holiness, and I will make myself known in the sight of many nations. Then they will know that I am the Lord.

—Ezekiel 38:18-23

ONCE RUSSIA AMASSES enough strength through the reacquisition of former Soviet territories, and the Islamist powerbrokers of the Middle East come into greater alignment with their objectives, the foundation will be laid for an attack on Israel. According to Ezekiel, when the time is right, God will put the thought into Russia's mind, and in the mind of her Islamic allies, to invade Israel.[50]

With the Saudis as an exception, Sunni and Shiite Islamic-controlled nations of the Middle East will join Russia in this conventional war, including Iran and Turkey. Great care will be taken to preserve the holy site of the Mosque of Omar, as well as the ports and resources of Israel's land. To do so would require restraint from the use of nuclear weapons. Ezekiel writes that God determined this invasion in advance with the intent, not only to inflict his punishment upon the enemies of Israel, but also to display his glory among the nations.[51]

The invasion will halt on the mountains of Israel when God sends a great earthquake, creates confusion within the ranks of the armies (causing them to turn their swords and weapons upon each other), and then pours down rain from heaven, mixed with hailstones and burning sulfur.[52] The soldiers will fall on the mountains, in the open fields, and along the coastlands of the Mediterranean. Their charred bodies will be left as carrion for vultures and animals.[53]

With our media reach today, this event will be witnessed by the entire world, making God's holy name known among the Jews. Nations, too, will acknowledge that God is the Holy One of Israel and no army can conquer him.

A fear of God and revival in Israel

With such a display of God's immense power, equal to the days of Exodus when God dealt with Pharaoh,[54] I believe a momentary fear of God and cautious respect for Israel will blanket the planet, long enough for many hearts to open and

---

[50] Ezekiel 38:1-13
[51] Ezekiel 38:23
[52] Ezekiel 38:18-22
[53] Ezekiel 39:4-5; 17-20
[54] Exodus 7-14

turn to Christ, including those among Arabs and Muslims. The doors to Russia and China will also be opened to the gospel, but only for a short time because the economic and geopolitical struggles that follow will harden hearts once more, and the love of many will grow cold.

As God makes known his glory through this divine intervention, I can imagine that the people of Israel will be shaken to the core in their beliefs, particularly the nationalistic Jews who are mildly religious, but don't know God. I can also see the Holy Spirit poured out upon the nation of Israel, igniting a desire to reexamine the Messianic claims of Jesus of Nazareth. Multitudes will experience revelation in the gospel accounts of Jesus and acknowledge him as their long-awaited Messiah. This is confirmed in Ezekiel's prophecy:

> I will make known my holy name among my people Israel. I will no longer let my holy name be profaned, and the nations will know that I the Lord am the Holy One in Israel. It is coming! It will surely take place, declares the sovereign Lord. This is the day I have spoken of.
>
> —*Ezekiel 39:7*

> I will display my glory among the nations, and all the nations will see the punishment I inflict and the hand I lay upon them. From that day forward the house of Israel will know that I am the Lord their God.
>
> —*Ezekiel 39:21*

> I will show myself holy through them in the sight of many nations. Then they will know that I am the Lord their God. I will gather them to their own land, not leaving any behind. I will no longer hide my face from them, for I will *pour out my Spirit* on the house of Israel, declares the Sovereign Lord.
>
> —*Ezekiel 39:27-29*

An opened highway

In addition to this revival in Israel, it's believed that an opened highway for the gospel will stretch from Egypt to Syria.[55] Syrians, Egyptians and Jews alike will worship *Jeshua*, the true Messiah of Israel.

Perhaps a demand for Bibles with New Testaments will increase among the Jews as many thirst to know more about Jesus of Nazareth. Christians in Israel, who have sown the seed of the gospel for decades, will rejoice as they reap their reward among their own people. The news will spread to Jews around the world, laying the groundwork for the two witnesses who will preach the gospel to the remnant of Jews when the Antichrist comes into full power.[56]

What an amazing time to look forward to. But this is only the beginning of the birth pains. More will come according to Jesus when he said:

> You will hear of wars and rumors of wars, but see to it that you are not alarmed. Such things must happen, but the end is still to come. Nation will rise against nation, and kingdom against kingdom. There will be famines and earthquakes in various places. All these are the beginning of birth pains.
>
> *—Matthew 24:6-8*

---

[55] Isaiah 11:16; 19:23
[56] Revelation 11

Chapter 9

Ten Kingdom Powers

> The fourth beast is a fourth kingdom [the Roman Empire] that will appear on earth. It will be different from all the other kingdoms and will devour the whole earth, trampling it down and crushing it. The ten horns are **ten kings** who will come from this kingdom.
>
> *—Daniel 7:23-24*

> The ten horns you saw are **ten kings** who have not yet received a kingdom, but who for one hour will receive authority as kings along with the beast [the Antichrist]. They have one purpose and will give their power and authority to the beast.
>
> *—Revelation 17:12-14*

THE BOOKS OF DANIEL and Revelation are companion books on end times. Both address the rise of the same ten kingdom powers predicted to emerge—in the last days—from its predecessor, the former Roman Empire. Though we can only speculate as to *how* they come into power, the aftermath of God's punishment upon Russia and its allies, could possibly be the point in time where this could happen.

Ezekiel says that God will send a great earthquake and torrents of rain, hailstones, and burning sulfur on Russia, on her troops, and on the many nations backing Russia.[57] Think about that for a moment. Think of the setbacks and the great

---

[57] Ezekiel 38:22

economic turmoil and chaos that will create. The world will not have just seen a good show and then go on with business as usual. These oil-producing countries will experience a huge loss of manpower. Oil fields will sit idle and shut down production. With the armies of Islamic countries and Russia decimated, political and violent uprisings will occur as rogue terrorists, despots, caliphs, and imams with the remnants of their factions, all fight to survive and regain control over weakened territories.

Western Europe, once serviced by Russia's oil and natural resources, will suffer serious setbacks from the loss of essential supplies and provisions. The world's stock market will reel and tumble. The propped up economies of every nation will implode under the weight and domino effect of this war. To survive the fallout, I can see the potential for nations moving toward interdependence within their own hemispheres. Travel by sea and air will struggle under the diminishing supply of oil and its skyrocketing prices.

Yes, this very well could be the time where a shift of power lays the groundwork for the ten kings spoken of by Daniel and John.[58] If that is the case, most likely (and logistically) on each hemisphere, a geopolitical shift will evolve toward regional and national treaties. These ten kingdoms will be equal in power; each led by a king who will rule over the weaker nations aligning themselves with the nearest and strongest economic power on their continent. Also, each king will govern states of third-world countries under their protection, requiring taxation and a pooling of resources from those lesser nations.

Given the tenuous economic nature of the times, the potential exists, also, for the ten kingdoms to make an egalitarian push toward financial and military strength while

---

58 Daniel 7:24; Revelation 13:1; 17:12

calling for equal distribution and peace. The much talked about world currency might become a reality during this stage, in order to balance the ebb and flow of world trade.

The Shiite Islamist movements in the Middle East will suffer a great setback in their caliphate goals, due to God's fiery decimation of their armies, weapons of mass destruction, and religious strongholds. But because the Sunnis of Saudi Arabia and the Emirates (UAE)[59] will have stood on the sidelines of the invasion[60] they could emerge into stronger positions of influence with the world's accelerating pace toward a one-world order.

Socialist governments, ruled by monarchs or totalitarian administrations will probably feign a kinder, gentler façade toward world peace, calling upon heads of states with nuclear arms to enter into a global treaty of nuclear disarmament, eliminating the destabilizing threat of future "dominant" superpowers. This would require a downsizing of conventional military weapons as well, perhaps by distributing them equally across the continents. If such a step toward deployment of equalized power occurs, it will set the stage for a one-world military under the Antichrist and his backing of the ten kings.

The role of socialism in the end times

Socialism will rise as the prominent ideology among the emerging generation of youth—seduced and drugged by the opiate of entitlement through government assistance. The inevitable and perpetual breakdown of such socialist programs will fuel more unrest in a world growing weary of politicians and broken promises.

---

[59] United Arab Emirates—a country located in the southeast end of the Arabian Peninsula. It borders Oman to the east and Saudi Arabia to the south. It also shares the Persian Gulf sea borders of Qatar and Iran.
[60] Ezekiel 38:13—Sheba and Dedan (Saudi Arabia).

The delusion and blindness to the lies of "socialism" will never be considered the culprit. Governments will be blamed for the mess, and riots will break out in the streets. Civil wars and factions will surge against the sovereign, nationalized governments of the ten kingdom equal-powers. This could trigger such a crisis of instability that a necessary alliance between the ten kings is generated to tamp down on the unrest. Marshall law could easily be imposed to unite the armed forces between the nations into a one-world armament to quell all sedition and sustain peace. Today's movies entertain us with similar plots depicting scenarios that aren't too far off the mark from what might happen down the road.

A world leader

As the economy worsens and food supplies diminish, the desperate conditions of a broken, dysfunctional world will demand the coronation of a world leader to preside over the ten-kingdom alliance, fix the economic mess, and restore peace to the planet. For Jews and Christians, such a person would be the Messiah. For Muslims, it begins with the return of Isa, our Jesus, who is considered a prophet in the Quran. They believe Jesus will assist the Mahdi when he arrives on the world stage. The Antichrist could use this belief to deceive Muslims by stating he's their Isa who will join the cause of their Mahdi to conquer and reestablish peace on the Earth. He could also deceive the Jews and Christians into believing that he's their long-awaited Messiah, a warning Paul gave Christians in Thessalonica about the end times, when he wrote:

> Don't let anyone deceive you in any way, for that day will not come until the rebellion occurs and the man of lawlessness [Antichrist] is revealed, the man doomed to destruction. He will oppose and will exalt himself over

everything that is called God or is worshiped, so that he sets himself up in God's temple, proclaiming himself to be God.[61]

The coming of the lawless one will be in accordance with the work of Satan displayed in all kinds of counterfeit miracles, signs and wonders, and in every sort of evil that deceives those who are perishing. They perish because they refused to love the truth and so be saved. For this reason God sends them a powerful delusion so that they will believe the lie and so that all will be condemned who have not believed the truth but have delighted in wickedness.

—2 Thessalonians 2:9-12

In the aftermath of the invasion of Israel, the world will fast track toward uniting politically, economically, and globally—out of necessity. It could be the tipping point toward a desperate, destabilized world, ripe for the scarlet-colored beast and his queen—the rising, harlot church.

---

[61] 2 Thessalonians 2:3-4

Chapter 10

The Harlot and the Beast

Then the angel carried me away in the Spirit into a desert. There I saw a woman sitting on a scarlet beast that was covered with blasphemous names and had seven heads and ten horns.

—Revelation 17:3-4

TO REIN IN the threat of anarchy and a devastated global economy, a movement could emerge among world religious leaders. Not just Catholic priests, not just Protestant ministers, not just Muslim imams, clerics, and caliphs, and not just Jewish rabbis, but *all* world religious leaders will step in to do something about the fallout. They will not sit idly by and allow monarchs, politicians, and government officials to run the show solo and destroy everyone and everything.

Throughout human history, all forms of government have had the influence of religion behind them and in them— in some way, shape or form. All governments and politicians take religion into account when running for office or running the office they're appointed to. Whether of God, or the gods of man, you can never separate religion and government from working hand in hand to either control or govern people.

Because man was made in the image of God, we were designed with a spiritual bent and desire to connect with our Creator. Satan has used that innate drive to distract us and offer us an alternative from the true God toward *his* gods and false religions. And when Satan couldn't sway God's people, he would simply join the club and corrupt the leaders. History reveals and confirms this. No religious or spiritual leader—whether of pagan origin, Hebrew origin, or Christian origin—has been immune to the Devil's schemes to use religion to seduce and control the world he relentlessly continues to control. The *spirit* of antichrist has been alive and well in this way and is the *spirit* behind all we see happening on the world stage today. Every detail, every scheme we're unaware of, every corrupt act going on in governments all over the world, including the United States, is taking us toward the embodiment of that *spirit*—who will be the Antichrist.

It's appropriate to believe, therefore, that at such a time of future upheaval as this, that religious leaders of the world—of all faiths—will flex their influence to replace the failed political systems with a more theocratic approach. I wouldn't be surprised, too, if they camouflaged their agenda through the guise of social justice.

The solidarity of these religious leaders will probably begin with a loose ecumenical movement to back a candidate they'll endorse and present to the world. Their campaign could start out focusing on the most prominent world leaders with socialist leanings. This won't be seen by the world as a "religious" undertaking, but rather a means of survival through a future world leader who can promise and create entitlement through equal distribution—i.e., social justice. And since socialism will have infiltrated most world religions by this time, including the churches of Christendom,[62] the idea will be easily embraced in such desperate times.

---

[62] Christianity will not embrace this campaign, Christendom will. Christendom is a politically oriented religion in the name of "church." Christianity is kingdom-oriented living in the "name" of Jesus for the "love" of Jesus.

A false messiah

Mesmerized by their candidate—the most charismatic, intelligent, religious and political figure ever to embody one man—the ten kings, and all world religions, could lay aside their differences and position him to lead the world. Not only will world religions succumb to the seductive powers of his deception, but one-third of the spiritual leaders and saints in the church will fall under the spell of his claim as the messiah of the Jews, and the messiah of the Christians. Even the Muslims could possibly be persuaded to see the Antichrist as their Isa of the Quran who is predicted to come and assist the Mahdi (the Guided One).

This false messiah will be no ordinary man, and I'm of the opinion that he won't be a politician, or an elected official. I believe he'll come upon the world stage from behind the scenes as the Devil incarnate. Historically, no other man—who has deceived the masses—will come close to the power and capability of this man. Only the most discerning saints of the Lord Most High will be able see him for who he is. No carnal, earthbound leader or body of leaders will be able to match wits with him. And no earthly figure will be able to work the false *signs* and *wonders* he'll have in his arsenal to deceive the world.[63] Satan himself will fully possess the spirit, soul and body of this powerful figure.

Adding to the Antichrist's deceptive prowess is another interesting element to seal the deal of his ability to deceive all religions and world leaders. The Bible says that God will assist in this process by sending a strong delusion among all who reject the truth[64] so that they will believe the Antichrist's claim of "messianic" status. No matter how fanatic and devout other religions are about their faith, including

---

[63] 2 Thessalonians 2:9
[64] 2 Thessalonians 2:9-12

Muslims, they'll not be able to escape the delusion apart from a genuine conversion to Christ.

I think it's highly probable that the Antichrist might come from Jewish descent, which would add to his leverage to deceive Muslims who believe in a Jewish Isa, and to deceive the Jews and nominal Christians who believe in a Jewish Messiah. Yet all of them will be very blind to the fact that the Antichrist is a *false* messiah.

A great falling away

Preceding the Antichrist's inauguration into world power, the Bible says that a great *falling away* of Christians will occur among those who have been nominal, cold or lukewarm in their faith.[65] Ill equipped in their knowledge of Scripture, they'll be easy targets to deceive, along with the rest of the world. The courageous, discerning and bold saints, who refuse to embrace the claims of the Antichrist, will be shunned, persecuted, and outlawed from practicing their faith, both publically and privately.

Today, we're witnessing such times of persecution against Christians more than ever. According to the organization, *Open Doors* (a ministry that serves and provides a global watch list of persecuted Christians), these statistics are listed:

- Each month **322** Christians are killed for their faith.
- Each month **214** Christian churches and properties are destroyed.
- Each month **772** forms of violence are committed against Christians (such as beatings, abductions, rapes, arrests and forced marriages).[66]

---

[65] 2 Thessalonians 2:3
[66] https://www.opendoorsusa.org/christian-persecution/

Under the authoritarian rule of the Antichrist, such statistics of persecution will expand throughout the rest of the world—exponentially. Because of this, many saints will succumb to state and social pressure to denounce Jesus Christ, and vow allegiance to the Antichrist.

Antichrist—person or spirit?

To address the teaching by some that the term "antichrist" is merely a force or a movement, the Bible is clear that he is a man.[67] The *spirit* of antichrist is already at work in the world,[68] parallel to the kingdom of darkness, which are the principalities and powers of the air and the spiritual forces of evil in the heavenly realms, all operating behind the atrocities already at play in this world.[69] But people will not line up to unite behind an "unseen" force. They want something more tangible.

People follow flesh and blood leaders who are the embodiment of an ideological movement. It is the *persona* of the Antichrist, including his unparalleled wisdom and strength as a leader, which will be his greatest strength. And when you top that off with the supernatural ability he'll possess to display lying signs and wonders—what unregenerate person can withstand his power?[70]

The False Prophet

Emerging alongside the Antichrist will be a False Prophet.[71] For reasons I'll address later in this book, I can see him acting as the Antichrist's prime minister over the ten kings of the emerging ten-kingdom empire. Like Joseph was to Pharaoh, the False Prophet will govern commerce and

---

[67] 2 Thessalonians 2:3
[68] 1 John 4:3
[69] Ephesians 6:12
[70] 2 Thessalonians 2:9
[71] Revelation 13:11

religion, and implement new laws and times—all set by the Antichrist.[72]

These two men will emerge out of the backrooms of religion, politics and socioeconomic structures—groomed and prepared for their debut as the solution to the world's problems. They'll advance their objectives through a one-world religion, one-world currency, one-world armament, and a one-world government, all laid at their feet by the alliance of ten-kingdom rulers in bed with the adulterous religious leaders of the world's harlot church. Her name is *Babylon.*

> One of the seven angels who had the seven bowls came and said to me, "Come, I will show you the punishment of **the great prostitute** [or harlot], who sits on many waters. With her the kings of the earth committed adultery and the inhabitants of the earth were intoxicated with the wine of her adulteries."
>
> *—Revelation 17:1-2*

> The woman was dressed in purple and scarlet, and was glittering with gold, precious stones and pearls. She held a golden cup in her hand, filled with abominable things and the filth of her adulteries. This title was written on her forehead:
>
> MYSTERY
>
> BABYLON THE GREAT
>
> THE MOTHER OF PROSTITUTES
>
> AND OF THE ABOMINATIONS OF THE EARTH.
>
> *—Revelation 17:4-5*

---

[72] Daniel 7:25

Chapter 11

The Sign of the Son of Man

> I watched as he opened the sixth seal. There was a great earthquake. The sun turned black like sackcloth made of goat hair, the whole moon turned blood red, and the stars in the sky fell to earth, as late figs drop from a fig tree when shaken by a strong wind.
>
> *—Revelation 6:12-14*

AS ALL OF THIS unfolds, after the invasion of Israel and before the Antichrist appears, I believe a *sign* will occur in the heavenlies and accelerate the political shift that's been happening toward a new world order.

Revelation 6 describes a sixth seal being opened on a seven-sealed document in the heavenlies.[73] The first five seals have already been opened and are not as obvious to the world—during their time—as this sixth one will be, yet to come. This seal will release the events of a monstrous global earthquake, followed by the sun turning dark, the moon turning blood red, and a deluge of meteorites raining down through Earth's atmosphere on all continents.[74]

I believe these cataclysmic signs will create urgency among the nations to award the ten-kingdom alliance with full authority toward establishing a one-world government. This will be the first of many "supernatural" events God will send, all coming like a falling row of dominoes—very big

---

[73] Revelation 6:12-13
[74] Revelation 6:12-13

dominoes. The succession of events after this one will shock the world, and usher in a great harvest of souls who will turn to God for deliverance.

These newly converted souls will be warned to resist the strong attraction and lure of the harlot church, which will exploit their zeal and ignorance by drawing them in with promises hard to refuse. Unbeknownst to them, the Antichrist will use this false church as an instrument for the mass *genocide* of unwavering Jews and Christians who reject his rule and claim to godhood. The apostle John describes the vision he witnessed of her in this way:

> I saw that **the woman** was drunk with the blood of the saints, the blood of those who bore testimony to Jesus.
>
> —*Revelation 17:6*

> In **her** was found the blood of prophets and of the saints and of all who had been killed on the earth.
>
> —*Revelation 18:24*

If you're there when it happens

Let's imagine for a moment, that you're experiencing that day of the great earthquake and the celestial signs that follow. Your entire house begins to shake. Pictures, knickknacks, and dishes rattle and fall off shelves and out of cupboards. Lamps tip over and shatter to the floor at the same time you're thrown from the chair. The floorboards screech where the nails are pulling away, groaning, rolling and shaking, making it impossible to steady yourself and regain equilibrium as you try to stand. The plaster and sheetrock in the walls and ceiling snap and pop, dropping dust and debris all around you.

A glance out your window reveals trees and telephone poles swinging back and forth like a metronome on a piano.

Your heart is pounding hard and you dare not move, because the rumblings of subsequent tremors persist, intermittently.

Suddenly, the sky darkens quickly into the blackness of night, like someone had thrown a blanket over the sun. You look outside through the window nearest you where the sun had shined minutes ago, but is now shrouded in a ghostly veil, like sackcloth.

From the corner of your eye, you catch a glimpse of a red hue of light coming through the hallway from the kitchen. The shaking has diminished enough for you to brave walking through the glass and debris on the floor. You approach the kitchen cautiously, avoiding the broken sheetrock with nails poking out, lying on the floor. A mild tremor rattles the house once more as you enter the kitchen. The entire room is bathed in an eerie, blood-washed stream of light coming through the window above the sink. A bright red orb in the black sky peeks just above the window's ledge—it's a blood moon, not a lunar eclipse—a supernatural *sign* of the Son of Man. You have a "knowing" in your spirit about this, but you can't process it, yet. Your pounding heart is bothering you.

Before you're able to reset your brain to deal with this unreality of darkness in the middle of the day—*and* this blood-red moon—suddenly a meteor streaks by the window in the sky, then another, and another until the whole sky is lit up with a meteorite shower. They're sizzling by, close by, crashing into buildings and homes around you. You're wondering when you're next, so you maneuver around the debris on the floor to get to the stairs to the basement where you can find cover.

While you were taking in the unprecedented display of signs and wonders, you were too distracted to notice the screams and cries filling the street in the neighborhood. Now in the basement, groping around in the dark, you hear them—clearly. The cries grow louder and more intense as the meteor shower diminishes and the aftershocks from the quake finally cease. You decide it's safe, so you push open the double doors from the basement to the world outside. The sky is still dark, the moon still red, but it casts enough light for a visual of your surroundings.

Houses on both sides of the street are flattened here and there. Some are still left half standing. Your neighbors are crawling out from under their flattened homes. Others are walking out of theirs. Cries for help are everywhere. The dim glow of the blood-red moon provides just enough light for everyone to inspect the damage to the street and homes. Chaos, panic, and death now confront you and them at every angle. Collapsed homes, cars upended in sinkholes, others swallowed up altogether. Where do you start?

This is what that day will bring. What *your* neighborhood will look like. And so will the next neighborhood, and the next—the next town and city, too, and the ones next to them. It'll happen all over Earth as the harbinger of impending doom and destruction.

Imagine what this will do to the electrical grid, as transmission lines fall, and power stations fail from broken dams and damaged nuclear reactors. Imagine a world without energy for computers, the Internet, or cell phones.

How will we live without radio, television, movies, the NFL, the MLB, the NBA, the PGA, the NHL, WCW, the Olympics, championship boxing, and NASCAR?

How will we entertain ourselves without Facebook, Twitter, email, Instagram, selfies, the World Wide Web, Xbox, PlayStation, news channels, and every other form of entertainment that relies on "electricity?"

We are a generation of techno junkies. How will we handle that? How will we charge up our hybrid cars? This is funny, but yet it's not, if we really go through this. We will be forced to have to find God's grace to live the way our ancestors used to—before technology.

The sign, the seal, and the secret weapon

The sixth seal in the sixth chapter of Revelation is the *sign* of the Son of Man, *symbolized* in the moon. As the moon reflects the light of the sun, so the Son reflects the radiance of his Father's glory.[75] As meteorites have marred the face of the moon (leaving craters), so the face of the Son of Man was marred and disfigured by the soldiers who carried out his execution.[76] As the face of the moon will turn to blood on that day, so the Son of Man had a blood-soaked face from the soldiers' beatings and the crown of thorns that pierced his brow. This is why this event is so symbolic. It will remind the world that the crucified King is about to return in great power and glory. The sacrificed Lamb of God, who died for a world that didn't know him. It'll be a wake-up call—an awakening that will eclipse the earlier revival that occurred after Israel's miraculous deliverance from the invasion.

Once this seal is opened, the seventh seal follows. And within the seventh seal are seven trumpets of judgments to come. When the seventh seal is opened, complete silence in heaven will occur for a half-hour.[77] After the silence, seven angels, who stand before God, will each receive a trumpet.[78] But before the first trumpet sounds, God will unveil his *secret* weapon—the glorious, triumphant church he's about to unleash on the Earth. She will bring good news to the lost, provide hope for the helpless, healing for the sick, food for the hungry, and help during the first wave of God's wrath upon planet Earth.

I believe that half-hour of silence in Revelation 8:1 represents the heavenly host standing in awe of the gloriously adorned bride of Christ who has made herself

---

[75] Hebrews 1:3
[76] Isaiah 52:13-14; Matthew 27:27-30
[77] Revelation 8:1
[78] Revelation 8:2

ready for her Bridegroom at the absolute perfect timing for her arrival—just before the seven trumpets sound.

> A great and wondrous sign appeared in heaven: **a woman** clothed with the **sun**, with the **moon** under her feet and a crown of twelve **stars** on her head.

—Revelation 12:1

Chapter 12

Four Winds and the 144,000

After this I saw four angels standing at the four corners of the earth, holding back the **four winds** of the earth to prevent any wind from blowing on the land or on the sea or on any tree. Then I saw another angel coming up from the east, having the seal of the living God. He called out in a loud voice to the four angels who had been given power to harm the land and the sea: "Do not harm the land or the sea or the trees until we put a seal on the foreheads of the servants of our God." Then I heard the number of those who were sealed: **144,000** from all the tribes of Israel.

—Revelation 7:1-4

THE SUN-CLOAKED darkness from the releasing of the sixth seal will soon pass and the light of day restored. The moon, also, will return to normal. The event of the *sign* of the Son of Man will leave its mark in the minds of Earth's inhabitants. The days before Christ's return are now short, and a shaken, confused and disparaged world will embark on a global effort to recover.

Four winds

In Revelation chapter 7, another global phenomenon takes place. If taken literally, it suggests that four angels restrain the meteorological patterns of the winds, preventing any wind from blowing across land, sea, or trees.[79] Some believe this could be a restraint of spiritual forces, and I would prefer to believe that, rather than the alternative when you consider the outcome of no wind across our planet. Is that even possible scientifically? Not likely, but with God, nothing is impossible; and if he means for this passage to be a literal event, then it will happen.

So let's entertain the thought of "literal" and imagine a world without wind. Wind causes the temperature to change, the waves to roll, currents to move through the ocean, rain clouds to move across land and sea, trees and plants to cross-pollinate, and the air to remain fresh and clear of pollutants. An extensive study of climatology and the subject of wind will astonish you as to just how important currents of air are to animals, people, crops, and life itself. Without wind, life will cease to exist in short order. So I hope it's *not* literal, because there are more than enough "literal" events to come in Revelation for the world to endure.

What's exciting to me, however, is what follows. Another angel says to the four angels not to harm the land, sea, or trees until a *seal* is placed on the foreheads of 144,000 servants.[80] This has great meaning! They're obviously selected for some divine purpose.

The 144,000

These servants in Revelation 7 are chosen from the twelve tribes of Israel[81] and receive a seal on their foreheads to protect them from the wind and/or trumpets that will harm the land, sea, and trees. Who these people will be has been a mystery to scholars for centuries. Some believe it's a

---

[79] Revelation 7:1
[80] Revelation 7:2-3
[81] Revelation 7:5-8—Judah, Reuben, Gad, Asher, Naphtali, Manasseh, Simeon, Levi, Issachar, Zebulun, Joseph, and Benjamin. *Note:* Ephraim and Dan are not included in this list.

symbolic number of God's people throughout history. Others believe that they're recent Jewish converts, or evangelists. Jehovah's Witnesses believe the 144,000 people are from their religion, i.e., men and women resurrected to heaven for eternity. Jehovah's Witnesses claim their religion and their Bible are the *only* legitimate expressions of God.

Let's observe the details of the verses in Revelation 7:2-3. First, the gender of these servants isn't mentioned; it reveals only an association with twelve different tribes of Israel listed in the Old Testament. Judah is the only tribe of Israel accounted for today, as the other tribes were lost and scattered throughout Europe. This happened when the lost tribes were captured and exiled by Assyria in the days of Hoshea, the last king of Israel.[82] So, Jews today are descended only from the tribe of Judah (with Benjamin and Levi mixed in because they didn't reject the house of David and join the ten northern tribes).

Undoubtedly, God knows the lost tribes of Israel. He can trace their DNA back through generations to the countries they migrated to. For example, Orthodox Jewish author, researcher and scholar, Yair Davidiy, believes that the lost tribe of Dan migrated north and settled in the lands of Denmark (the Danes), Ireland, and Wales.[83]

In light of this fact, I find it difficult to embrace that all 144,000 mentioned are Jewish evangelists when only 12,000 of them are listed as being from the tribe of Judah.[84] Jews today are descendants of Judah, not the other eleven tribes, mentioned.[85] The apostle James addresses all the tribes in the introduction of his letter:

---

[82] 2 Kings 17:1-23
[83] Yair Davidiy, *The Tribes: The Israelite Origins of Western People*, 4th ed. (Jerusalem: Russell-Davis Publishers, 2011), 179-212.
[84] Revelation 7:5
[85] Revelation 7:4-8

> To the **twelve tribes** scattered among the nations: Greetings.[86]

If eleven of the tribes were lost at the time of his writing, why didn't James just address the Jews? Because James was addressing the *heritage* of the descendants of the twelve tribes scattered across the nations. They would receive the gospel then, just as James' message does for us, wherever we are in the world.

Depending on our ethnic roots, you and I may possess the DNA of one of these lost tribes, even the DNA of the Jews who were scattered throughout Europe, Africa, and Asia after the dispersion in A.D. 70-73. Today, there is even a DNA test that allegedly determines if you're a Hebrew descendent. So I believe that these individuals in these twelve tribes of 12,000 not only possess the natural bloodline of the tribes of Israel mentioned here, but they're also from the spiritual DNA of the Holy Spirit as saints selected out of the church.

So who might these servants be and what is their purpose? Why call them out specifically to be sealed at this time before the Antichrist is revealed and placed in power?

These questions will be addressed later, but suffice it to say for now that they're sealed and protected from incurring any harm from the ensuing events of the judgments ahead, and the persecution of an angry, hateful, frightened world.

The multitudes in heaven

In Revelation 7, following the description of the twelve tribes of Israel, we witness a scene in heaven of an innumerable host of martyrs from every nation, tribe, people and language. It shows them standing in white robes before the throne of God and the Lamb (Jesus), and all are carrying palm branches, shouting with one voice:

---

[86] James 1:1

> Salvation belongs to our God, who sits on the throne, and to the Lamb.[87]

These martyrs will come out of the time of great persecution under the oppressive rule of the Antichrist and the murderous, bloodthirsty harlot church.[88] Here they're shown to receive a promise of eternal bliss in the company of the Lamb of God. Never again will they hunger or thirst, or experience the scorching heat of the sun. He will wipe every tear from their eyes, and they will have the incredible honor of serving God day and night in his temple.[89]

> Then one of the elders asked me, "These in white robes—who are they, and where did they come from?"
>
> I answered, "Sir, you know."
>
> And he said, "These are they who have come out of the great tribulation; they have washed their robes and made them white in the blood of the Lamb."
>
> **—Revelation 7:13-14**

---

[87] Revelation 7:10
[88] Revelation 17:6
[89] Revelation 7:9-17

Chapter 13

Enter the Bride

Christ loved the church and gave himself up for her to make her holy, cleansing her by the washing with water through the word, and to present her to himself as a radiant church, without stain or wrinkle or any other blemish, but holy and blameless.

—Ephesians 5:25-27

Let us rejoice and be glad and give him glory! For the wedding of the Lamb has come, and his bride has made herself ready.

—Revelation 19:7

AFTER THE INSERTION of the parenthetical events in Revelation 7, John picks back up in chapter 8:1-5 with the opening of the seventh seal containing seven angels with seven trumpets. Before the first trumpet is blown, a half-hour of silence occurs, followed by an angel holding a golden censer at the golden altar before God's throne.

After the angel is given incense to offer up with the prayers of the saints, he takes the censer and fills it with fire from the golden altar. Then he hurls the censer to the Earth where peals of thunder and flashes of lightning rumble in tandem with another earthquake.[90] The verses in this passage contain so much hidden truth; we'll need to address

---

[90] Revelation 8:1-5

what's behind them to unpack the mystery of the bride of Christ.

The high priest and the Day of Atonement[91]

To start with the symbolic significance of this imagery, we must go back to the Old Testament where Israel observes an annual event called the "Day of Atonement" (Yom Kippur). On this day, and only on this day, the high priest, totally dressed in white garments, would go behind the veil of the Most Holy Place in the Tabernacle of Moses.[92]

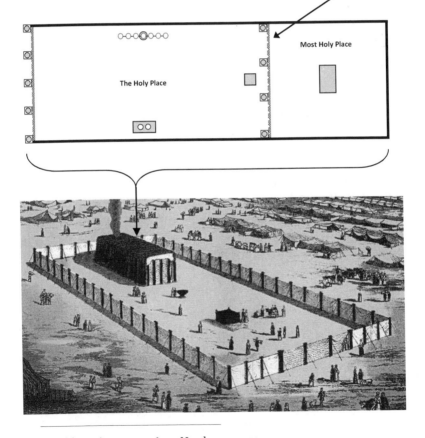

---

[91] Leviticus 16:2-34; 23:26-32; Numbers 29:7-11
[92] Exodus 26:1-37; 36:8-38

With him he carried a golden censer of burning coals and two handfuls of incense to throw on the coals so that the room would be filled with a cloud of smoke. This shielded the high priest from God's blinding light that emanated from beneath the shadowing wings of two cherubim facing the cover of the Ark. This cover, or lid, was called the *mercy seat.*[93]

With one hand the high priest swung the censer to fill the room with incense. With the other, he took the blood from the sacrificed bull and sprinkled it on the front of the atonement cover (mercy seat) beneath the cherubim. He then sprinkled the blood seven times before the cover. By this act—done once for himself, then again for the people— his sins and Israel's sins were all atoned for. Only by blood could the high priest survive the radiant presence of God in the Most Holy Place. Without the blood of the bull, he would have died before the ark.

During the atonement ceremony, all of the Israelites waited outside in front of their tents in silence, anxiously hoping that God would pardon the high priest and themselves for their sins of the past year. As God accepted

---

[93] Exodus 25:10-20; 37:1-9

the offering—in that brief moment—the priest and all of Israel stood blameless, holy, and pure before God. Their sins were covered over, and they began their new year as redeemed people.

Later in this chapter, we will examine the language of this event and its symbolic application to the most exciting and important scene of the last days: the unleashing of the bride of Christ.

Here comes the bride

The apostle Paul asserts in his letter to the Ephesian church that a *profound mystery* is coming, symbolized in the marriage between a man and a woman. This mystery will be enacted on the day when Christ presents to himself a holy, radiant bride without stain or blemish.[94] This is a bride who is *pure*—inside and out—tainted no more by the effects of sin or a sin nature. These words used to describe the bride are similar to the words used by Peter to describe the nature of Jesus: *a lamb without blemish or defect.*[95] Paul, in his (alleged) letter to the Hebrews, uses similar words for Jesus as he did for the bride in Ephesians:

> Such a high priest [Jesus] meets our needs—one who is holy, blameless, pure, set apart from sinners.[96]

Just as God presented Eve to Adam as a commensurate bride *without* sin, so Christ—the last Adam[97]—will present to himself a bride, commensurate to himself, *without* sin; not *after* he returns, but *before* the Antichrist is revealed. John, in the vision he received in Revelation, elaborates on this cameo of a perfect, sinless bride. He describes the portrait of

---

94 Ephesians 5:25-27; 32
95 1 Peter 1:19
96 Hebrews 7:26
97 1 Corinthians 15:45

a glorious woman who is clothed with the *sun*, the *moon* under her feet, and a crown of twelve *stars* on her head.[98] So what does this celestial vision symbolize?

The celestial adornment

In the beginning, God created the sun, moon, and stars to serve as *signs* to mark the seasons, days and years.[99] They will also serve as signs in the last day's events of the sixth seal,[100] and as symbolic *signs* in relation to the triune nature of God. The sun, moon, and stars each represent one of the members of the Godhead bodily. Here's how it works.

The **sun** symbolizes God the Father. He is the Father of lights, sustainer of all life on Earth, and doesn't change like shifting shadows.[101]

The **moon** is a reflection of the sun's radiance in the night sky, and symbolizes Jesus, who came as the true light that shines in the darkness[102] and is the exact reflection and representation of the Father's being.[103]

The **stars** symbolize the Holy Spirit who lives in all who are born again through faith in Jesus Christ and his atoning work on the cross. God's redeemed sons and daughters are called children of light,[104] who shine as bright stars in a dark, lost world.[105] The light doesn't come from them, but from the Holy Spirit who dwells in them.

---

[98] Revelation 12:1; *compare with* Song of Songs 6:10
[99] Genesis 1:14-19
[100] Matthew 24:29; Mark 13:25; Luke 21:25; Revelation 6:12-13
[101] James 1:17
[102] John 1:3-9
[103] Hebrews 1:3
[104] Ephesians 5:8
[105] Daniel 12:3; Philippians 2:15; Hebrews 11:12

Interesting how Paul prayed for the saints at Ephesus that they would grasp the width, length, height and depth of Christ's love, and also personally experience this love that surpasses all knowledge.[106] It is a knowledge that promises God's children may be filled to the "full measure" of *all* the fullness of God in the same way Jesus—in his earthly body—was filled with *all* the *fullness* of the Godhead.[107]

Though we haven't yet attained the measure of that fullness, Jesus is the prototype of God's ultimate plan for the church to possess such a measure in the last days.

Jesus, the prototype, came as the first fruit—a glorious, radiant, *sinless* Bridegroom. In the last days, he will unleash a glorious, radiant, sinless bride upon the world. A bride who is commensurate to his own power and authority, confirming God's Word she'll preach with *signs* and *wonders*.

This picture of a woman clothed with the **sun**, the **moon** under her feet, and a garland of twelve **stars** on her head is a symbol of the church in the last days, filled with *all* the *fullness* of the Godhead bodily.

A church with limited power

Why a bride commensurate to the fullness of the measure of the stature of Christ?[108] Why a bride without sin? Well, might I ask, "Why not?" How else could the bride of Christ carry—responsibly—the *unbridled* power of the Holy Spirit?

The reason the Father gave Jesus the Spirit *without limits*[109] is because his Son—unlike us—was *without sin*. In Christ there was *no* sin nature, and in keeping with Old

---

[106] Ephesians 3:16-19
[107] Ephesians 4:12-13; Colossians 2:9-10
[108] Ephesians 4:13
[109] John 3:34—For since He Whom God has sent speaks the words of God [proclaims God's own message], God does not give Him His Spirit sparingly or by measure, but boundless is the gift God makes of His Spirit! (Amplified Bible)

Testament requirements for the high priest, he can only marry a *pure virgin* from among his own people. Yes, Christ, our High Priest must marry a *pure virgin* (spiritually),[110] so as to not be unequally yoked to a bride with defects.[111]

As mentioned earlier, Adam was created *without* a sin nature. The sinful nature entered his body through disobedience to God and, by his disobedience, brought sin into the world and death to all.[112] Jesus, however, as God in human flesh, came into the world *without* sin. Unlike Adam, Jesus obeyed the Father in everything, never sinned once, and brought life into the world by the shedding of his own blood. The sinless Son of Man was completely led by the Holy Spirit and walked in unlimited power because he was *without* sin.

In his perfect, sinless state, Jesus did nothing to serve himself, but did everything for his Father's glory and eternal purposes. Can the same be said of God's people today? We who call ourselves the church, Christ's bride?

It isn't difficult to recognize that the church is filled with carnal saints, selfish ambitions, worldly standards, political correctness, disunity, quarrels over trivial matters, and *selective* acts of obedience to God. Nothing has changed since the early church. Paul's letters to the Corinthian church addressed sin, scandals, sexual immorality, false teachings, immature behavior, greed, covetousness, and pride. Jesus, also, addressed similar sinful deeds through John's seven letters to the churches in Asia Minor.[113] The church wasn't perfect or without fault then—and it isn't still today.

So when will there ever be a bride for Jesus described like the one in the Bible, who has made herself ready;[114] a

---

[110] 2 Corinthians 11:2
[111] See Leviticus 21:13-15 with 2 Corinthians 6:14
[112] Romans 5:12-13; 18-19
[113] Revelation 2-3
[114] Revelation 19:7-8

bride who is commensurate to the stature of her Bridegroom?

How, if ever, will God be able to trust the imperfect, carnal church today, with the same *limitless* power he granted to his Son? In its current state, the church isn't glorious, radiant, or triumphant enough to command the respect of the world. It was the same way for the members of the early church in the book of Acts[115]—they had their own issues of carnality. The world today mocks the church as hypocritical, irrelevant, and out of touch with life.

The Laodicean church

In his vision in Revelation, John is instructed to provide the following message to the church in Laodicea:

> These are the words of the Amen, the faithful and true witness, the ruler of God's creation. I know your deeds, that you are neither cold nor hot. I wish you were either one or the other! So, because you are *lukewarm*—neither hot nor cold—I am about to spit you out of my mouth. You say, "I am rich; I have acquired wealth and do not need a thing." But you do not realize that you are wretched, pitiful, poor, blind and naked. I counsel you to buy from me gold refined in the fire, so you can become rich [spiritually]; and white clothes to wear, so you can cover your shameful nakedness; and salve to put on your eyes, so *you can see.*
>
> *—Revelation 3:14-18*

It is believed by some scholars that the church of Laodicea depicts the era and traits of today's church. Given what we know, this could be a fair description. Like the Laodiceans, there are those in the church today who think they are spiritually rich and need nothing—but, in reality,

---

[115] Acts 2:42-47; 4:32-35; 5:12-16, 42; 9:31; 11:21; 12:24; 14:3; 19:11

they are lukewarm. They may think they're clothed in God's glory today—but, in many churches of Christendom, the members are no more clothed in glory than the emperor in Hans Christian Andersen's tale: *The Emperor's New Clothes.*

Andersen tells of a fashion-obsessed emperor who is deceived by a tailor into believing that he is wearing the finest of clothes, invisible to his own eyes, but seen by others. The "others" go along with the ruse, afraid to speak out and offend him. But to their surprise, the deceived emperor calls for a parade to display his fine, new (invisible) outfit. During his march through streets the deception is ousted by a small child who shouts, "But he isn't wearing anything at all!"

Many today—"church-attendees" or good, conservative, "religious" folks—believe they're wearing Christ's clothes of righteousness. But like the child in Hans Christian Andersen's tale, Jesus sees the *naked* truth. And so does the Devil.

The great apostasy

Since our human bodies haven't been *fully* redeemed, yet—that is, to the stature of a glorious church, without blemish[116]—many blood-washed saints, in the last days, will be lulled to sleep through their lukewarmness, self-indulgence and complacency.

Paul says that in the last days, people will be lovers of pleasure rather than lovers of God, having a *form* of godliness but denying its power.[117] Some will even abandon their faith, following deceiving spirits and things taught by demons.[118]

They'll not recognize that the tailor (the Antichrist) will deceive them into wearing an *invisible*, nonexistent garment

---

[116] Romans 8:18-25 with Ephesians 4:13; 5:27
[117] 2 Timothy 3:4
[118] 1 Timothy 4:1

of righteousness that is s*elf*-righteousness. Their "perceived" righteousness will be man-made.

In his letter to the Thessalonians, Paul warns that this will happen to a significant percentage of last-day Christians. He calls it the *apostasy*, or the great falling away. Here are his words in the Amplified Bible:

> Relative to the coming of our Lord Jesus Christ (the Messiah) and our gathering together to [meet] Him, ... Let no one deceive or beguile you in any way, for that day will not come except the *apostasy* comes first [unless the predicted great falling away of those who have professed to be Christians has come], and the man of lawlessness (sin) is revealed, who is the son of doom (of perdition) [Dan 7:25; 8:25; 1 Tim 4:1.].[119]

This is a serious picture painted here for all Christians and forces us to examine the present condition of our soul and spiritual life. Are we healthy and discerning enough to avoid being in this group of emperors?

This is a question I have to ask myself.

Jesus adds his own prediction to this when he warned that many will turn away from the faith and betray and hate each other in the last days.[120]

He continues to say that many false messiahs and false prophets will appear and perform great signs and miracles to deceive even the elect, if that were possible.[121]

According to Paul, the Antichrist will be able to perform all kinds of counterfeit signs and wonders.[122] And because of the increase of wickedness in the last days, the love of many

---

[119] 2 Thessalonians 2:1, 3 (Amplified Bible)
[120] Matthew 24:10
[121] Matthew 24:24-25
[122] 2 Thessalonians 2:9

will grow cold—unless they stand firm in their faith to the end.[123]

Lukewarm, cold, and deceived Christians in the last days will be candidates for the *apostasy*[124]—the great falling away of Christians from the faith. I have reason to believe, from studying the Scriptures, that the number of apostates could be as high as one-third of the Christian population (I'll address that later in chapter 23).

Think of it—one-third of believers in the world whose love for God and each other will go from being lukewarm to cold. It's startling, yes, but not beyond the realm of possibility when you consider how many backslidden Christians you and I have seen walk away from the faith since their initial salvation experience. I still remember their faces and grieve.

Not the same fate, however, for the bride of Christ. The oil in her lamp—which keeps her light burning—will be full and ready when her Bridegroom comes.[125] We've heard often how a bride looks so *radiant* when she walks down that aisle. I believe her radiance comes from a heart burning with passionate love for the one she's about to marry—an unquenchable love that no other man can lure her away from; that is, unless she comes down the aisle with a divided, lukewarm heart, easily turned away by another man. Or, in the case of an *apostate*—another religion, another messiah, or another spiritual lover called pride, greed or lust.

When Jesus returns for his bride, he'll know her love as intimately as she prepares herself to know him. This is why

---

[123] Matthew 24:12-13
[124] *Apostasy:* 1: renunciation of a religious faith. 2: abandonment of a previous loyalty: defection (Merriam-Webster Dictionary). It is a revolt against the truth of God's word by a believer.
[125] Matthew 25:1-13

he'll say to the five virgins, who let their oil run dry, "Truth be told, I never really *knew* you."[126]

Don't give up—there's hope

There is good news, however, and it's a hope that the creation groans for—i.e., the manifestation of the *mature* and *prepared* sons and daughters of God.[127] These particular saints will be revealed to the world and come from among those who wait in eager expectation for his promise to us to possess his full stature and unlimited, Holy Spirit power. These saints won't buy into the deception of a man-made glory that denies the *power* of God.

These saints will be fully aware of their nakedness and speak to the fact that they are as incomplete, wretched, pitiful, poor, blind, and naked as the deceived emperor. Therefore, they'll see what's coming, repent, become hot (zealous for Christ) and buy gold that's been refined in the fire.[128] The result of their clear-sightedness and penitence will be a capacity to hear and open the door to Jesus—to let him come *fully* into their hearts, into every nook and cranny of their lives, dining with him at the table of intimacy.[129]

These are the ones who will have their nakedness covered with white clothes and *overcome* the lies of the world and the Antichrist—the great deceiver.

Overcomers

The bride will have many traits, one of which is that of an *overcomer*. She'll overcome many things because her heart is so in love with Jesus, nothing will stand in her way. The word "overcome" is a qualifier for special treatment given by

---

[126] Matthew 25:12
[127] Romans 8:19-21
[128] Revelation 3:17-18
[129] Revelation 3:20

Jesus, and what he's looking for when he returns to examine the church. To each of the seven churches he said this, "To him who *overcomes* [and does my will to the end], I will give...."[130] The gifts Jesus promised to give *overcomers* in the seven churches were:

- The right to eat of the tree if life in the paradise of God
- No participation in the second death
- Hidden manna and a white stone with a new name
- Authority over the nations
- The bright and morning star
- White clothes
- A permanent name in the Book of Life
- A permanent place as a pillar in God's temple with the name of God, the city of God (Jerusalem), and the new name (of the Lord Jesus Christ) all written on them
- The right to sit with Jesus on his throne

I believe these same gifts will apply to the church today, for God rewards those who seek him diligently and are faithful.[131] This requires nothing less than whole-hearted devotion to Christ. Jesus tells the seven churches[132] to *overcome* temptations, testing and specific issues, or the consequences will be that they'll not receive the gifts he's promised to overcomers. His letters were addressing serious matters in those churches; matters the church still struggles with today. But as Jesus admonished the seven churches, then, he's still requesting of us:

> He who has an ear, **let him hear** [take heed to] what the Spirit says to the churches.[133]

---

[130] Revelation 2:7, 11, 17, 26; 3:5, 12, 21
[131] 1 Samuel 26:2; Hebrews 11:6
[132] Revelation 2-3
[133] Revelation 2:7, 11, 17, 29; 3:6, 13, 21

And if this isn't enough for you and me to sit up and take notice, if we still aren't listening, perhaps James' admonition might help amplify the *why* we need to listen:

> Do not merely listen to the word, and so deceive yourselves. ***Do what it says***. Anyone who listens to the word but does not do what it says is like a man who looks at his face in a mirror and, after looking at himself, goes away and immediately forgets what he looks like. But the man who looks intently into the perfect law that gives freedom, and continues to do this, **not forgetting what he has heard, but doing it**—he will be blessed in what he does.[134]

And Jesus seals this thought with his last words of the Sermon on the Mount:

> Therefore everyone who hears these words of mine and **puts them into practice** is like a wise man who built his house on the rock. The rain came down, the streams rose, and the winds blew and beat against that house; yet it did not fall, because it had its foundation on the rock.
> But everyone who hears these words of mine and **does not put them into practice** is like a foolish man who built his house on sand. The rain came down, the streams rose, and the winds blew and beat against that house, and it fell with a great **crash**.
> *—Matthew 7:24-27*

"Crash" is the operative word for those who don't listen, pay attention, and do what the Bible says. Kind of like "crash" and "burn." So if you want to be an overcomer and not crash and burn, be a doer of the Word of God and not a hearer only.

---

[134] James 1:22-25

A commensurate bride for Jesus

If the church today isn't *commensurate* to the stature of Jesus, her Bridegroom, how can she rise to the occasion?

The day I married my wife, I watched her come down the aisle toward me, lovely and radiant. She didn't show up in bib overalls, clunky mountain boots, and a flannel shirt—like when I first met her. She also didn't walk down the aisle with a mudpack on her face and her hair rolled up in curlers. Instead, she prepared herself to be beautifully adorned for her bridegroom on our wedding day.

Today the church still bears the stain of the sin nature. Though adorned externally, it is the *internal* beauty[135] Christ wants to find when he comes. At the risk of being redundant, the church isn't prepared to meet her Bridegroom, and hasn't been for nearly two thousand years. In fact, she is incapable of being ready, apart from a divine intervention significant enough to complete what God has begun in her. Yes, we are made righteous by the blood of Jesus, judicially, which gets us into heaven. But we aren't sanctified enough *internally* to find ourselves in the bridal chamber.

Christ's bride will be a perfected bride, clothed in the fullness of the Triune God, as indicated in the symbolic language of Revelation 12:1. She will come out of the redeemed of all nations and will have made herself ready as a candidate for the bride company.[136]

A light in the darkness

There's something about a wedding that brings momentary light amidst the darkness around us. There's joy, there's celebration, there's the couple getting married who are focused only on each other—not the problems of the

---

[135] 1 Peter 3:3-4
[136] Revelation 19:7-8

world. The wedding of Christ to his bride will also be a time of great joy, but it will take place when the world is drinking from a cup filled with its own abominations.

Immediately after the marriage is consummated, the sounding of trumpet judgments will follow through Revelation 8 and 9. Justice and retribution will break loose, and darkness will grow darker. It will be like the prophet Amos described of the last days:

> Woe to you who long for the day of the Lord!
> Why do you long for the day of the Lord?
> That day will be darkness, not light.
> It will be as though a man fled from a lion only to meet a bear, as though he entered his house and rested his hand on the wall only to have a snake bite him.
> Will not the day of the Lord be darkness, not light—pitch-dark, without a ray of brightness?
>
> *—Amos 5:18-20*

During times like these, a light will shine out of darkness. The glorious, radiant church will appear like the beacon of a lighthouse to assist the lost during the waves of judgments. While God's justice and retribution pounds the Earth and its inhabitants, people will be converted and saved, and just in time, before the seven *bowls* of wrath are poured out in the final hour upon those who reject the gospel and accept the mark of the beast.

Chapter 14

The Day of Atonement

IF THE THEORY OF a *sinless* bride is true, then when might we expect such a transformation? As I briefly introduced in chapter 13, the clues are found in the "language" of Revelation 8:1-5.

The words *golden censer, golden altar, smoke of incense,* and *before the throne of God,* all describe the Feast of Tabernacles[137] in the Old Testament. This is the third of three annuals feasts for Israel and is celebrated in the fall on the tenth day of the seventh month of the Jewish calendar. This tenth day is called the "Day of Atonement."[138] I'll share more about the three feasts in the next chapter.

As stated in chapter 13, this "day" is the only time of the year when the high priest entered behind the veil (curtain) of the Most Holy Place and stood before God's shekinah glory. A brilliant light emanated from between the wings of the two cherubim, which were fashioned out of one solid piece of gold, including the lid of the Ark of the Covenant. It was on the lid (the mercy seat) of the Ark where the blood of a sacrificial bull was sprinkled to atone for his sins and his family's sins.[139] It was here in the Most Holy Place where the priest could stand in the presence of God protected by the

---

[137] Leviticus 16:1-34; 23:26-32; Numbers 29:12-39; Deuteronomy 16:13-17
[138] Leviticus 16:1-34; 23:26-32—called "Yom Kippur" today.
[139] Exodus 30:10; Leviticus 16:11-14

blood, which atoned for his past year's sins and rendered him "righteous" before God.

Also on the Day of Atonement, when the blood was brought from the sin offering into the Most Holy Place, the priest took the golden censer and filled it with burning coals from the golden altar of incense, standing before the curtain, which hid the Ark. He sprinkled two handfuls of holy incense on the burning coals in the censer. This created a shield of smoke to protect his eyes from the blinding light of God's presence. He then entered behind the curtain into the Most Holy Place with the smoking censer. He sprinkled the blood of the sin offering with his finger *once* on the mercy seat (the atonement cover), then *seven* times before the mercy seat for his own sins. He returned then to the Outer Court to offer another sin offering on the bronze altar—this time the offering of a goat. He then went back into the Most Holy Place to repeat all of the steps of his first offering and sprinkled the blood from the goat to atone for the year's accumulated sins of the Israelites.[140]

What does this have to do with the bride?

The "Day of Atonement" language of the Old Testament is comparable to what John uses in Revelation 8, beginning in verse 3 with an *angel* who is standing at the golden altar with the golden censer and incense. This angel was given a similar task to what occurred on the Day of Atonement; a task that belonged to *no other* than the high priest.

The Greek word used by John for *angel* is "aggelos" and can also be translated "messenger," or by implication—"pastor." The *angels* of the seven churches, to which John wrote, were literally the messenger-pastors of those churches.[141] Since Jesus is the only legitimate and eternal

---

[140] Leviticus 16:12-13
[141] Revelation 2-3

High Priest in the New Testament—after the order of Melchizedek[142]—it is safe to assume that this *angel* isn't some randomly elected angel God pulled from the ranks, but rather a *messenger-pastor*, that is, Jesus himself who is called "the *messenger* of the [new] covenant"[143] and the "chief *shepherd* of our souls."[144] Christ can, therefore, be seen in Revelation 8:1-5 as the High Priest of the *heavenly* tabernacle—the blueprint God gave Moses to build the *earthly* tabernacle.[145] I believe Jesus is shown here in these verses as the *mediator*[146] and *intercessor* of the church,[147] offering up the smoke of incense with the prayers of the saints before the glory of God's throne.

As our High Priest in the heavenly sanctuary, Jesus fills the censer with fire and hurls it to the Earth, creating thunder, flashes of lightning, and another great earthquake. Perhaps this could represent a prelude to the seven trumpet judgments about to take place.

Silence in heaven

Let's take a look for a moment at the thirty minutes of *silence* in Revelation 8:1. Why is this mentioned?

The Day of Atonement was considered the most solemn event of the year. According to Alfred Edersheim,[148] the high priest stood alone in that room, separated from the people outside. He placed the golden censer between the two gold-layered poles used to carry the Ark. Left in the rings, the poles were perpendicular to the Ark. He put the incense into his hand, and threw it on the coals of the censer. He waited

---

[142] Hebrews 7:11-28; 8:1-6
[143] Malachi 3:1
[144] 1 Peter 5:4 with Mark 14:27; John 10:1-16; Hebrews 13:20; 1 Peter 2:25
[145] Hebrews 8:5 and 9:23-24
[146] Job 33:23; 1 Timothy 2:5; Hebrews 8:6; 9:15; 12:24
[147] Hebrews 7:25
[148] Alfred Edersheim, *The Temple: Its Ministry and Services* (Grand Rapids, MI: Eerdmans Publishing Company, 1982), 313-314.

until the smoke filled the Most Holy Place, and if all went well, after he was done, he emerged safely from the inner sanctuary.

While the incense was being offered in the Most Holy Place, the people outside drew back from the Tabernacle, and worshiped in *silence*. When they saw the high priest emerge from the sanctuary, they knew that the service had been accepted. I believe it is this *silence* that coincides with the thirty minutes of silence in Revelation 8:1.

Just as the people worshipped in silent reverence when the high priest offered the incense before God on the Day of Atonement, so shall there be a reverent silence among heaven's witnesses when Jesus, our High Priest, stands before the throne of God in the heavenlies. But why does this happen if there is no sin in heaven to atone for? I would suggest this activity John describes is for a very special event that the atoning work of the cross paid for *in advance*. That event is a wedding.

Day of Atonement's symbolism

The symbolism of the Day of Atonement in the Old Testament points to four specific actions in Revelation 8:1-5.

First, the priest—a man with sinful flesh—meets face-to-face with God **behind the veil** of the Most Holy Place.

Second, he stood **without sin** before God because of the atoning work of the sin offering of blood from a sacrificed bull.

Third, the blood was sprinkled **one** time on the mercy seat, and **seven** times before the Ark where he stood. Numbers have symbolic meaning in the Bible. **One** stands for "unity" and **seven** stands for "completion, perfection, and maturity."

Fourth, there was **silence** from Israel observing reverently outside the Tabernacle, as the event of "man meeting God" took place in the holiest place on Earth, where no other than the high priest could go.

If Christ is going to present to himself someday, a holy, blameless, perfect bride, without the stain of sin and commensurate to the stature of his own sinless nature, then what other place in the Bible could that happen than in this passage of Revelation 8:1-5? The language is pretty clear and I don't believe this takes place *after* Christ returns, I believe it happens *before*.

Let's apply these four Old Testament actions now to John's vision with Day of Atonement language. This suggests to me that to consummate the marriage between Christ and his bride, the time will come when the bride will meet her Bridegroom face-to-face, that is, she'll become *one* (united) with him *behind the veil*. It is at this point and time in the Revelation, that she receives her divine transformation of becoming a *sinless* bride so as to be compatible, commensurate, and completely perfect for Christ. With a play on words, this is the day of "at-**one**-ment" for the Bridegroom and his bride.

The thirty minutes of *silence* in heaven could represent a time when all eyes are on the bride, her Bridegroom, and the consummation of their marriage—the profound *mystery* that Paul spoke of in Ephesians 5:32.

In some mysterious work of grace on God's part, she stands *face-to-face* with deity, *without* sin in glory, able to become *one* with her Bridegroom in complete and perfect maturity, observed in *silence* by a host of angels and the redeemed of all ages.

This, I believe, is the event represented in the parable of the ten virgins, or those members of the body of Christ who are prepared to meet the Bridegroom:

The [five] virgins who were ready [with their lamps full of oil] went in with him [the bridegroom] to the wedding banquet. And the door was shut.[149]

The bride and the great harvest

Following the Day of Atonement, four days were set aside to harvest the corn, wine, and oil. *Four* is the symbolic number of the Earth. I believe these four days of harvest symbolize the bride's primary assignment—to reap the greatest world harvest of souls through an unprecedented display of *signs* and *wonders*. What better time than this for the radiant bride of Christ to arrive, fully equipped to take on the task of hope and deliverance to a world brought to its knees in the final hour.

During the time of the coming seven trumpet judgments, God has no intention of leaving the world without hope and deliverance. His *secret weapon* won't be an escaping, whimpering, hanging-on-by-a-thread, milk-toast church. Instead, she'll be a victorious, triumphant church, grabbing the attention of the entire world through her miraculous abilities by operating on the level and power of Jesus himself. Jesus predicted this would happen when he said:

I tell you the truth, anyone who has faith in me **will do what I have been doing. He will do even *greater* things than these** [miracles I have been doing], because I am going to the Father. And I will do whatever you ask in my name, so that the Son may bring glory to the Father. You may ask me for anything in my name, and I will do it.[150]

On that day of "at-**one**-ment" in Revelation 8:1-5, the sinless bride of Jesus will be so completely tuned in to the

---

149 Matthew 25:10 (Bracketed words added by author for clarity.)
150 John 14:12-14

Holy Spirit's voice,[151] she can ask Jesus for anything and he'll do it because it's accurately in line with the Holy Spirit's prompting. This is what the crown of *twelve* stars on the woman represents in Revelation 12:1. The number *twelve* is the symbolic number of "spiritual, governing authority;" and the *stars* represent the Holy Spirit within every born-again believer. In her *sinless* state, the bride will walk in perfect alignment with the governing guidance of the Holy Spirit, just as Christ did when he walked this Earth. The Holy Spirit will rest as a crown upon the queen of King Jesus.

For such a time as this, the bride of Christ will meet a great need on Earth. A miraculous need created by the horrific judgments of the seven trumpets; a supernatural need for food, water, and miraculous healings; and a supernatural need for resurrections of the dead among those who will die from the destructive events to come. Through this ministry of the bride, millions of souls will be saved, and the prodigals will return home to the Father.

But while the light of the gospel grows brighter and brighter, the love of many will still grow colder and darker. They will harden their hearts against God, as Pharaoh and the Egyptians had done when the ten plagues came upon them.

---

[151] John 14:12

Chapter 15

Introduction to the Feasts

BEFORE WE LOOK INTO to the sounding of the seven trumpets, I wish to complete this picture of a *sinless* bride by introducing the symbolism embedded in the three feasts of Israel. In each of these feasts God conceals significant *spiritual truths*, as reflected in what King Solomon had said:

> It is the glory of God to *conceal* a thing, and the glory of kings to _discover_ it.[152]

Memorize this saying below when it comes to discovering symbolism in the Old and New Testaments of the Bible:

> The New is in the Old <u>concealed</u>,
> The Old is in the New <u>revealed</u>.
>
> The New is in the Old <u>contained</u>,
> The Old is in the New <u>explained</u>.

When I was first introduced to the concept of a glorious church, triumphant in the last days, I couldn't imagine it possible. Ever since I was saved, I've grown much in knowledge, faith, and intimacy in the Lord. I also know that God's pleasure with me isn't based on works, but by faith in the atoning work of Christ's blood.

---

[152] Proverbs 25:2

However, I can't escape the fact that my sin nature still holds me back from the potential God knows I'm capable of, that is, a place of complete abandonment to his will. Oh how I want that, but I have never experienced it on a level I know it could be. Four decades after my conversion, I'm still deficient in my efforts to attain such abandonment. And though sin no longer reigns over my life, *remaining* sin still keeps me from the place I long to go.

I want to see more power released in my life. I want to cast out devils with a word, heal the sick, the lame, the blind, the deaf, and the mute. I want to raise the dead back to life and multiply fishes and loaves to feed the hungry—just as Jesus did. I want to see the gospel preached with power, accompanied and confirmed with miracles, signs and wonders like in the early days of the apostles. And though I've experienced a small measure of that—here and there—as a pastor, it pales in comparison to that of the apostles and the early church.

I praise God for today's saints, churches and missionaries that have experienced miracles accompanying the gospel. I've seen the documentaries of such places, studied the extraordinary lives of great healers and miracle workers, listened to healing seminars, and read books on how to pray for and receive healings. But when all is said and done, the church as a whole is still more power*less* than it is power*ful*, and is limited in its range to attract attention on a global scale.

Achilles' heel

In the past, many miracle-working preachers, who've seen thousands healed during their ministries, have had their Achilles' heels. How often have we read the accounts of many who succumbed to pride, selfish ambitions, sexual immorality, larceny, strange doctrines or questionable methods, all of which stained the integrity of the gospel? Such supernatural movements surrounding these preachers came and died out because of the backlash from preachers who denounced the scandals and extremes of those ministries and movements.

By blaming "Pentecostalism" as the perpetrator of fanatical extremes and scandals, cessationist[153] pastors felt justified in their suppression of the flow of the Holy Spirit, and backed their actions with doctrines to support it. Such efforts have created splits, in which new denominations emerged embracing the gifts of the Spirit in venues where they were free to seek God for more power.

I have lived long enough to watch many of these "renewal" movements come and go. Preachers find themselves on the crest of a wave when the Holy Spirit moves and they rise with that wave of popularity. But with power comes pressure that tests us, and many have failed and crumbled under the stress attached with fame and the handling of supernatural power.

We are all but flesh wrapped around a carnal, sinful nature. The sinful nature always desires what is contrary to the Spirit and the Spirit what is contrary to the sinful nature.[154] They are in such conflict with each other that we become blocked in our efforts to bring God's glory to its fullest extent on Earth. How will we ever be able to fulfill bringing God's kingdom to Earth as it is in heaven? Exactly as it is in heaven—not merely a percentage of it.

Collateral damage and compromise

When leaders of dynamic churches or "renewal" movements fall, collateral damage follows. Foundations are

---

[153] **Cessationism** in Christianity is the doctrine that apostolic gifts ceased with the original twelve apostles.
[154] Galatians 5:17

shaken, people are hurt, and many become cynical and leave the church altogether. When the church is rocked by scandals because of highly visible religious figures, the world takes notice and gloats, once again, over the hypocrisy. Then they parade the hypocrisy across the screens of Hollywood, in the news, on nightly shows, and on sitcoms—all creating a deeper divide of an "us *versus* them."

In response to the scandals, the church becomes more like the world to help the world become more like us, but never enough to become a threat to the Devil or the world. The *apostate* church of the last days will take on a *form of godliness,* but deny the power of the Holy Spirit. The apostate church will shave back moral standards and Holy Spirit power in an effort to reach the lost through reason, relativism and relationship.

Such an effort compromises the whole gospel message in order to reach the lost by "being relevant." Instead of the church setting the standards of godliness and righteousness, the world sets the standard for the church. Instead of the church being *salt* and *light* to influence the world to raise its standards, we put a bushel over our light so as to not offend the world.

The approach of the early church

The early church, however, took a different approach—one that came through a demonstration of *power.*

> For we know, brothers loved by God, that he has chosen you, because our gospel came to you not simply with words, but also *with power,* with the Holy Spirit and with deep conviction.[155]

> —*Paul*

---

[155] 1 Thessalonians 1:4-5

My message and my preaching were not with wise and persuasive words, but with a *demonstration* of the Spirit's *power*, so that your faith might not rest on men's wisdom, but on God's *power*.[156]

—*Paul*

This is the dichotomy that troubles me. I love the church and, despite her defects, have served it for more than forty years. I also love God's people and pastors. I desire to make no judgment of their hearts, because God alone knows motive and intent. And though there are no perfect churches, God still uses his church and the gospel is still presented through the message of the cross.

But where is the *power* of the early church today? Why do we struggle so to return to the days of the miraculous? Yes, we see a glimmer of hope in some pockets of Christianity experiencing God's power, but will it ever be enough to make a global impact? This is my struggle.

The body of Christ today is divided over whether the power in the early church is still needed. This division creates an "us *versus* them" mentality, and Jesus warned that a kingdom divided against itself will be ruined, and a house divided against itself will fall.[157] This hinders the spreading of the gospel and is the reason why the church remains power*less* in the eyes of the world.

Paul indicated to the Ephesians that *before* we become mature—to the fullest extent of Christ's stature—we will first be united in the faith and knowledge of the Son of God.[158] Given the current status of the church, Paul's prediction would require a major miracle because we *aren't* united in doctrine, faith and the knowledge of the Son of God, and it's been that way from the beginning. I see no other way for the

---

[156] 1 Corinthians 2:4-5
[157] Luke 11:17
[158] Ephesians 4:13

church of the last days to walk in unity and power unless God does something so amazing, so brilliant, and so supernatural in the church that no power or kingdom on Earth can deny it.

Hope from the three feasts

Despite my troubles and struggles concerning the church, I find hope in the symbolic gems found in the three feasts. Through these hidden gems, the concept of a *sinless* bride becomes more real every day. It encourages me to see the potential of a glorious church—despite her current condition.

In a bride with no sin nature, there'll be no more envy, strife, or immaturity. She'll be able to preach the gospel with power through a *third* work of grace that comes through the Day of Atonement in the Feast of Tabernacles. That momentous work of grace in the church will remove carnality, divisions, selfish ambitions, pride, quarrels, and the restrained freedom of the Holy Spirit.

The clue to the timing of that event rests in understanding how all three feasts apply to the church's experience. You received a preview of this in the last chapter regarding the Day of Atonement. I want to expand that horizon to the other two feasts to complete the full picture.

I invite you to prayerfully commit these new thoughts to God; and as we begin the next phase of our journey through this book, remember again that...

> The New is in the Old <u>concealed</u>,
> The Old is in the New <u>revealed</u>.
>
> The New is in the Old <u>contained</u>,
> The Old is in the New <u>explained</u>.

Chapter 16

The Three Feasts of Israel

"Blessed—happy, fortunate [to be envied]—are the people who know the joyful sound [who understand and appreciate the **spiritual blessings** symbolized by the **Feasts**]; they walk, O Lord, in the light and favor of Your countenance." —*Psalm 89:15* (*Amplified Bible*)

MANY YEARS AGO, a man from New Zealand came to the church I attended in Anchorage before I was sent out to plant my first church. He was a seasoned veteran in the kingdom of God and apostolic in nature. He taught the most amazing revelations about the three feasts of Israel, which opened up a whole new world of understanding for me in how the bride fits into the end-time picture. In this chapter we'll analyze the details of each feast and then apply their symbolism to the experience of the church within the church age, and the end of time.

The Feast of Passover

Passover is the first feast, which took place in the *first* month of Israel's calendar year during the time of their "barley" harvest. This feast commemorated Israel's deliverance on the fourteenth day of the month when God struck down Egypt's firstborn.[159] There are three feasts within this Passover feast (*see* Leviticus 23:4-22). They are:

1) Feast of Passover (14th day)—*verses 4-8*
2) Feast of Unleavened Bread (15th-21st days)—*verses 9-14*
3) Feast Day of the Sheaf of the Firstfruits—*verses 15-22*

The Feast of Pentecost

Pentecost is the second feast, which took place in the *third* month of Israel's calendar year during the "wheat" harvest. Pentecost means "fiftieth." This feast originated on the *fiftieth* day after the children of Israel left Egypt, where they stood before God at the foot of Mt. Sinai and received the Law and the Ten Commandments.[160] This occurred exactly seven full weeks after the third Feast Day of the Sheaf of the Firstfruits of Passover. [161]

The Feast of Tabernacles

Tabernacles took place—after the dry season—in the *seventh* month of Israel's calendar year, during the "fruit" harvest of corn, wine and oil. It originates with the celebration of the fruit harvest in the Promised Land (in Canaan) after forty years of wilderness wanderings. Like Passover, there are three parts to this feast (*see* Leviticus 23:23-44). They are:

1) Feast of Trumpets (1st day of month)—*verses 23-25*
2) Day of Atonement (10th day)—*verses 26-32*
3) Feast of Tabernacles (15th-21st days)—*verses 33-44*

Within all three feasts of Israel, seven distinct feasts are celebrated. From a distance, you see three feasts, but up

---

[159] Exodus 11-13
[160] Exodus 19 and 20
[161] Exodus 19

close there are actually seven. It's the same with the rainbow. From a distance you see the three primary colors of *red*, *yellow*, and *blue*; but up close, there are actually seven colors—red, orange, yellow, green, blue, indigo, and violet. This is why a closer look at the feasts reveals more beneath the surface. So let's keep searching; there's a pot of treasure at the end of this rainbow.

Natural and spiritual truths

The Old Testament **contains** the *literal* and *historical* accounts of the feasts. The New Testament **explains** the *spiritual truths* fulfilled in their symbolism.[162] Let's examine the chart below to see how the three feasts *progress* from the Old Testament to the New Testament:

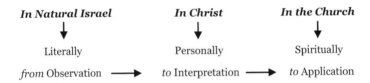

In Natural Israel	*In Christ*	*In the Church*
↓	↓	↓
Literally	Personally	Spiritually
from Observation ⟶	*to* Interpretation ⟶	*to* Application

Paul said in his letter to the Romans that everything written in the past was written to teach us, so that through patience and the encouragement of the Scriptures we might have hope.[163] Understanding what is written about the feasts in the Old Testament fills me with great hope for the church. That's why I find it so relevant to share the symbolism with you in context of the bride's ministry.

Here's the pattern

1) The feasts are fulfilled **literally** in the Old Testament for us to <u>observe</u> as a historical fact.

---

162 Psalm 89:15 (Amplified Bible)
163 Romans 15:4

2) The feasts are fulfilled in Christ **personally** in the New Testament, because in his life all the Law, the Psalms, and the Prophets are fulfilled.[164] Therefore, Christ is the infallible *interpretation* of the three feasts fulfilled in his life as the **Passover** Lamb on the cross, the Baptizer in the Holy Spirit at **Pentecost**, and the High Priest of the Day of Atonement in **Tabernacles**.

3) The feasts are fulfilled **spiritually** in the church by *application*. **Passover** is our salvation experience, the *first* work of grace; **Pentecost** is our spirit-filled experience, the *second* work of grace; and **Tabernacles** has yet to be experienced, but will be the *third* work of grace—a sinless perfection by an act of God's sovereign infusion. Let's look more closely at the historical details, one at a time.

Fulfillment of the feasts *in natural Israel*

Passover	Pentecost	Church in the Wilderness	Tabernacles
Egypt	Mt. Sinai	40 years of Wanderings	Promised Land

God fulfilled his promise to Israel that he would deliver them from Egypt. He instructed them to take a year-old male *lamb*, without defect, on the tenth day and then slay it on the fourteenth day. They were to take the blood of the lamb and put it on the doorposts, and the beam above the door, as a sign. When the Lord came through Egypt that night and saw the blood, he would **"pass over"** the marked house and not strike down the firstborn male of the homes protected by the blood on the doorframes.

God then led Israel out of Egypt through the Red Sea. Fifty days later, in the third month (**Pentecost**), they arrived safely at the foot of Mt. Sinai where they received the Laws of God through Moses. They remained there for one

---

[164] Luke 24:44; Romans 10:4

year and constructed the Tabernacle of Moses for God. They set out for Canaan then and, near the border, sent twelve men ahead, one from each tribe, to spy on the land.

Ten of the spies came back with a negative report, filling Israel with doubts about going into the Promised Land. Because of their unbelief, God turned them back to the desert to wander (as the church) in the wilderness for forty years until that generation died out and a new generation emerged.

Joshua became Moses' successor and led them into the Promised Land to conquer it, settle it, and then begin to celebrate the Feast of **Tabernacles**. From then on, God required celebrating all three feasts annually—in the Promised Land—to commemorate their deliverance, God's provision, and his atoning work through animal sacrifice.

The feasts fulfilled *in Christ* toward the church

Passover	*Pentecost*	Church Age	*Day of Atonement*
Gospels	Acts	Epistles	Hebrews/Revelation
Lamb of God Sacrifice	Baptizer in the Holy Spirit	High Priest Intercessor/Sanctifier	Bridegroom Appearing

Besides being part of Israel's culture and religious duties, the three feasts were symbolically fulfilled in the *person* of Christ and his *relationship* to the church. Note the chart above and we'll look carefully at each one.

First, in the four gospels, Jesus fulfilled the Feast of **Passover** by becoming the ultimate sacrifice for our sins. John the Baptist indicated this when he pointed Jesus out to his disciples and said, "Look, the *Lamb of God,* who takes away the sin of the world."[165]

In the book of Acts, Jesus fulfilled the Feast of **Pentecost**. God told John the Baptist, "The man upon

---

[165] John 1:29

whom you see the Spirit come down and remain, is the same who will *baptize with the Holy Spirit.*"[166] Jesus told his disciples to remain in Jerusalem until they were *baptized* with the Holy Spirit and with power.[167] After he ascended into heaven, he sent the Holy Spirit on the Day of Pentecost where they were gathered together in an upper room.[168]

Paul taught in Hebrews that we have a permanent *High Priest* in Christ who lives to intercede for those who seek God.[169] Jesus taught in Matthew that the Bridegroom will come for those who are prepared to meet him.[170] And, as mentioned before, Paul taught that Christ will present his wife to himself as a radiant church, without stain or wrinkle or any other blemish, but holy and blameless[171] (the same description used for Jesus in 1 Peter 1:19 and Hebrews 7:26).

The three feasts are in the Law of Moses and Christ came to fulfill *all* of the Law in himself.[172] So the first two feasts were fulfilled in Christ as our Passover Lamb, as our Baptizer in the Holy Spirit, and as our High Priest Intercessor.

The last feast (Tabernacles) will be fulfilled when Christ—our Bridegroom—returns for a spotless bride—completing all three feasts in his relationship to his church.

The feasts fulfilled in the church's experience

Passover	Pentecost	Church Age	Tabernacles
Gospels	Acts	Epistles	Hebrews/Revelation
Salvation	Spirit Baptism	Decline to Restoration	Prepare/Unity/Perfect
First work of grace	Second work of grace	Dark Ages to the Reformation	Third work of grace
"Spring Rains"		"Dry Season"	"Autumn Rains"

---

[166] John 1:33
[167] Acts 1:4-6; 8
[168] Acts 1:12-14; 2:1-4; 16-18
[169] Hebrews 7:25
[170] Matthew 25:10
[171] Ephesians 5:25-27
[172] Matthew 5:17; Luke 24:44

This is the ultimate outcome of the feasts and why they relate to the concept of a bride *without* a sin nature who will be able to walk one day in the fullest measure of God's anointing and power. It is this *mystery* miracle of the bride company that will change the world and bring about the greatest harvest of souls ever imagined. And this movement won't stop until the last person—who wants to be saved—can be saved. This is the "profound mystery" that Paul spoke of; the experience the church has not yet received, but is destined to receive when that time and "day" arrive.

The *day* of Passover arrived in A.D. 30 and the world could be saved from sin and born again—that remains in place to this day.

The *day* of Pentecost arrived fifty days later in A.D. 30 and the Holy Spirit was poured out upon the believers. The gift of the Spirit that came on them in Acts chapter 2 can be received—that also remains in place to this day.[173]

The only *day* of the three feasts that's left for the church to experience is the *Day of Atonement* on the "tenth day" of the Feast of Tabernacles. There's no place in church history where this feast has occurred, but as surely as the church experienced the first two feasts on the exact **day** they were scheduled to occur, so shall the church experience the third feast's work of grace on the exact **day** of the "Day" of Atonement.

The first two works of grace

Passover—Jesus was born of the Spirit at his birth and separated unto God's purpose for his life. If Jesus is the firstborn, the first fruit, the prototype and model for us who are partakers of his divine nature,[174] then we are born of the Spirit and separated unto God's purpose for our lives. This

---

173 Acts 2:38-39
174 2 Peter 1:4

salvation is our "**Passover**" experience and God's *first* work of grace. The disciples experienced their Passover in the gospels.[175]

Pentecost—Jesus was anointed when the Holy Spirit came upon him in the form of the dove.[176] We, too, are anointed by the Holy Spirit when he comes upon us.[177] This is our "**Pentecost**" experience and God's **second** work of grace. The disciples experienced their Pentecost in the book of Acts,[178] fifty days after they were born again in the Spirit, because the day of Pentecost had to occur as the appointed "day" for the outpouring.[179]

The church age

The strength and power of the early church diminished as the church declined into the Dark Ages. This became the "dry season," the "no rain" era, the time of "wilderness wanderings," and the time where a "famine of the Word" prevailed.

Passover	Pentecost	Church Age	Tabernacles
Gospels	Acts	Epistles	Hebrews/Revelation
Salvation	Spirit Baptism	Decline to Restoration	Prepare/Unity/Perfect
First work of grace	Second work of grace	Dark Ages to the Reformation	Third work of grace
"Spring Rains"		"Dry Season"	"Autumn Rains"

However, God is faithful to preserve a remnant of his people from generation to generation. Each generation of people operates and ministers in the light of their understanding during the days of their pilgrimage. This will

---

[175] John 20:22
[176] Matthew 3:16; John 1:32-33
[177] Luke 24:49; Acts 1:4, 8; 2:1-5
[178] Acts 2
[179] John 20:22

continue until God restores every truth lost, from the time of the early church to the final generation of God's remnant in the last days.[180]

The three feasts in the feast of tabernacles

1) Feast of Trumpets (1st day of the month)—*Lev. 23:23-25*
2) Day of Atonement (10th day of the month)—*Lev. 23:26-32*
3) Feast of Tabernacles (15th-21st of the month)—*Lev. 23:33-44*

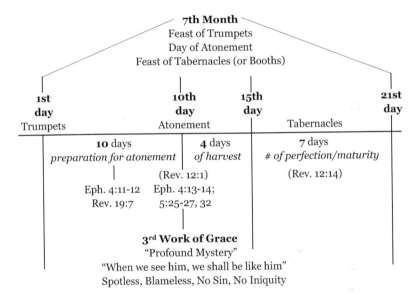

The priests blew their trumpets on the first day of the seventh month to announce the "New Year" day of Israel's "civil" calendar. This was called the *Feast of Trumpets*. This announcement initiated ten days of preparation for the Sabbath of all Sabbaths, the *Day of Atonement*. On the Day of Atonement, all Israel came together in unity for atonement for sins. The high priest first offered up a bull sacrifice to atone for *his* sins and *his* household, by

---

[180] Acts 3:21—"He [Jesus] must remain in heaven until the time comes for God to restore everything."

sprinkling the animal's blood on the mercy seat. Then he offered up a goat sacrifice, repeating the same act of sprinkling blood to atone for the sins of the people.

The Day of Atonement was followed by the completion of the fruit "harvest" for the next four days. The fifteenth day began the week of the *Feast of Tabernacles* (or *Booths*). Israel fashioned huts out of branches and leaves for shelter to inhabit for *seven* days to celebrate the harvest as a memorial to God's provision during the forty years of their wilderness wanderings.

The *trumpets* blown by the priests are the harbinger of the Day of Atonement. They alert the people that they have ten days to prepare their homes by removing all leaven and anything unholy. During this time they were to examine their lives, prepare to stand accountable before God, and pray for mercy. If the tabernacle sacrifices conducted by their mediator, the high priest, were accepted by God, then their sins from the previous year were covered and forgiven.

It is possible that the church is experiencing this Feast of Trumpets period today. It is a time to receive the wake-up call to examine our lives and prepare for the "**day**" of the ***third*** work of grace, when Christ gathers his bride and perfects her.

After the Day of Atonement, Israel took the next four days to gather in the fruit harvest of corn, oil and wine ("four" is the symbolic number for the world, as in four corners of the Earth). After the dry, summer season, God brought forth a "double portion" of rain to accelerate the crop's growth in the fall to be finished in time for the harvest. After they were done with the harvest, they spent the next *seven* days celebrating around their primitively fashioned booths.

Later, we'll examine when the bride experiences her "Feast of Booths." It is then, after the great harvest, that she'll be taken to a place out of harm's way and the *seven* bowls of wrath; a place where she will celebrate the *completion* of the greatest harvest of souls in human history.

The great and final harvest

Imagine a world ravaged and falling apart from the events of the sixth seal (Rev. 6:12-14) and the seven trumpets (Rev. 8:6-9:21). It will look like a scene out of a sci-fi movie.

Imagine the hunger, the devastation, the injured, the sick, the dying, the hopeless and despairing. Then imagine inserting millions of saints into that scene who are carrying the full, anointed power of Christ.

But let's not stop there, because it gets even better.

The "third" work of grace

Remember when I shared that once the *first* and *second* feasts of Israel were fulfilled in the church spiritually, everyone could have that same experience from then on?

That also applies to the *third* feast. Imagine that sinless stature and limitless power, exponentially multiplied by everyone who is saved because they, too, can step into that *third* work of grace, as it was and still is with the *first* and *second* works of grace.

Imagine the testimonies of the supernatural healings, the supernatural feeding of the hungry, and the signs and wonders that will turn the hardest of hearts into converted believers and followers of Jesus. Redeemed people, even those converted from powerless world religions, fanatical jihadists, witch doctors and sorcerers, will step into instant maturity and power in the Holy Spirit.

The "process" of sanctification will be shortened. God will do an instantaneous work because the need will be "now" and the need will be great. God's secret weapon—his spiritual bride and her offspring (or spiritual children)—will be unleashed upon the Earth to bring in that great and final harvest of God. This is what I continue to prepare for. This is what motivates me to be ready and teach others to get ready for—that "**day**" the church is going to experience.

I pray the church will experience the *call* to this profound mystery, a building *anticipation*, a holy *unrest*, a taste here and a taste there of God's power (though it's merely a *trickle* compared to the "gusher" that's coming).

If we are honest with ourselves, the church as we know it today isn't a glorious church—yet. It is fraught with compromise, lethargy, and an entitlement spirit, because we retain the law of sin within our flesh that contends with the law of God in our minds.[181] It won't remain that way, however, and it can't remain that way if the world will ever be reached in that last great harvest.

God has a plan for the end of the age—where the plowman will overtake the reaper and the planter will overtake the treader of grapes.[182] Where Joel's prediction of a "double portion" of rain will come in time for the fall harvest.[183] Where the bride shall leave her bridal chamber to be consummated with her husband in full glory,[184] so that she may be unleashed upon the Earth to reveal the *divine romance* God has planned for his Son *before* time began. This divine romance—between Christ and his bride—will complete the fullest expression of God's love to the world since the **day** of the cross.

---

[181] Romans 7:25; Galatians 5:17
[182] Amos 9:13
[183] Joel 2:23-24
[184] Psalm 45 with Joel 2:15-16

Chapter 17

Revealing the Divine Romance

THE BOOK OF REVELATION is a book of revealing. The word "revelation" actually means: *revealing* or *unveiling,* like the unveiling of a statue for the first time in public. Many think of Revelation as mostly a book about judgments, but it is more than that; it is a book about contrasting characters of good and evil, where good prevails and evil is overthrown.

Jesus Christ, the Son of God, is the primary character *revealed* in this book in a variety of ways. He is revealed as the Lamb slain *and* the Lion of Judah, as the King of Kings *and* our eternal High Priest, as the First and Last *and* the Alpha and Omega, as the Living One who *was* dead *and* is now alive forevermore, as the Defender of truth *and* the Judge of the wicked, as the High Priest-Angel with the smoking censer *and* the Mighty Angel with the little scroll, as the Lamb to open the seven-sealed scroll *and* the Rider on the white horse, as the one called Faithful and True *and* the Word of God, as the Root and Offspring of David *and* the Bright and Morning Star.

All of these names referring to Jesus are found in the words of John's prophecy and visions. Is it any wonder that it's called "The Book of the *Revealing* of Jesus Christ?"

But there's so much more about Jesus in this book.

He conquers Satan and chains him in the Abyss. He conquers the Antichrist and throws him into the lake of fire. He conquers the harlot church, the oppressor and persecutor of his saints. He conquers *every* enemy, including sin, death and the grave. He is the triumphant victorious King who will set things right, and then establish a perfect kingdom on Earth to rule and reign for a thousand years. But there's one very important part to not overlook in this prophetic story called "the Revelation of Jesus Christ."

Jesus is *revealed* as the Bridegroom and lover of his bride. Not only does he marry her, he empowers her. He assigns her to his cause, and then he protects her until his return where she joins him at his side through the millennial reign and eternity.

Understanding the culmination of this *eternal* romance between Christ and the church will help us make sense of all the terrifying subplots depicted in the symbolism, judgments, and plagues in Revelation. Without the love story of all love stories playing out in the darkest hour of history, we would never understand the importance of the blessings to come in the end.

So, Revelation isn't only a revealing about God's future wrath—it's a revealing about his love in the final hour. It isn't only a revealing about the deserved punishment of the wicked—it's a revealing about God throwing a lifeline to the lost through the bride, in one last effort to deliver us out of a world careening toward destruction.

Same plot, divine package

In every great romance is an adventure. In a romantic adventure you have three primary characters—a male protagonist (the hero), a woman (the heroine), and the antagonist (the villain).

In the high-tech, graphic film industry today, blockbuster movies throw these characters into a plethora of packaged plots. We've witnessed a super hero vs. a super villain, a cowboy hero vs. an outlaw (or alien), a martial arts hero vs. a martial arts villain, a good cop vs. a bad cop, a super black-ops soldier vs. a corrupt government with an evil president, a mutant hero vs. a mutant villain, a fairy tale hero vs. an evil witch or wizard, a good vampire vs. a bad vampire, a genius detective vs. a genius nemesis—and the list goes on. Same plot, different package.

Throw into the plot a beautiful woman with a touch of *moxie* and *mystery,* and you've got a great story. Instead of a damsel in distress, she's a confident, capable woman who partners with the hero in his effort to defeat an adversary who attempts to conquer the world and rule it like a god (or he thinks he's God).

The plot usually unfolds with mayhem and destruction, cruel and brutal injustice, a number of setbacks and overwhelming odds for the hero and heroine to plow through.

The villain typically leverages manpower and wealth to achieve his objective. Of course, the hero and heroine are the underdogs who encounter corrupt government officials, crooked politicians, ambitious corporations, gun-toting street gangs, religious fanatics, alien invaders, or black-ops organizations that stand in their way (through the story) of taking out the mastermind.

Despite the odds, we, the audience, hunker down and hang on for the ride because we know it'll end well for our heroes. We're intrinsically wired to want it that way, which is why Hollywood provides the same action-packed plot, in another newer, more advanced, hi-tech package. We're okay with the new twist in the plots and the mesmerizing graphics, as long as the story ends with *justice.* We hang on for that point in the story when the hero and heroine finally discover the weakest link in the plan, confront the mastermind, and defeat the villain in an *epic* battle that saves the world!

When the show is over, and the credits are rolling, we leave the theater satisfied that our investment of time and money was worth it. The show ends as it should have. Justice prevailed, the villain was destroyed, and the hero and heroine were vindicated and will now live happily ever after. Life is good.

In the early days of film, the package wasn't so elaborate. The villain wanted a woman who didn't want him, but he took her anyway. A hero comes along, discovers the damsel in distress, makes several attempts to rescue her until he succeeds, and then defeats the villain. They ride off into the sunset and live happily ever after. Much simpler but still the same plot. Good versus evil—good wins out.

People love stories where the guy gets the girl and the villain's defeated. But the adventure is even more fun when the heroine possesses *moxie* and *mystery*. Such is the plot in the book of Revelation, where the bride is not helpless or weak, but smart, bold, and *very* capable.

Revelation's love story

The love story in the backdrop of Revelation is an actual *future* event, not fiction. Satan, the antagonist, will incarnate the soul and body of the Antichrist. He will use this man of lawlessness, this son of perdition, to rule the world's governments, economies, militaries and wealth. He will empower him with the ability to work counterfeit miracles, signs, and wonders in which to deceive the nations. The Antichrist will hold all the leverage and possesses all the power and wealth to accomplish his nefarious plot.

Satan's prime objective is to dethrone the Son of God as the King of Kings and Lord of Lords. He intends to replace him with the Antichrist who will enslave the hearts and souls of men and women to worship, not only him, but also Satan. His elaborate scheme will engage the services of corrupt officials in world governments, world religions, and militaries to serve as pawns in this game of thrones.

God, of course, won't be mocked, for this true story includes a hero and a heroine. The Son of God will be joined by his bride, who will assist him in aiding the lost through the devastation and destruction. The war between good and evil—God and Satan—will create global collateral damage. No one will go untouched by what transpires. There'll be no place to hide from it, not even for the "preppers." The whole Earth is the battleground, and the planet will groan and travail as a scorched Earth, until justice is met. The purpose of God's coming judgments will be threefold: 1) to thwart the efforts of the Antichrist at every turn, 2) to set the stage for a wake-up call, and 3) for righteousness to shine.

The main weapon in God's arsenal will be the heroine-bride. Upon the consummation of her marriage to Christ on the Day of Atonement, she'll be equipped to confront the Antichrist. Her hero-king will watch from his throne at the Father's right hand while interceding for the saints. The King's bride will lead the army of God, like Joan of Arc who led the campaign of the French King Charles VII to drive out the English. King Jesus will overthrow Satan's plan to possess every soul in the human race. His bride will accomplish globally what he could only do regionally when he was on Earth.

Back in the land of Israel, during the Roman occupation, Jesus deployed seventy-two disciples two by two to perform healings, miracles, and deliverances. He also sent his twelve to do the same and report back to him about their successes. But his reach was limited. He had one human body, himself, and twelve disciples, who were neither born again, nor endued with the power of the Holy Spirit. They only shared in the anointing of Jesus, but didn't possess it. Also, the timing was premature for Christ to release an army that could conquer the world, not with weapons of destruction, but with weapons of love.

Christ's kingdom is a peaceful kingdom—one that began with a band of twelve apostles. Since then, it has grown to more than two billion adherents, nearly two thousand years later. But this army of saints is still hindered by the "limitations" of being an imperfect, carnally challenged church.

The exciting truth that remains hidden to many in the book of Revelation is the *unveiling* or *revealing* of a bride company that will possess the truest expression of the kingdom of her King that will have ever existed in the history of the church. She'll have no other lovers, no other distractions, and no sin nature to contend with. She'll be insanely pure, incredibly prudent, and divinely powerful—armed to the teeth with every gift of the Holy Spirit operating at maximum capacity.

Most importantly, she won't be a small band of saints as in the beginning; she'll be an army of millions, suddenly appearing on every island and continent throughout the world. And in the wake of her mission, millions will be converted to experience the same *third* work of grace and the same level of power she will possess.

As in any romantic-adventure, this woman (the bride-heroine) is a necessary part of the story in the backdrop of the prophecy. This might be a very big reason why John promised we'd be blessed if we read this book—blessed because it not only unveils the many faces of our Lord Jesus Christ, but also the redeeming role of his *unveiled* bride.

Blessed is the one who reads the words of this prophecy, and blessed are those who hear it and take to heart what is written in it, because the time is near.

—Revelation 1:3

Chapter 18

The First Four Trumpets

> When he opened the seventh seal, there was silence in heaven for about half an hour. And I saw the seven angels who stand before God, and to them were given seven trumpets.
>
> *—Revelation 8:1-2*

TRUMPETS IN THE BIBLE are symbolic of two things: judgment and blessing. Though these seven trumpets are about judgments, there is a *blessing* that comes with the results—i.e., a great harvest of souls.

At the opening of the seventh seal, the intercessory prayers of our High Priest and the prayers of the saints precede the blowing of these trumpets.[185] If we are in the last days, this intercession might coincide with the rise of the 24/7 prayer movements in the last twenty years. In response to these prayers, God not only answers with judgments, but also with blessings—perfect judgments and perfect blessings—because *seven* is the symbolic number in Scripture of *perfection* and *completion*.

The trumpet *judgments* will be attention-getting events that will humble and break down the walls of the complacent and prosperity-minded traits of the Laodicean church. The *blessings* will come by way of "opened ears" to what the Spirit is saying both to the church and to the lost about the

---

[185] Revelation 8:1-5

gospel. It is a fact that whenever severe trouble occurs, people tend to look to God for help. As it's been said, *"There are no atheists in foxholes."*

The bride will be released in power to step in and respond to the judgments by pointing people to God through the signs, wonders, and miracles that will confirm the gospel's message.

The book of Revelation doesn't elaborate on the details of these trumpet events, but they'll be clear and will come at a steady pace. The time lapse between each judgment is unknown, but it's possible they'll leave a short window for recovery between each event. Each trumpet, however, will herald such severe judgments on our planet that "normal" will cease to exist in our world.

Hail and fire—mixed with blood

Keep in mind as we go through the trumpets that not every picture in Revelation is symbolic. In the case of the trumpets, these are actual events that will occur—as real as the plagues God sent upon Egypt to deliver the children of Israel.

The sound of the *first* trumpet will bring a deluge of hail and fire, mingled with blood. This judgment will burn up a **third** of the Earth's vegetation.[186] To lose a third of our planet's vegetation is to a lose a third of the Earth's oxygen supply.

For example, one mature tree converts enough carbon dioxide into oxygen to supply two to ten people a year. Humans inhale *oxygen* and exhale *carbon dioxide*, whereas trees and plants do the opposite—they absorb carbon dioxide and produce oxygen. Without vegetation there would be no oxygen for us to breathe.

---

[186] Revelation 8:7

In addition to the loss of oxygen, consider how the plague will ignite rampant wildfires, which will be virtually impossible to control. Homes and cities will be lost, bankrupting insurance companies. In Revelation, it says that *all the grass* will burn up, grass needed to feed our livestock.

The Earth will already be reeling from the aftermath of the global earthquake caused by the opening of the sixth seal. And the famine—which first began when the *third* seal was opened—will compound exponentially. With the heavy losses of crops, grass and fruit, food prices will soar worldwide as supplies diminish and demand increases.

Enter the bride who, like Jesus, will be able to multiply the smallest amount of food to feed thousands of people. Miracles similar to the two fish and five loaves that fed the five thousand will occur. People will hear about this and will travel to wherever food can be found.

No one will be left untouched by this plague. Everyone will be impacted, just as Isaiah the prophet predicted when he said:

> See, the Lord is going to lay waste the earth and devastate it; he will ruin its face and scatter its inhabitants
> — it will be the same
>> for priest as for people,
>> for master as for servant,
>> for mistress as for maid,
>> for seller as for buyer,
>> for borrower as for lender,
>> for debtor as for creditor.
>
> The earth will be completely laid waste and totally plundered. The Lord has spoken this word.
>
> The earth dries up and withers, the world languishes and withers, the exalted of the earth languish.[187]

---

[187] Isaiah 24:1-4

A blazing asteroid and blood

The sound of the *second* trumpet will hurl a mountainous, blazing meteorite (or asteroid) from space into the sea. A **third** of the ocean will turn into blood, destroying a third of the sea creatures.[188]

Imagine the deep blue seas of the Atlantic turning scarlet with blood, down to the very depths of the oceanic trenches below the surface. All living creatures will suffocate and their carcasses will float to the surface. As they decay, the smell of blood and rotting flesh will be unbearable. The propellers of ships in the harbors and on the sea will become jammed and unable to move through the carnage. It will become the all-time greatest marine disaster, shutting down a third of the world's trade and naval operations.

When God sent the first plague upon Egypt, it turned the water of the Nile, the canals, ponds, streams and reservoirs into blood. Water contained in every bucket and vessel also turned to blood. The fish died, the river reeked, and they could only find water by digging along the banks of the Nile. As the plague in Egypt was a *literal* event, so will the plague of the second trumpet.

But still, there's hope. Perhaps the Lord will assign members of his bride to strategic ships on the sea or in shipping ports and naval bases. As Jesus operated in the gift of miracles by turning water to wine, perhaps saints will perform the miracle of turning blood back to water. Signs and wonders will occur wherever necessary to confirm the gospel.

Wormwood and polluted water

The sound of the *third* trumpet brings another great star, like a blazing torch, hurling toward the Earth. This asteroid

---

[188] Revelation 8:8-9

is given the name, "Wormwood," which means *undrinkable.* It will strike land instead of the sea, and poison a **third** of the rivers and springs, killing any living creatures that drink from them.[189]

Let's add up everything that's happened so far to the planet. We've got earthquakes, increased famine, a *third* of the Earth's vegetation burned up, a *third* of the ocean's waters turned to blood, a *third* of the ships and shipping industry destroyed, and now—the most critical and necessary of all elements for human and animal survival—a *third* of the water supply turned bitter and deadly.

I am not a scientist or an astronomer. I don't have the background necessary to understand what might happen on impact when an asteroid hits or explodes above ground. I've seen movies and read articles about it, but since we haven't observed, on a grand scale, an asteroid of such magnitude, can anyone know exactly what will occur?

The largest impact of an asteroid recorded in history occurred in 1908 in Russia. It was called the *Tunguska Event.* The explosion—estimated to be the strength of 10-15 megatons of TNT—knocked over some 80 million trees covering an area of 830 square miles. The shock wave would have measured at 5.0 on the Richter scale, capable of destroying a large city.[190]

Perhaps an eyewitness account of this event can give us a look into such an experience. Here's the testimony of S. Semenov, as recorded by Leonid Kulik's expedition in 1930:[191]

> At breakfast time I was sitting by the house at Vanavara Trading Post [*65 kilometers/40 miles south of the explosion*], facing north. [...] I suddenly saw that

[189] Revelation 8:10-11
[190] See http://en.wikipedia.org/wiki/Tunguska_event
[191] N.V. Vasiliev, A.F. Kovalevsky, S.A. Razin, L.E. Epiktetova (1981). *Eyewitness accounts of Tunguska (Crash).* Section 6, Item 4.

directly to the north, over Onkoul's Tunguska Road, the sky split in two and fire appeared high and wide over the forest [*as Semenov showed, about 50 degrees up— expedition note*]. The split in the sky grew larger, and the entire northern side was covered with fire. At that moment I became so hot that I couldn't bear it, as if my shirt was on fire; from the northern side, where the fire was, came strong heat. I wanted to tear off my shirt and throw it down, but then the sky shut closed, and a strong thump sounded, and I was thrown a few meters. I lost my senses for a moment, but then my wife ran out and led me to the house. After that, such noise came, as if rocks were falling or cannons were firing, the earth shook, and when I was on the ground, I pressed my head down, fearing rocks would smash it. When the sky opened up, hot wind raced between the houses, like from cannons, which left traces in the ground like pathways, and it damaged some crops. Later we saw that many windows were shattered, and in the barn a part of the iron lock snapped.

I'm sure that the asteroid described in the third trumpet is much stronger and larger than the Tunguska event. And when it comes to supernatural judgments brought on by God, nothing is off the table. He can do whatever he wishes, like cause an asteroid to make water undrinkable when it hits the planet.

Another opportunity for the bride

In the Old Testament, men from a nearby city approached a prophet named Elisha. They complained to him about their polluted water supply. Elisha requested they bring a bowl of salt to him. He took the salt to the spring and threw it into the bitter waters, which were then miraculously made drinkable.[192]

---

[192] 2 Kings 2:19-22

I've tasted salt water and it's not good to drink. However, salt can be used as a purifying agent. Symbolically, it shows how God can use something uncommon to make something pure. This literal event in the Old Testament is a clear example of the ability God will give the bride to turn embittered, poisonous water into sweet, purified water.

What a beacon of hope she'll be to the dying and thirsty souls of people without drinkable water. She'll be able to say what Jesus declared to the masses, "If anyone is thirsty, let him come to me and drink."[193] Of course, Jesus meant the spiritual water of life he would give. But the water the bride will offer has a double meaning: she'll be able to offer not only natural water, but the spiritual water Jesus promised to the woman at the well—the water of *eternal life*.[194]

> Everyone who drinks this [natural] water will be thirsty again, but whoever drinks the [spiritual] water I give him will never thirst. Indeed, the water I give him will become in him a spring of water welling up to eternal life.   —*Jesus*

The sun, moon, and the stars

The sound of the *fourth* trumpet will strike the sun, moon and stars, causing a **third** of the day and night to become completely pitch black.[195]

A third of a 24-hour cycle is eight hours, resulting in *four* hours of each day, and *four* hours of each night cloaked in complete darkness. Four is the symbolic number for the Earth (i.e., four corners of the Earth). It was on the *fourth* day of creation that God created these lights as *signs* to mark the seasons, days and years.[196]

---

[193] John 7:37
[194] John 4:13-14
[195] Revelation 8:12
[196] Genesis 1:14-18

To play this out visually, let's imagine that four hours before the sun sets a thick blanket of darkness descends and remains in place until four hours after the invisible setting of the sun. Not a fraction of light will appear in the sky—no dusk, just complete and utter darkness. Light will only come from candles, fire, battery operated lights, or electricity (that is, if we still have power from the electrical grid). This darkness will cover the entire planet, not just a third of the planet. It also appears this will continue for a short time since the fourth bowl of wrath that comes later, includes using the sun for judgment on the ungodly.[197]

This won't be the first time God has used supernatural signs in the heavenlies to get the world's attention. We see several accounts like this in the Bible. In Egypt, the ninth plague covered the land in thick darkness before God delivered Israel.[198] In Jerusalem, at the crucifixion of Jesus, darkness covered the land for three hours from noon to three,[199] and under the sixth seal, the sun will turn black like sackcloth.[200]

If God can cause the sun and moon to stand still at midday, for nearly 24 hours at Joshua's command,[201] then it is safe to assume the Earth literally stopped rotating. And if God could give Hezekiah a sign by causing the sun's shadow on a stairway to go backward ten steps,[202] then it is safe to assume the Earth literally reversed its rotation, momentarily.

Both are extreme miracles—so for God to create a supernatural cloak of darkness as a trumpet *sign* to the world, that won't be a challenge in the least. After all, the prophet Joel predicted this would happen:

---

[197] Revelation 16:8-9
[198] Exodus 10:21-23
[199] Matthew 27:45; Luke 23:44-45
[200] Revelation 6:12
[201] Joshua 10
[202] Isaiah 38:1-8; 2 Kings 20:1-11

In the last days, God says ... I will show wonders in the heaven above and signs on the earth below, blood and fire and billows of smoke. The sun will be turned to darkness and the moon to blood before the coming of the great and glorious day of the Lord. And everyone who calls on the name of the Lord will be saved.[203]

Jesus confirmed Joel's prophecy, too, about the last days when he said:

There will be signs in the sun, moon and stars [heavenlies]. On the earth, nations will be in anguish and perplexity at the roaring and tossing of the sea [by the tidal waves created by the great earthquake]. Men will faint from terror, apprehensive of what is coming on the world, for the heavenly bodies [including the Earth] will be shaken.[204]

So how does the bride fit in with this trumpet judgment? I can't say she'll create supernatural light to counter the darkness; but she can, as Jesus did, be *in* the world as a light that shines in the darkness ahead.[205] Read carefully the following verses regarding the saints of God being likened unto light.

Daniel 12:3-4

Those who are wise will **shine like the brightness of the heavens,** and those who lead many to righteousness, like the stars forever and ever.

Acts 26:16-18

I [Jesus] have appeared to you [Paul] to appoint you as a servant and as a witness of what you have seen of me and

---

203 Acts 2:17, 19-20; Joel 2:30-32
204 Luke 21:25-26 (Bracketed words added by author for clarity).
205 John 1:9; 3:19-21; 5:35; 8:12; 9:5; 11:9-10; 12:35-36, 46

what I will show you. I will rescue you from your own people and from the Gentiles. I am sending you to them *to* **open their eyes and turn them from darkness to light**, and from the power of Satan to God, so that they may receive forgiveness of sins and a place among those who are sanctified by faith in me.

Ephesians 5:8-11

For you [saints] were once darkness, but **now you are light in the Lord**. Live as children of **light** (for the fruit of the light consists in all goodness, righteousness and truth) and find out what pleases the Lord.

1 Thessalonians 5:5-6

You [saints] are all sons [and daughters] of the **light** and sons [and daughters] of the **day**. We do not belong to the night or to the darkness.

With these Scriptures in mind, the bride and her offspring will have enormous opportunities during these trumpets to preach the gospel to the world. Throughout the literal darkness of the fourth trumpet, they can be lights, bringing the world to the ultimate light of Jesus.

With her anointing of power on the same level as Christ, her unwavering faith, her message of love, her supernatural provision of food and water, her miracles of healings, and her untold tens of thousands of resurrections from the dead, who (but the hardest of hearts) could resist such a display of God's love at a time when nations are in anguish, people's hearts are failing for fear, and others are fainting from terror, apprehensive about what is happening to the world?

Who else could accomplish such a great harvest but Christ's glorious bride who will lead many to righteousness? When you look closely at the doomsday message of Joel, he caps off the bad news with this good news:

And everyone who calls on the name of the Lord will be saved.[206]

Closing thoughts

I believe the book of Revelation can be taken literally with its symbolism describing *actual* events. I also believe the Revelation is a book of *linear* events leading up to the second coming and beyond. The only "overlapping" events in the book are the segments or scenes taking place *simultaneously*, just as each of the four gospel accounts covered the same three-and-one-half-year ministry of Christ.

Some gospels exclude sections or stories of each account, while one or the other gospels fill in the gap. For example, many of the things that Christ said in John's gospel were excluded in the other three. Matthew, Mark, Luke and John each addressed different audiences by focusing on the Jews and/or Gentiles. Each presented Christ with a different emphasis on his identity—as *King* in Matthew, as a *Servant* in Mark, as the *Son of Man* in Luke, or as the *Son of God* in John.

Mark's gospel was simple and concise telling Christ's story. Luke's gospel was detailed and precise offering more of a historical account of the facts. Matthew was less concerned with the chronological order of events and highlighted Old Testament prophecies fulfilled in Christ in an effort to persuade Jews that Jesus of Nazareth was the true Messiah-King. John mentions fewer accounts than those found in the other gospels, but he reveals Jesus more as the Son of God and as deity, revealing the Father's traits and love to the world through Christ's *personhood*.

I say all this to show that the book of Revelation's portrait of Jesus in the last days is just as *linear* and revealing of Christ's nature and activity as the gospel

---

[206] Acts 2:17, 19-20; Joel 2:30-32

accounts of his first coming. But just as each gospel emphasized some stories and events more than others, so will each chapter of Revelation—in a linear fashion—present a picture of last-day events happening simultaneously with other events presented in the Revelation.

For example, the book of Revelation speaks frequently of a three-and-one-half-year period of time with phrases such as: *42 months, 1,260 days,* or *a time, times, and a half of time*. Scholars concur that these phrases all refer to a three-and-one-half-year period of time. And to go a step further, I believe they refer to the *same* time period, not two, three-and-one-half-year periods back to back.

Because the book of Revelation is a chronological order of events (in my opinion), I believe chapters 1 through 10 all happen *prior to* the last three-and-one-half years leading up to Christ's return. If this is true, then may I suggest that chapters 11 through 19 each present a different picture of *an* event or events taking place somewhere within the same three-and-one-half years—either at the beginning, during, or in the end.

If you will try to follow me in this logic, then the rest of my book will make sense to you. This thought is also consistent with the idea that if Christ ministered for three-and-one-half years in the gospels, then is it possible that the culmination of the gospel will end in judgment upon those who reject the message of the cross during the *last* three-and-one-half years of human history?

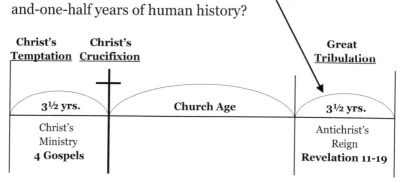

Why the first four trumpets?

> The coming of the lawless one [Antichrist] will be in accordance with the work of Satan displayed in all kinds of counterfeit miracles, signs and wonders, and in every sort of evil that deceives those who are perishing. ***They perish because they refused to love the truth and so be saved.***
>
> For this reason God sends them a powerful delusion so that they will believe the lie and so that all will be condemned ***who have not believed the truth*** but have delighted in wickedness.
>
> —*2 Thessalonians 2:9-12*

The purpose of the first four trumpets is to awaken the world's conscience, judge the unrepentant, and serve as a *sign* that the end of the age has come. Jesus will deploy his bride company throughout the world to be lights that shine in a very dark time. Those who are open to receive her message and love the *truth* will be saved, join her company of new converts, and receive the *third* work of grace that she walks in.

Those who do *not* love the truth, but delight in their wicked ways will harden their hearts, and God will harden their hearts, as well,[207] just as he hardened Pharaoh's heart.[208] He also hardened the heart of the Jews who refused to receive their Messiah, so that the Gentiles might be saved, and then they, too, would be grafted back in.[209] He will harden the hearts of the unrepentant wicked in the last days, in order to display his power through his bride, so that his name might be proclaimed in all the Earth, just as he did with Pharaoh when he displayed his power through Moses.[210]

---

[207] 2 Thessalonians 2:11-12
[208] Romans 9:17-18; Exodus 4:21; 7:3; 14:4, 17
[209] Romans 11:25
[210] Romans 9:17

The trumpets will accelerate and force the ten equal-powers to become an alliance of ten kings, who will back the rise to power of the Antichrist.

The purpose of the trumpets will also force a decision among the inhabitants of the Earth—to repent and be saved or believe the lie of the Antichrist. Those who eventually embrace the Antichrist will suffer the same judgment as the rest of the deceived world under the three remaining trumpets and the seven bowls of wrath.

> As I watched, I heard an eagle that was flying in midair call out in a loud voice: "Woe! Woe! Woe to the inhabitants of the earth, because of the trumpet blasts about to be sounded by the other three angels!"
>
> —*Revelation 8:13*

Chapter 19

A Sample of the Bride's Ministry

BEFORE I COMMENT on the last three of the seven trumpets, I'm going to insert a fictitious account taken out of my coming revised novel called, *The Unveiling*. I will show you one of my characters named, Whitney, who is a member of the bride company operating in the limitless power and anointing of the Holy Spirit. So please shift your brain from reading nonfiction to putting yourself into Whitney's shoes as a member of the bride of Christ on an assignment.

WHITNEY PASSED THROUGH the barren square of the city where a mixture of snow and soot had blanketed the cars, trees and buildings. Little activity appeared on the streets— the cold weather had driven everyone inside.

The college town of Canterton, located fifty miles from ground zero, had survived the asteroid. The megaton-sized blast had damaged homes and buildings beyond repair, leveling many to the ground. The previous earthquake from the sixth seal had so badly weakened infrastructures that they crumbled to the ground like toothpicks. The once-active city, which Whitney had enjoyed since her freshman year, was reduced to the likes of a ghost town, similar to so many other cities in the country.

As she left the city square, she moved quickly toward the low-rent district, where many lived after the job market crashed. She passed by numerous homes that had been stripped of wood siding for fuel. Active smoke stacks or chimneys meant signs of life inside, but they were few.

People who weren't prepared or informed about the poisoned waters of Wormwood, died in their homes from drinking the water supply they had drawn from rivers, streams and ponds. The stench of death escaped from the lifeless homes, though the frost-bitten air had kept much of the smell at bay.

Whitney scanned the rooflines for signs of rising smoke from an active fire. She knew she was on the right street and nearing the address she had seen on the mailbox in the vision she received.

She finally located the house, stepped onto the porch and knocked on the door. No smoke was ascending from the chimney. The pitter-patter of feet could be heard inside running to the door. The doorknob jiggled as if the occupant on the other side struggled to open it. Finally, the click of the releasing lock and a slowly opened door revealed a soot-faced child of about four years. The girl's aqua-blue eyes peered curiously through the narrow opening. Brushing back a golden lock of her hair she asked, "Are you here to help my mom?"

Whitney knelt down to her eye level and smiled, "Yes, I am. And who might you be?"

"Hannah."

"Well it's nice to meet you, Hannah," Whitney said softly, extending her leather-gloved hand, palm up. "Is it all right if I come in and see what we can do for your mom?"

The toddler looked at Whitney's hand, then into her eyes, and back at her hand again. She nodded, opened the door wide and grabbed Whitney's hand, pulling her inside. Whitney closed the door behind her and rubbed her arms.

"So where is your mother?" she asked, with the steam of her breath still noticeable.

The girl pointed to the sofa by the fireplace where her mother lay motionless. "She isn't talking," Hannah said. Her eyes welled with tears and trickled down her cheeks, leaving thin, white trails through the dirt on her face.

Whitney removed her gloves and walked to the couch. She leaned over to touch the still figure. The body was cold and stiff. She lifted her stance and looked at the child, staring at her mother. "How long has she been like this, Hannah?"

"Since yesterday morning."

"And what's your mom's name?" Whitney asked, noticing the tipped over glass on the floor beside the couch.

"Her name is Mary," she said, rubbing the back of her hand across her runny nose. "Can you wake her up?"

Whitney bent down and grabbed the empty glass. "Did your mother drink some water last night?"

Hannah nodded and said, "From the icicle she got outside. She heated it on the stove for us to drink."

Whitney took Hannah's cold, tiny hands in hers and asked, "Do you know who Jesus is, Hannah?"

"No, but mom said we should pray to him before she fell asleep."

Whitney swept the girl into her arms and onto her lap as she sat down on the edge of the couch. "Well then, why don't you and I finish your mother's prayer and ask Jesus to wake her up? Would you like that?"

"Yes," Hannah said, squeezing Whitney's hand.

Whitney leaned over to push back the curly lock of hair covering Mary's face. "Your mom is very pretty," she said, trying to hold back her tears. "She has hair like yours doesn't she?"

Hannah smiled and nodded. "She liked to brush it all the time."

Whitney chuckled and gently pulled back the blanket that had covered Mary's chest. She laid her hand over the still heart and said, "Hannah, I want you to lay your hand where my hand is and we'll ask Jesus to wake her, okay?"

"Can he do that?"

"Yes, sweetie, he can."

Hannah looked at her mom and placed her soiled, tiny hand on Whitney's.

"Father," Whitney began, "you sent me here to help Hannah and her mom. I know you're not done with Mary, and her daughter needs her, too. So, Mary, in Jesus' name, rise up now and embrace your daughter."

Immediately, the body jerked and startled Hannah. She pulled her hand away and watched her mother's eyelids flutter and open. "Oh! Oh!" Hannah shouted, "He did it! Jesus did it!"

Mary sat up, gasping for air in deep long breaths until her breathing became steady. She sat in a daze for a moment, staring across the room as though struggling to recall her surroundings. Then she turned her gaze toward Hannah.

"Momma!" Hannah cried as she climbed from Whitney's lap and threw herself into her mother's arms.

Whitney got up and moved quietly to the end of the couch as Mary and Hannah repeatedly kissed each other's cheeks, eyes, forehead and mouth. This was the part she enjoyed and had witnessed many times since her encounter with Jesus that night.

Whitney stood quietly by until she felt it appropriate to make her presence known, "Hello, Mary, my name is ..."

Mary jumped and clutched Hannah to her chest. "Who are you?"

"Mommy, it's okay," Hannah said, placing her hands on her mother's cheeks. "That's Whitney."

Whitney stepped closer and extended her hand, "Mary, I'm sorry to frighten you. Hannah let me in. I came to help."

Mary frowned and shook her head, so Whitney continued with, "God sent me here in answer to your prayers. I saw you in a vision drinking the poisoned water from that icicle you melted. It immediately entered your bloodstream and killed you. God told me to come heal you and here you are, back from the dead with the living, with a very excited daughter. So, how do you feel?"

Mary relaxed her grip on Hannah, moved to the edge of the couch and put her feet on the floor. She then touched her forehead with the back of her hand. Her eyes opened wide as she said, "My fever ... it's gone!" She immediately stood and examined her arms and legs, which were previously too weak to use. "How is this possible?" she laughed. "I'm completely healed!" She looked back at Hannah and began to weep.

"Mommy, are you okay?" Hannah asked.

"Yes, dear, mommy's okay." Mary sat down and hugged her little girl. She then looked up at Whitney with trails of tears on her face. "When I gave Hannah our last drop of fresh water," she said, "I took the icicles from the roof outside and boiled them for drinking water. It never occurred to me that the fallout would be in the icicles, too. It was our last hope for survival since the asteroid hit. I don't remember anything after I tested it because I immediately grew weak and delirious with fever. I had instructed Hannah that if anything happened to me, she was forbidden to touch the water. I started to pray with her, then everything went black."

"You died," Hannah said, grabbing her mother's arm.

Mary took her hand and said, "Yes, sweetie, I know—"

"Is she an angel?" Hannah asked, pointing at Whitney.

Mary looked gratefully at Whitney and smiled. "She's certainly an angel to us. Jesus answered our prayers before we even asked him and he sent us this wonderful new friend."

Whitney smiled and clapped her hands. "Okay then," she said with her frosty breath and a twinkle in her eye, "Let's get a fire going in here because it's freezing. Then you can take me to your kitchen and wherever it is you store your water in bottles. We're going to fill them up and I'm going to pray over each one so they're permanently healed and pure. We don't need you revisiting this tragedy. And while we're at it, let's check out your cupboards to make sure they're full of food again. You two look a little gaunt under those baggy clothes and I'm sure you're as hungry as I am."

Mary and Hannah stared at Whitney for a moment in stunned silence. Then Hannah said, "Can Jesus do all that, too?"

Whitney laughed and said, "My dear, Hannah, I can't wait to show you and your mom everything Jesus can do."

Chapter 20

Signs and Wonders of the Bride

WITHOUT GOING FURTHER into this story, let's assume that raising a dead mother to life, purifying her water supply, and multiplying her food was only part of the good news.

Perhaps Mary wasn't a Christian, but she looked to Jesus for help despite her past understanding of him. Surely Hannah would have known about Jesus if her mother had been a Christian. So she and Hannah desperately needed someone to show them the way, but it began with their urgent need, brought on by the trumpet judgments that gave God the opportunity to show his greatness, love and compassion through Whitney. Since the prime objective of the bride will be to win souls to Christ, miracles will open doors and hearts to receive the gospel.

In Acts 10, Peter was in Joppa, at the home of a tanner named Simon. While praying on the rooftop, Peter fell into a trance and received a vision from God. In Caesarea, 30 miles north along the coastland, a centurion named Cornelius had received an angelic vision about Peter and sent three men to retrieve him. Peter received an important message in his vision, which included an assignment from God to go with these men to the home of a Roman centurion—a Gentile.

When Peter arrived with his men and heard how an angel had visited Cornelius, he presented the gospel for the first time to the Gentiles. As Peter shared the story of Christ and his resurrection, they received his message, became born again, and spoke in tongues—*before* Peter finished his message. This shocked Peter and the other Jews who were with him. They simply couldn't deny that God had just given the same gift to the Gentiles as he had to the Jews on the feast day of Pentecost—Cornelius and his household received both the *first* and *second* works of grace, *simultaneously.*[211]

Other incidents of conversions in the book of Acts show these works of grace received *sequentially.* First, came their born-again experience (Passover), and sometime later, their Pentecost experience, evidenced by speaking in tongues. But, here in Cornelius' house, both were received at the exact same time. So Peter had no choice but to baptize them right away in water.

Given this account of an early church experience, it isn't without reason that the same experience can happen to everyone who receives the message of Christ in the last day's gospel blitz upon a lost and turbulent world. Only this time they'll receive, not *one* work of grace, not *two* works of grace, but all *three* works of grace. The miracles and actions recorded in the book of Acts will be even greater in the last days through the bride's ministry.

As in the case of Peter, God sent him and Cornelius a vision that would connect them together and fulfill his kingdom purposes of bringing the gospel to Gentiles. Cornelius, a devout and prayerful man, needed salvation. He needed someone who could show him how to be saved through the message of the cross. Peter presented the good news and the whole household believed and received salvation.

In my fictitious demonstration of Whitney's anointing and power as a member of the bride, she had received an assignment from God in response to the prayers of an unsaved mother dying from the waters of Wormwood. Think

---

[211] Acts 10:1-48

of the magnitude of that one assignment for a moment. Put yourself in Whitney's place, imagining yourself bringing that gift of life. Now take this one story and multiply it all over the world through the glorious bride who has millions of members being directed by the Holy Spirit and carrying out *their* miracle-working assignments. Such an encounter with a person like Whitney would no doubt result in a household of new converts to Christianity. And the family members of that household would experience all *three* works of grace, simultaneously—Passover, Pentecost and Tabernacles. Every new convert will become the "offspring" of the bride's ministry, walking in the same power God displayed in Whitney.

Why is it so important that all *three* works of grace are given immediately? Because the army must be equipped with a completely unwavering, active faith to operate in everything God assigns them to do. No time for basic training. The warrior-bride's new converts will be inducted into her Bridegroom's army *sanctified* and *sinless*. Receiving the experiences of Passover, Pentecost and Tabernacles will be essential to bombard the world with the good news. The world will be in a full-blown state of survival, which will necessitate instant maturity to quickly advance the gospel and assist the wounded, the poisoned, the dying, the dead, the hungry and the lost.

But while the harvest ingathering grows powerfully and exponentially, a growing threat looms on the horizon. Once the Antichrist comes into full power, backed by the ten-kingdom rulers, the new world religion, and a one-world military, Christians and Jews will become the target of their wrath—blamed somehow for the devastation of the world.

Until then, however, the fields are still ripe. Imagine the impact of such a harvest. Millions within the ranks of the bride recruiting millions of new converts who not only receive a *sinless* nature, but also are equipped with the Holy

Spirit's anointing to heal the sick, give sight to the blind, hearing to the deaf, voice to the mute, legs to the lame, life to the dead, restored minds and memories to the mentally ill, fresh water from the polluted waters, and small food rations multiplied to feed not just thousands, but millions of starving people. What an army! What an incredible harvest we have to look forward to! Would the current condition and faith level of the church today be able to produce such a harvest? Not without the supernatural power of God.

Nothing I've depicted in the story of the previous chapter is unfamiliar to accounts seen in the Old and New Testaments. Why should we believe in a lesser scenario, like the cessationists who teach that the gifts of the Spirit ceased with the early church apostles, and that God no longer performs miracles today? Who can claim, with any authority, that God won't do this again when the Bible declares:

> The Lord does *whatever* **pleases** him, in the heavens and on the earth, in the seas and all their depths.[212]

If it pleased God to make man in his likeness and in his image as *sinless* human beings *before* Adam fell, why wouldn't it please him to make the bride and her offspring sinless and commensurate to Christ's stature, so that she can blast the world with a message backed by incredible feats?

Why wouldn't it please God to use signs and wonders? He sent them to Pharaoh and his gods in Egypt. He bestowed his Son with them to reveal his kindness. And, he backed the gospel of the apostles and early church with signs and wonders and miracles.[213] Why would he break the pattern he used throughout the Bible to reach the world in its darkest hour?

---

[212] Psalm 136:5
[213] Mark 16:19-20

Atheists, agnostics and nonreligious people, as well as those involved in world religions, scoff at our intellectual debates about theology and doctrine—and they aren't impressed. Muslims, too, aren't impressed with our message because their Jesus (Isa) will return to assist the Twelfth Imam or last caliph to become their future messiah. But if you perform healings, signs and wonders in the name of Jesus Christ—now then, you've got their attention!

How much more powerful can the gospel be, than through *signs* and *wonders* confirming that Christ has risen from the dead and is coming soon? Some believe that our technological advancements in social media are sufficient enough to bring in the last great harvest of souls. Not that it can't to some degree since that's our *present* condition, but what if there will be no access to technology after the great earthquake followed by the judgments of the first four trumpets? What if the electrical grid is knocked out?

Even if we had electricity and technology in some parts of the world, would using it to present the gospel change more minds than it already does now? Or would the circulating reports of millions of converts, brought to Christ through miracles, really grab people's hearts? I'll place my bet on the latter.

The Spirit and the bride say, "Come!"
—Revelation 22:17

Chapter 21

The Fallen Star

WE ARE NOW in chapter 9 of Revelation, which is preceded by this warning:

> As I watched, I heard an eagle that was flying in midair call out in a loud voice: "Woe! Woe! Woe to the inhabitants of the earth, because of the trumpet blasts about to be sounded by the other three angels!"[214]

The first four trumpets deal with judgments on the Earth, but the fifth trumpet is an actual "revealing" of a person—not another asteroid or comet—but a person who is *deceived* and fallen from a position of great heights.

> The fifth angel sounded his trumpet, and I saw a *star* that had **fallen** from the sky to the earth.[215]

A fallen star

I remember when my dad woke me up one summer night and drove my siblings and me to the country to witness a meteor shower. That was my first experience to see what dad said were stars falling from the sky.

Stars are mostly used in the Bible to symbolize people or spiritual beings such as Lucifer, angels,[216] Jesus,[217]

---

[214] Revelation 8:13
[215] Revelation 9:1

Abraham's spiritual descendants,[218] messengers, spiritual leaders, saints,[219] or fallen saints who, like *wandering* stars, have left the orbital path of their heavenly position.[220]

Several theories exist about the identity of this particular "star" heralded by the fifth trumpet. Let's first set aside the thought of it being another asteroid, because this star describes a *person*, not an object. Some believe it's Lucifer, others believe it's a mighty angel; but I'm of the opinion it's someone who comes from a high-ranking position of spiritual authority. Here's why.

Not only are individual numbers symbolic in the Bible, but also numeric "patterns" based on the order of certain events. For example, we'll consider the numeric pattern of **three**, **twelve**, and **one** according to the "order" of events that have transpired in heaven, in Israel, in the gospels, and—possibly—in the last-days' church. Read closely:

- *The Heavenly Order*—here we see three: the Father, Son, and Holy Spirit; twelve archangels according to Jewish tradition; and one archangel is *fallen*: **Lucifer**.

- *Israel's Order*—here we see three: the Father, Son, and Holy Spirit; twelve sons of Israel (Jacob); and one son is *fallen*: **Reuben**.

- *The Gospel's Order*—here we see three: the Father, Son, and Holy Spirit; twelve apostles of Jesus; and one apostle is *fallen*: **Judas Iscariot**.

- *The Last-Days' Church Order*—here we see three: the Father, Son, and Holy Spirit; twelve last-days' apostles (perhaps symbolized by the twelve stars

---

216 Isaiah 14:12-14; Luke 10:18; Job 38:7; Psalm 148:2
217 Revelation 22:16
218 Genesis 15:1-5
219 Daniel 12:3; Philippians 2:15; Revelation 1:16
220 Daniel 8:10; Jude 13; Revelation 12:4

crowning the woman in Revelation 12:1); and <u>one</u> is *fallen*: the **Antichrist**.

Notice what every "fallen one" in the list of numeric patterns has in common—they've *all* been deceived.

The Antichrist is the *antithesis* of Jesus Christ, holding *contrasting* similarities. For example, Jesus is the Son of God; the Antichrist is the son of Satan. The public ministry of Jesus covered three-and-one-half years; the worldwide rule of the Antichrist will also cover three-and-one-half years. Jesus had twelve apostles including Judas (the son of perdition) who fell away and betrayed him; in the last-days' church, I believe Jesus will have twelve living apostles on Earth, and the man of lawlessness, the son of **perdition**, (perhaps) a fallen apostle who betrays Christ and his church.

Thus we have this *pattern* of "order" in four places:

Heaven	Three	—Father, Son and Holy Spirit
	Twelve	—Archangels — according to Jewish Tradition
	1 <u>Fallen</u>	—the archangel, Lucifer (son of the morning)[221]
Israel	Three	—Father, Son and Holy Spirit
	Twelve	—Sons of Israel (Jacob)
	1 <u>Fallen</u>	—Reuben (lost his rights as the firstborn)[222]
Gospels	Three	—Father, Son and Holy Spirit
	Twelve	—Apostles of Jesus
	1 <u>Fallen</u>	—Judas Iscariot (the son of **perdition**)[223]
Last Days	Three	—Father, Son and Holy Spirit
	Twelve	—Last-Day Apostles (crown of twelve stars)[224]
	1 <u>Fallen</u>	—the Antichrist (the son of **perdition**)[225]

---

[221] Isaiah 14:12—"How are you fallen from heaven, O Lucifer, son of the morning!"

[222] Genesis 35:22; 49:3-4; 1 Chronicles 5:1

[223] **Perdition**—means to have lost something, utter destruction, eternal damnation; Judas is called the son of **perdition** by Jesus (John 17:12).

[224] Revelation 12:1—the glorious bride of Christ. "Twelve" is the number of spiritual and governmental authority in the Bible.

[225] The Antichrist is called the son of **perdition** by Paul (2 Thessalonians 2:3).

I believe the **star** of the *fifth* trumpet is the Antichrist, because he opens the shaft to the *Abyss*.[226] This can be determined by comparing this "star" to the "beast" (or Antichrist[227]) that comes out of the *Abyss* in Revelation 11:7.

I believe the Antichrist is given a key under the *fifth* trumpet in order to unleash demonic principalities and powers upon the Earth, *before* his debut to the world. During this five-month period of torment upon the Earth's inhabitants, the Antichrist will be able to position himself (behind the scenes) by brokering deals with the ten-king alliance and their emerging kingdoms. He'll also have time to align himself with top-ranking religious leaders among world religions, financial moguls, crime lords, kingpins, government officials, political and national leaders, and high-ranking military leaders (both rogue and official).

With a world drowning in chaos, the timing will be perfect for presenting himself as the solution for survival. In the wake of the first four trumpets, followed by the demonic hordes, the world will cry, "Uncle! We give! Who else but *this* man can lead us out of our mess?"

Five months of torment

Among the events of the fifth trumpet, the fallen "star" is given a key to unlock the shaft of the Abyss and release locust-like demons that will torment the ungodly for *five* months. I believe they're literal. The Scriptures say an angel-king from the Abyss, called "Destroyer,"[228] will lead them. The scorpion-like sting of these creatures will be so painful that the afflicted will seek death, but death will elude

---

[226] *Abyss*—the underworld realm of spirits.
[227] Revelation 13:1-8
[228] In Hebrew—*Abaddon* (destruction); in Greek—*Apollyon* (destroyer).

them.[229] This is only the *first* of three woes the eagle warns is coming upon the Earth.

I've been stung by bees, hornets, wasps, sea urchins and even the pectoral barb of a catfish fin—but never a scorpion. The venom of the catfish barb was the most painful I had ever experienced—so painful it felt like my thumb was going to fall off. I couldn't find relief fast enough. And if the puncture of a catfish barb in my hand can hurt that bad, I can't imagine how tormenting the sting of a scorpion is. I've heard it's excruciating.

The good news, however, is that the bride and all the saints will not be stung when these creatures arrive. We've been marked with a seal on our foreheads, and no demon can hurt us.[230] Even more good news is the fact that the bride's power will be able to heal the ungodly that are tortured by these demons, just as Jesus delivered the demoniac from his tormenter, Legion.[231]

On a side note, I've often wondered how a plague of stinging demons could benefit the Antichrist, that is, if he is the one who opens the Abyss to release them. Perhaps in his own deception, he might think it would slow down the momentum of the bride's harvest. Or by adding this nightmarish experience to the horrific global mess, it might accelerate the rush to place the world into the hands of a messiah—himself.

The great apostasy

As demonstrated earlier, during the time of the seven trumpets, a great harvest of souls will occur. But while the light of the gospel grows brighter, darkness and wickedness

---

[229] Revelation 9:1-11
[230] Ephesians 1:13; Revelation 7:3; 9:4
[231] Mark 5:1-17

will increase and the love of many will grow cold, including the love of Christians.[232]

A great falling away of believers, called the *apostasy*, will increase throughout the trumpet judgments *before* the Antichrist makes his debut. By the time he steps out on the world stage, backslidden believers will make up *one-third* of all spiritual leaders in the church, including *one-third* of those who follow these spiritual leaders in their churches.

This visual of the future is demonstrated in Revelation 12:3-4 where Satan (as an enormous red dragon) sweeps *a third* of the stars out of the sky and flings them to the Earth.[233] I don't believe these are Satan's fallen angels, as some teach from a historicist view, but fallen "stars" of saints who, like the Antichrist, will fall into great deception. These apostates will succumb to the world's sevenfold ideologies[234] within the political and economic stratagem of the ten-kingdom alliance already under way.

Spiritual leaders, and the saints who follow them, will abandon their faith, giving heed to seducing spirits and doctrines of demons.[235] Because of their delusion and willingness to believe a lie, they'll be overcome by the imposing charm, charisma, authority, wisdom and supernatural power of the Antichrist, who is backed by the ten world equal-powers, including an ecumenical one-world church.

Paul predicted this would happen in his letter to Timothy when he said:[236]

---

[232] Matthew 24:12
[233] Revelation 12:3-4
[234] The seven heads on the red dragon represent seven world empires—Egypt, Assyria, Babylon, Medo-Persia, Greece, Rome and the new world order of ten kings led by the Antichrist. Each world empire represents ideologies that will blend and culminate into the last-days' empire of the Antichrist.
[235] 1 Timothy 4:1
[236] 1 Timothy 4:1-2; 2 Timothy 3:1-5

The Spirit clearly says that in later times *some will abandon the faith* and follow deceiving spirits and things taught by demons. Such teachings come through hypocritical liars, whose consciences have been seared as with a hot iron.

But mark this: There will be terrible times in the last days. People will be ... lovers of pleasure rather than lovers of God—*having a form of godliness* but *denying its power.*[237]

Paul predicted this same *apostasy* in his letter to the church of Thessalonica:

Brothers and sisters, we have something to say about the coming of our Lord Jesus Christ and the time when we will meet together with him. ... That day of the Lord will not come until **the turning away from God** happens and the Man of Evil, who is on his way to hell, appears. He will be against and put himself above anything called God or anything that people worship. And that Man of Evil will even go into God's Temple and sit there and say that he is God.[238]

The reason I'm so passionate about teaching and equipping others to become disciples is because of this dire warning God gives his saints about **apostasy**. No leader or saint is immune from this possibility, which is why the book of Revelation, and Paul's repeated admonitions, compel me to present this truth as a reality we can't ignore. As we end this chapter about the thought of a "fallen" apostle, consider these warnings from Paul for yourself. They're not put in the Bible just for your neighbor or the person who sits next to you in the pew. They're in there for you and me.

---

[237] 2 Timothy 3:1-5
[238] 2 Thessalonians 2:1, 3-4 (New Century Version)

1 Corinthians 10:12

If you think **you** are standing firm, *be careful* that **you** don't fall!

1 Timothy 4:16

Watch ***your*** *life* and doctrine closely. Persevere in them, because if **you** do, **you** will save both **yourself** and your hearers.

Hebrews 2:1

We must *pay more careful attention*, therefore, to what **we** have heard, so that **we** do not drift away.

Hebrews 3:2

See to it, brothers, that none of **you** has a sinful, unbelieving heart that *turns away* from the living God.

Chapter 22

Conviction or Preference?

I WANT TO INSERT a thought here before we go to the next event in Revelation. In the previous chapter, I mentioned that God issues a dire warning to those who succumb to apostasy. But how does that happen? Nobody just wakes up one morning and says, "I think I'll figure out a way to abandon my faith so I can be deceived by false ideologies, demons, or the Antichrist." I've never met anyone like that, have you?

Deception develops, oh so subtly—like the proverbial slow-cooking frog in the kettle—and mostly without our knowledge until someone or the Holy Spirit points it out. People who are deceived don't think of themselves that way, nor be aware of it if they were. So what lays a foundation for becoming deceived, and how can we catch it before it becomes entrenched in our spirit? There are many root causes for deception, but I want to focus on the word, "relativism."

Relativism is the philosophical term for people who believe there is no absolute truth—which means no system of *proclaimed* truth is more valid than another because there's no objective standard for truth. Truth becomes *relative* to the culture and environment of each social group. Therefore, all morals and ethics are *relative* to the constructs of what each society deems as moral or ethical.

For example, one culture esteems women as human beings, whereas another culture believes women are mere possessions and they serve at the pleasure of the owner. However, if a man *prefers* that women be free and equal in opportunity to men, then he might *prefer* to live in a society relative to that belief. If he believes the other way, then he might *prefer* to live in a country with an ideology, religious system or cultural *preference* that leans in that direction.

In its basic form, relativism is the "party line" of *preference*. It floats upon the waves of popular opinion. Rudderless and without an anchor—it gradually drifts from the shoreline toward an endless sea of confusion. Preference is *not* the way of a Christian whose convictions are grounded in the standards and principles of God.

In chapter 3 of the book of Daniel, three exiles from Judah refused to join the party of *preference*. Here's what happened. Nebuchadnezzar, the king of Babylon, had invited every official in his kingdom to the dedication of a 90-foot statue made in his likeness. Skilled musicians, with six different instruments, sounded the call to bow and worship the image. But these exiles did not.

It was *preferable* to bow for those who valued their lives—an expedient gesture to avoid dishonoring the king and incurring his wrath. Whoever had their own gods could simply "pretend" to worship the king's image and avoid the consequences—i.e., just flow with the crowd and bow like everyone else. This mindset is a *preference* for beliefs that are "negotiable."

The three exiles—Shadrach, Meshach, and Abednego—were among the highest-ranking officials in the Babylonian province, put there by the king himself sixteen years earlier. Yet they refused to bow. Their convictions superseded political expediency. Their God, the true God, required that none of his people should bow or worship the image of any created thing.[239]

Threatened by the king with fire, these men boldly declined the offer for a second chance and placed their trust in God. Enraged, the king heated the flames seven times hotter, so hot that it killed the guards when they threw the men into the furnace.

Relativism (preference over conviction) would try to reason with Shadrach, Meshach, and Abednego and say, "What's the big deal? Why spoil the party? What will it hurt? Are your beliefs so important you're willing to die over a little bowing?" Nothing, however, could persuade them to love their lives more than their love for God. They refused to denounce him.

The moment we attempt to save face or save our place in life over conviction is the moment we yield to *relativism*. The disciples of Jesus were persecuted and martyred for their convictions. Jesus Christ, the Messiah, the Son of the living God held their hearts with such conviction they never flinched in the face of death.

In the last days, another Nebuchadnezzar-like king—the Antichrist—will rise to rule a global empire. Like the Babylonian king he, too, will have a statue made in his likeness and command every knee to bow and worship it or die. Those who don't will lose their heads.[240]

How will our conviction hold up under such pressure? Will relativism have us *prefer* not to bow in order to save ourselves? Or will we stand up to the ruler of that day and say, "No thanks—I'm ready to meet Jesus."

Christians of *preference* (negotiable beliefs) cannot be Christ's disciples or overcomers because true disciples will carry unyielding convictions in the face of death. They'll do

---

[239] Exodus 20:3-5a
[240] Revelation 13:11-17

so because they have determined that *to die is gain*—long before the test of conviction comes knocking at their door.

> If anyone comes to me and does not hate ... **even his own life**—he cannot be my disciple.
>
> —*Jesus*[241]

> Whoever loses his life for my sake will find it.
>
> —*Jesus*[242]

> They overcame him [Satan] by the blood of the Lamb and by the word of their testimony [conviction]; **they did not love their lives so much** as to shrink from death.
>
> —*Revelation 12:11*

---

[241] Luke 14:26
[242] Matthew 10:39b

Chapter 23

A Third of Mankind

> The *sixth* angel sounded his trumpet, and I heard a voice coming from the horns of the golden altar that is before God. It said to the sixth angel who had the trumpet, "Release the four angels who are bound at the great river Euphrates." And the four angels who had been kept ready for this very hour and day and month and year were released to kill a third of mankind.
>
> —*Revelation 9:13-15*

WE COME NOW to the plague of the sixth trumpet and *second woe* upon the Earth. The unique thing about this trumpet is that a voice from the horns of heaven's *golden altar of incense* gives the command to release four angels at the Euphrates upon evil mankind.[243]

In the Tabernacle of Moses, the golden altar of incense stood before the veil hiding the Ark of the Covenant. Its four horns were sprinkled with blood every year on the Day of Atonement.

This action symbolized the high priest's intercession of God for mercy and a pardon for man's sins. In Revelation 8:3, prior to the sounding of the seven trumpets, incense and

---

[243] Revelation 9:13

prayers for all mankind are being offered to God at this golden altar before his throne in heaven.

Since that time of prayer at heaven's golden altar, five trumpets have sounded to release severe judgments upon the Earth while the bride ministers to present Christ to the world in the most effective and merciful way. Despite the love and mercy of God being extended to the lost—through his glorious bride—billions of souls will still harden their hearts to the message of the cross and refuse their opportunity for pardon.

For the sixth trumpet,[244] the cry from the horns of the golden altar isn't for mercy this time—it's for judgment. As the blood of Abel's voice and the voice of the martyrs under the fifth seal cried out for God to avenge their deaths,[245] the voice from the horns of the golden altar now releases vengeance upon the willful ungodly who reject the merciful blood of Jesus, and the saints who interceded on their behalf.[246]

These four fallen angels have been kept bound (since Lucifer's rebellion) at the river Euphrates from the Garden of Eden where Satan deceived Eve. Now they're released to lead 200 million mounted troops of demonic creatures. These creatures will slay *a **third*** of mankind. Not the saints or those who are yet to repent and be known by God, but the relentlessly unrepentant souls of the ungodly.

Global data organizations estimate that more than 200,000 people are added daily to the world's population. As of this writing, there are 7.25 billion people in the world and research indicates 8.25 billion by 2025. Religious data places the adherents of Christianity at approximately 2 billion. It's the largest and fastest growing religion in the world with a

---

244 Revelation 9:1
245 Genesis 4:10; Luke 11:51; Hebrews 12:2; Revelation 6:9-11
246 Revelation 8:3-4

projection of 2.6 billion by 2025. The creatures won't harm the true believers among those 2.6 billion people. That leaves the remaining 5.6 billion unbelievers vulnerable to the attacks. If this happened today with these statistics—not including the great harvest that will occur under the bride's ministry—then one-third of the remaining 5.6 billion unbelievers would be 1.8 billion people slain by the creatures. That would be more than the population of China (1.3 billion) or India (1.2 billion), the two largest populations in the world.

This means each demonic creature of the mounted troops will kill at least nine people. And for those who don't have eyes to see or ears to hear the message of the cross—they will shake their fists at God and still not repent.[247]

Here is the vision that John saw of these creatures, a description that sounds like something from the imagination of a special-effects team for a science-fiction movie. The difference being, *this isn't fiction.*

Their breastplates were fiery red, dark blue, and yellow as sulfur. The heads of the horses resembled the heads of lions, and out of their mouths came fire, smoke and sulfur. A third of mankind was killed by the three plagues of fire, smoke and sulfur that came out of their mouths. The power of the horses was in their mouths and in their tails; for their tails were like snakes, having heads with which they inflict injury.[248]

Notice the contrast between these creatures and the demonic creatures of the fifth trumpet. The first wave of demons stung and tormented their victims for five months, but those who were stung couldn't die.

---

[247] Revelation 9:20-21
[248] Revelation 9:17-19

The mounted troops of these demonic creatures, however, will kill people with the smoke, fire and sulfur breathed from the mouths of lion-headed horses. Their snake-like tails with heads will inflict terminal injury. These predators from hell will *stalk* their prey and smell out the hate and fear of the ungodly who defiantly refuse to stop their worship of demons, murders, sorcery, witchcraft, sexual immorality and thefts.[249]

The writer of Hebrews warns of such a time of judgment when he said:

> See to it that you do not refuse him who speaks. If they [Israel] did not escape when they refused him who warned them on earth, how much less will we, if we turn away from him who warns us from heaven? At that time his voice shook the earth, but now he has promised, "Once more I will shake not only the earth but also the heavens." The words "once more" indicate the removing of what can be shaken—that is, created things—so that what cannot be shaken may remain.[250]

This will be a time of great shaking. One-third of the created things of Earth have already been removed, and one-third of mankind will be removed next, like wheat sifted through a sieve.

The bride and her offspring will continue to shine at this time while the world's population of the wicked is whittled down to 4 billion unbelievers. They will set their faces like flint against God and his ambassadors, and be more hateful and vengeful than ever, ready to be rid of all Christians and Jews. For now, however, the burnings or burials of 1.8 billion people must be attended to. Revenge will come later.

---

[249] Revelation 9:20-21
[250] Hebrews 12:25-27

It's necessary to remember that the plagues of all six trumpets will occur *during* the time of the bride's supernatural ministry. She'll operate within the context of a world under siege by God's judgments. In the meantime, behind closed doors in the "back room," a world leader is being groomed to rescue and deliver the Earth from its desperate condition. By the conclusion of the sixth trumpet, the stage will be set for the Antichrist to play his hand. The world's religious leaders and the ten-king alliance will move toward inaugurating him as an emperor-king—ruler of the religious, political, and economic factions all gearing up for survival.

Because of the mounting hatred toward the God of Christians and Jews, the wicked ungodly will target them as the source of the world's problems. They'll blaspheme and annihilate them with the full endorsement of the Antichrist when he comes into power. These times will occur under the period of the *seventh* trumpet when it "begins" to sound, and will continue to sound, throughout the forty-two months (or three-and-one-half years) of the Antichrist's reign.

The Bride's Ministry/Harvest Time	*Antichrist's Reign*	
Trumpet Judgments — Revelation 8-9	**42-month period**	
• *1st Trumpet* – **1/3rd** Earth	Rev. 11	
• *2nd Trumpet* – **1/3rd** sea	Rev. 12	
• *3rd Trumpet* – **1/3rd** rivers and springs	Rev. 13	
• *4th Trumpet* – **1/3rd** sun, moon, stars (darkness)	Rev. 14	
• *5th Trumpet* – **Fallen Star**/Abyss/demonic hordes		Rev. 15
• *6th Trumpet* – **1/3rd** mankind killed/4 evil angels		Rev. 16
	Rev. 17	Rev. 18
• *7th Trumpet* **Sounds**	- - - - - - - - - ➤	

Chapter 24

The Angel and the Little Scroll

So I went to the angel and asked him to give me the little scroll. He said to me, "Take it and eat it. It will turn your stomach sour, but in your mouth it will be as sweet as honey." I took the little scroll from the angel's hand and ate it. It tasted as sweet as honey in my mouth, but when I had eaten it, my stomach turned sour. Then I was told, "You must prophesy again about many peoples, nations, languages and kings."

—Revelation 10:9-11

BETWEEN THE SIXTH seal and the seventh seal, Revelation chapter 7 inserts events preceding the opening of the seventh seal containing the seven trumpets.

Now we arrive at another insertion of events in Revelation chapter 10, between the sixth trumpet and the seventh trumpet containing the seven bowls of wrath. Revelation 10 prepares us for all the subsequent events occurring simultaneously during the final three-and-one-half years before the battle of Armageddon and the return of Christated. It looks like this:

- Revelation 6 – 1st through **6th seal** opened
- Revelation 7 – <u>parenthetical</u> events *before* the 7th seal
- Revelation 8 – **7th seal** opened containing the 7 trumpets

- Revelation 9 – 1st through **6th trumpets** sounded
- Revelation 10 – <u>parenthetical</u> events *before* the 7th trumpet
- Revelation 11-19 – **7th trumpet** events of the last 3½ years

The messenger-angel with a scroll

Chapter 10 begins with a mighty angel coming down from heaven. Read John's vision and see if you recognize this angel based on the adjectives used to describe him:

> He was robed in a **cloud**, with a **rainbow** above his head; his face was like the **sun**, and his legs were like **fiery** pillars. He was holding a little scroll, which lay open in his hand. He **planted** his right **foot** on the sea and his left **foot** on the land, and he gave a loud shout like the roar of a **lion**. When he shouted, the **voices** of the seven thunders spoke.
>
> —*Revelation 10:1-3*

Most expositors agree that this is the Lord Jesus Christ. I believe that, too, when you see the description of his title, clothing, head, face, legs, feet, hands, and voice—all of which match the biblical descriptions of his nature, character, and authority in other parts of the Bible.

As for the *seven* thunders, their meaning is not mentioned, but they are loud and perhaps as loud as the roar of a large waterfall.[251] Perhaps the idea behind the seven thunders is that of "completing" the period of the trumpet judgments and beginning the period of the "great" tribulation as the *seventh* trumpet "begins" to sound.

The "sevens" in Revelation

Seven is the prominent number in the book of Revelation and symbolizes *finality, completion, maturity,* and *perfection.* In Revelation there are *seven* churches, *seven* spirits, *seven* seals, *seven* trumpets, *seven* thunders, and *seven* bowls of wrath. This suggests that Revelation's theme

---

[251] Revelation 1:15

is about wrapping up, finalizing, and completing all things pertaining to Earth in its unredeemed state.

Along with this theme of "completeness" we see how God deals with two categories of people: the *ungodly* and the *godly*. Ungodly people become completely wicked, stubborn, and cold-hearted toward God, whereas the godly become completely mature, equipped, perfected, and preserved. [252]

The ungodly are "incrementally" destroyed throughout the events of the trumpets and seven bowls of wrath. And the wicked who survive the trumpets and the bowls, are *completely* destroyed at the time of the war against Jesus when he returns.[253] At the end of Revelation, the ungodly are *completely* separated from God for all eternity.[254] The godly, however, are *completely* sold out to Jesus until the end of their lives in the last days, after which they are resurrected into *complete* redemption, eternal bliss, and a life with God— never to be oppressed again by the wicked.[255]

The little scroll

The little scroll laying open in the hand of Jesus is only mentioned in one other place in the Bible. In the Old Testament, Daniel declares that God's words on a scroll are to be "closed up and sealed till the time of end."[256] Here, it's opened by Christ, who alone is worthy to do so.

The vision of John in Revelation 10 matches the vision in Daniel 12 in regard to the time period of Revelation,[257] the end of time. Now that the scroll is opened, the *seventh* trumpet "begins" to sound and "continues" to sound during the last three-and-one-half years of human history. The New

---

[252] Compare with Daniel 12:9-10
[253] 2 Thessalonians 1:6-10; 2:8
[254] 2 Thessalonians 1:9-10; Revelation 20:11-15
[255] Revelation 5:9-11; 7:9-17; 15:2-4; 20:4; 22:1-5
[256] Daniel 12:9
[257] Daniel 12:1-10

King James Version says: "In the "**days**" of the sounding of the seventh angel..."[258]

In Daniel chapter 9, the prophet was shown a timeline of 490 years or 70 weeks of years.[259] The first 486½ years or 69½ weeks of Daniel's prophecy stretches from the decree of Cyrus, the Persian king,[260] to the day of Christ's crucifixion in A.D. 30.[261] Detailed events of that time period we're given to Daniel and confirmed later by Jesus, who also predicted the destruction of the city by Prince Titus,[262] plus the *signs* of the times occurring in the last days.[263] Jesus also fulfilled Daniel's vision of the Messiah (the Anointed One) who would be cut off and crucified for our sins in A.D. 30.[264]

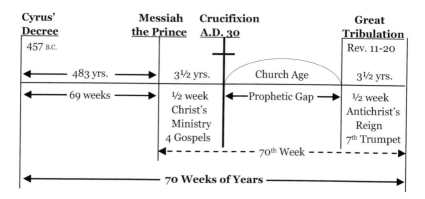

As mentioned earlier, the contents of Daniel's 70-week prophecy provide specific details for the events of the first 69½ weeks, up to the cross. Daniel didn't, however, provide

---

[258] Revelation 10:7

[259] Daniel 9:20-27—1 day equals a year, 7 days equals a week of 7 years, and 70 weeks equals 7x7 weeks of 490 years. Notice the use of "sevens"— the symbolic number of completion and finality.

[260] Daniel 9:25 with Isaiah 44:24-45:4; 2 Chronicles 36:22-23; Ezra 1:1-4

[261] Daniel 9:25-27 with Isaiah 53:8, 12

[262] Daniel 9:26—The people [Rome] of the ruler [Titus] who will come will destroy the city [Jerusalem] and the sanctuary [Herod's Temple]. Luke 21:20-24—about Titus in A.D. 70.

[263] Luke 21:25-28—the signs of the last days.

[264] Daniel 9:26; Isaiah 53:8

details for the *last* three-and-one-half years—the *last* half week of the 70th week. Again, the vision given to Daniel specified that the scroll was to be closed up and sealed, not to be understood until the time of the end days.[265]

Revelation is the only other book in the Bible that mentions a period of three-and-one-half years and is, therefore, the most logical fulfillment of the last half week of Daniel's 70th week. There aren't "two" distinct periods of three-and-one-half years in Revelation. Instead, they are one and the same period in *every* place Revelation mentions the time covered in the *last* half week of Daniel's prophecy during the Great Tribulation. Here is where this period is mentioned in Revelation:

Revelation 11 — mentions *42 months*[266] and *1,260 days.*[267]

Revelation 12 — mentions a period of *1,260 days*[268] and *a time, times, and half a time.*[269]

Revelation 13 — mentions *42 months.*[270]

It's important to note going forward that we'll focus on chapters 11 through 20 of the book of Revelation and present the details of all the events leading up to the second coming of Christ. Revelation's events aren't random. The book is an actual *linear* account—from chapter 1 to 22—of the events of the last days.

So each chapter mentioned above (Revelation 11, 12, and 13) have timeframes that cover the *same* three-and-one-half years of the Great Tribulation.

The *first* half week of Daniel's 70th week is found in the period of the three-and-one-half-year public ministry of

---

[265] Daniel 12:4, 9
[266] Revelation 11:2
[267] Revelation 11:3
[268] Revelation 12:6
[269] Revelation 12:14
[270] Revelation 13:5

Christ. Examine and study again the chart below to establish a visual for the rest of the story.

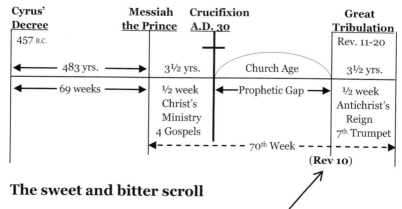

The sweet and bitter scroll

In Revelation 10, John is told to take the scroll from the angel's hand and eat it. It tastes sweet, like honey, but turns bitter in his stomach. He's then told to prophecy about many, peoples, nations, languages, and kings[271] found in the final story of history.

John then begins to prophesy—in detail—about the events covering the last one-half week or three-and-one-half years. Immediately after the parenthetical chapter of Revelation 10, John picks up where Daniel left off and now provides the specifics found in Revelation 11 through 19.

The "mystery" of God

Before we leave chapter 10 of Revelation, let's look closer at verse 7:

> In the **days** of the sounding of the *seventh* angel, when he is about to sound, the **mystery** of God would be

---

[271] Revelation 10:8-11

finished [completed], as He declared to His servants the prophets.[272]

The word "mystery," in this verse comes from the Greek word, *musterion*, which denotes the idea of something that can only be known by divine revelation, but won't be made known until God's appointed time to those illumined by the Holy Spirit to see it. It is truth revealed.

Throughout the Bible, God had declared to his servants, the prophets, that a "mystery" or "secret" is being withheld or *hidden* in Scriptures through types and shadows,[273] until the real thing comes along and is finished—or completed.[274]

The prophets of old received prophetic visions and dreams of future events they didn't understand completely or, in most cases, see them come to pass. But they were moved by the Holy Spirit to write down these "mysteries."[275]

One such *mystery* is the incarnation of God made flesh, who lived among us.[276] Another *mystery* is that of the Holy Spirit, living in the spirits of the redeemed.[277] Another *mystery* is that of the marriage between Christ and his bride, the church.[278] Another *mystery* is that Jew and Gentile would become one in Christ.[279] Then you have the *mystery* of iniquity where Satan incarnates the man of lawlessness.[280]

All of these "mysteries" come to completion and are finished by the time the angel begins to sound the seventh trumpet, which launches the world and the church into the three-and-one-half-year period of the Great Tribulation.

---

[272] New King James Version
[273] Types and Shadows—symbols concealing truths within events, persons, places, or objects that are fulfilled in the same categories in the future.
[274] 1 Corinthians 2:6-10
[275] 2 Peter 1:20-21
[276] 1 Timothy 3:16 with John 1:1, 10, 14
[277] Colossians 1:27;
[278] Ephesians 5:23-33
[279] Ephesians 3:2-6
[280] 2 Thessalonians 2:7

But one mystery still remains, which is the "mystery" of the bride of Christ and her *manchild*.[281] That requires an entire chapter we'll address later.

Here's what we have so far visually:

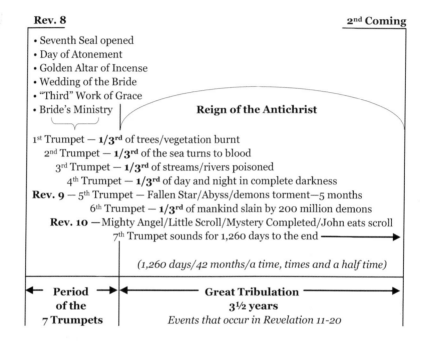

Rev. 8   **2ⁿᵈ Coming**

- Seventh Seal opened
- Day of Atonement
- Golden Altar of Incense
- Wedding of the Bride
- "Third" Work of Grace
- Bride's Ministry   **Reign of the Antichrist**

1ˢᵗ Trumpet — **1/3ʳᵈ** of trees/vegetation burnt
2ⁿᵈ Trumpet — **1/3ʳᵈ** of the sea turns to blood
3ʳᵈ Trumpet — **1/3ʳᵈ** of streams/rivers poisoned
4ᵗʰ Trumpet — **1/3ʳᵈ** of day and night in complete darkness
Rev. 9 — 5ᵗʰ Trumpet — Fallen Star/Abyss/demons torment—5 months
6ᵗʰ Trumpet — **1/3ʳᵈ** of mankind slain by 200 million demons
Rev. 10 — Mighty Angel/Little Scroll/Mystery Completed/John eats scroll
7ᵗʰ Trumpet sounds for 1,260 days to the end ⟶

(1,260 days/42 months/a time, times and a half time)

⟵ **Period** ⟶ ⟵ ————— **Great Tribulation** ————— ⟶
of the   **3½ years**
7 Trumpets   *Events that occur in Revelation 11-20*

---

[281] Revelation 12:1-5

Chapter 25

The Temple and the Outer Court

BY NOW, THE WORLD has been reeling from the terrifying, disruptive period of the seven trumpets. The ten kings with their kingdoms and the world religious leaders have all been aligning themselves with each other to survive the aftermath.

But one significant component remains and that is to put a face to this alliance of a new world order. They must find the most wise, powerful, and charismatic leader on earth. Scripture calls this person the Antichrist, and the next three-and-one-half years will be his time to govern as a king above all kings.

Before we consider the specifics of the role he plays in the last days, let's take a look at what's happening to the church *before* he comes into power.

The church is measured

Now that John has eaten the little scroll of Daniel, he begins to prophesy about the events transpiring in Revelation 11, 12, and 13—all taking place at the beginning of the sounding of the seventh trumpet; the beginning of the Great Tribulation. The bride's ministry of gathering in the harvest is ending because the world, under the reign of the Antichrist, will rise swiftly to persecute and destroy the church.

Before this occurs, however, John is given a vision in Revelation chapter 11—marking the start of the final pages of human history. The last days' church is being measured by the standards of the High Priest Jesus—just as he examined the *seven* churches[282] of the early days' church. Here's what John saw:

> I was given a reed like a **measuring rod** and was told, "Go and measure the **temple of God** and the **altar**, and count the **worshipers** there. But exclude the **outer court**; do not measure it, because it has been given to the **Gentiles**. They will trample on the **holy city** for **42 months**."[283]

The Bible says judgment begins at the house of God,[284] and this language of measuring the New Covenant temple[285] is symbolic. John is not the measuring a "literal," brick-n-mortar temple, he's measuring a *spiritual* temple, the church.

The reed given to John is likened to God's disciplinary rod[286] used to judge his church. The one who gives him this measuring rod is Jesus, the angel-messenger in Revelation 10. This vision is an extension of the same vision John just received in chapter 10 and is now carried over into the first and second verses of Revelation 11. This still falls in the parenthetical realm *between* the sixth and seventh trumpets.

The golden altar and the worshipers

In the passage above, two things are measured, the temple (the church) and the golden altar, which symbolizes the prayers of the worshippers (or saints) in the temple. As the buildup to the Great Tribulation begins to wrap up, the

---

[282] Revelation 2-3
[283] Revelation 11:1-2
[284] 1 Peter 4:17
[285] 1 Corinthians 3:16-17; 6:19; 2 Corinthians 6:16; Ephesians 2:21
[286] Job 9:34; 21:9; Psalm 23:4; Ezekiel 40:3; Micah 6:9

bride and her offspring, with the rest of the church, have filled the temple with the incense of their prayers.[287]

So what are these prayers about? I believe they're prayers for the remaining lost souls of the Gentiles whose salvation window is closing,[288] *and* they are prayers for the Jews who are about to experience an awakening to Jesus their Messiah.

They could also be prayers for the church whose members are about to go into the Great Tribulation period and be martyred. As Jesus prayed for strength in the garden of Gethsemane, preparing to go through the suffering he was about to endure,[289] so will the church seek God for strength as her time of suffering approaches. These will be the future martyrs mentioned in Revelation 6:9-11 and 7:9-17.

The unmeasured Outer Court

The measuring of the temple and altar is symbolic in regard to *who* will be ready. Notice the Outer Court is not measured, because there is nothing there to measure. I believe it's because the saints in the Outer Court are those who didn't measure up to the stature of Christ—perhaps because they had lost their first love. They sat on the sidelines as those who bore no fruit[290] and, therefore, have nothing to show or account for in their walk as Christians.[291]

They are "non-overcomers" like those mentioned among the seven churches of Asia Minor. They had either left their first love, maintained their controlling legalism, or embraced false doctrine, choosing political correctness over truth. These are the unprofitable and unreliable servants who hid their gifts from the world. They are the spiritually dead and lukewarm who will be cast out into outer darkness, where the

---

[287] Compare Revelation 8:3-4
[288] Luke 21:24; Romans 11:25
[289] Luke 22:40-44
[290] Matthew 7:19-20; Luke 13:6-9; John 15:5-6; Romans 7:4; Colossians 1:10
[291] 1 Corinthians 3:10-15

light of the "radiant ones" once shined, but are replaced with these who will experience a weeping and gnashing of teeth.[292]

They are among the five foolish virgins who lacked enough oil in their lamps to go out and meet the Bridegroom on the Day of Atonement, before the sounding of the trumpets. They went to buy oil, but returned too late for the wedding and lost their window of opportunity to be in the bridal chamber for the consummation.[293] They are still saved, as virgins[294]—but no longer betrothed in this hour, for they were foolish virgins. They will remain saved as long as they hold fast to their faith and aren't swept away into the great deception and apostasy.[295] But they will go into the Great Tribulation where they'll need to recover their first love, first walk, and initial faith in Christ to survive the great deception. The bride company will escape the three-and-one-half years of the Great Tribulation—the weeping and gnashing of teeth period—but her offspring of new converts and reformed, remaining saints will become targets of martyrdom.[296]

To arrive at this interpretation we must go back to the Outer Court in the temple of the Old Testament. It was a place of *blood, fire* and *judgment of sin.* Unwilling animals were tied to the horns of the Bronze Altar where they were sacrificed and burned on the altar's grate. Such will be the time under the Antichrist and his regime. Human sacrifices will become the bloody sport of choice before the jeers and cheers of bloodthirsty crowds, like in the days of the Roman Colosseum where Christians were martyred.

---

[292] Matthew 25:14-30
[293] Matthew 25:1-13
[294] 2 Corinthians 11:2-4
[295] 2 Corinthians 11:3-4; Galatians 1:6-9; Colossians 1:21-23; 2 Thessalonians 2:3, 9-12; 1 Timothy 4:1; Hebrews 10:26-31, 36-39; 1 Peter 4:17-19; 2 Peter 2:20-22; 3:8-12, 17; Jude 3-4, 12-13
[296] Revelation 12:6, 13-17

During the last three-and-one-half years, the Holy Spirit will withdraw his restraint against wickedness on the Earth and allow the church to be given over to the ungodly Gentile-controlled world, just as Christ was given over to the Gentiles for their hour and power of darkness.[297]

The Gentiles will control the "holy city" of Jerusalem, no longer holy but devoid of God's presence and glory.[298] It will become the Antichrist's city,[299] the capital of religion—a one-world religion. It will be neither Christian nor Jewish, but a false, bloody, blasphemous, idolatrous religion, backed by the political capital of Babylon.

The offspring (new converts) of the bride and the "outer-court" saints (who return to their first love) will be beheaded for refusing to embrace the political and religious agenda of the new world order. There'll be no compromise, no in-between, and no "can't we all just get along" negotiations. We'll either be with them or against them, and death is the only alternative to not joining their club. There'll be no "moderate" Christians during this time; we'll either be all in with Jesus, or all in with the world.

Three categories of "thirds"

By now you have probably noticed that *a third of this* and *a third of that* has been mentioned often in Revelation. It's a biblical equation that surrounds the symbolic number *three* and is the number of "divine completeness and perfect testimony."

One-third of a whole pie leaves two-thirds. Two-thirds of a whole pie leaves one-third. The Father is *a third* of the members in the Godhead, the Son is *a third* of the members in the Godhead, and the Holy Spirit is *a third* of the

---

[297] 2 Thessalonians 2:7-8; Luke 22:53
[298] Revelation 11:8
[299] Daniel 11:41, 45

members in the Godhead. All three persons of the Triune family make the Godhead complete as one. The Father and the Holy Spirit are invisible and remain invisible, while the Son became visible to us in his manifested body on Earth.

God made us in his likeness. He made us *tri*-part beings with a body, soul and spirit.[300] When all three parts of our being are healthy, we're complete. Our soul and our spirit are invisible; our body, which houses the soul and spirit, is visible. God wants the same for his spiritual body, the church—i.e., to be healthy and complete. However, the sin remaining in our souls hinders us from complete perfection and maturity. As in all defects or dysfunctions in our natural bodies, some members of the spiritual body, the church, are weaker than others. That has been the case for church since its inception.

Many letters from Paul address such weaknesses. He repeatedly encourages us to not weaken in our passion, to not quarrel with each other, to not yield to sexual immorality, and to not be self-centered, but serve one another. Paul and other writers in the New Testament speak to these issues and more, all of which suggest that *some* members are weaker than others (see Romans 14).

Jesus, too, addressed problems in the churches of Asia Minor, with some surprisingly strong warnings, like, "Jezebel, I'll kill your children if you don't stop fornicating and committing adultery."[301] In both the gospels and Revelation, Jesus warns us about "unacceptable" behavior as citizens of God's kingdom and the consequences such behavior will produce, *if* we don't turn from our sins.

I remember the first time I read the description of Jesus in the opening chapter of Revelation. He has blazing eyes

---

[300] 1 Thessalonians 5:23
[301] Revelation 2:20-23

and fiery glowing feet! This describes the appearance of someone I wouldn't want to have upset with me.

Jesus also spoke in a parable about *levels* of growth or maturity in our lives, determined by four different types of soil and the amount of crops they did or didn't produce. The "productive" individuals were found with a return of thirtyfold, sixtyfold, or a hundredfold.[302]

It's true that some of us will produce more fruit than others, while others produce nothing at all. It all comes down to how faithful we've been in the little things.[303] Jesus and Paul warned us that, in the end, our behavior and productivity in God's kingdom will be examined. We'll receive an accounting of what we've produced with God's gifts and the investments he's made in our lives.[304] This is what's happening here at the measuring of the temple and the altar, and the "non-measuring" of the outer-court saints.

I believe that the church of the last days will fall into three distinct *thirds*:

1/3rd — makes up the saints who fall away (Great Apostasy)

1/3rd — makes up the unprepared saints (Five Foolish Virgins)

1/3rd — makes up the Bride of Christ (Five Wise Virgins)

If you and I are alive at that time, will we be ready for the Bridegroom? Will we be found faithful and productive servants? Or will we be found abandoning our faith to preserve our lives, rather than keeping our faith for the sake of him who died for us?

When the dragon's tail sweeps *a third of the stars* of the sky to the Earth, will we be among those *stars* on that day when Jesus measures the temple and the golden altar? And

---

302 Matthew 13:22-23
303 Matthew 24:45-46; 25:21-23
304 Matthew 12:36; Luke 16:2; Romans 14:12; Hebrews 4:13; 13:17; 1 Peter 4:5

in the measuring of his temple (the church), Jesus will be looking for a faithful, passionate bride to separate her from the lethargic, complacent members of the church body.

The tabernacle and the temple

The tabernacle and temple in the Old Testament were both constructed with three compartments: the *Outer Court,* the *Holy Place,* and the *Most Holy Place* (see the tabernacle and the temple in the "Charts" section at the back of the book).

The schematics for both dwellings were given by God and precisely constructed to every minute detail. To Moses he gave the plans for the Tabernacle that had been patterned after the one in heaven.[305] To David he gave the plans for the temple and for his son, Solomon, to build it.[306]

The function of each compartment in these dwellings symbolizes the spiritual condition of three categories of the church in the last days. First, let's take a look at what each compartment had in the tabernacle and the temple:

- In the **Outer Court**—blood, sacrifice and judgment
- In the **Holy Place**—communion, fellowship and incense
- In the **Most Holy**—God's glory, presence, Day of Atonement

Apply this now to John's temple vision in Revelation 11, preceding the Great Tribulation. Since the falling away of *a third* of the saints occurs *before* the appearance of the Antichrist, we won't include them in this application as a third category. Instead, the surviving members of the church will be made up of these three compartments, corresponding to the symbolic interpretation of the temple vision.

Compare this next list with the list above:

---

[305] Hebrews 8:5; Exodus 25-40
[306] 1 Chronicles 22-29

- **Outer Court**—foolish virgins and unproductive saints
- **Holy Place**—worshipers at the altar and productive saints
- **Most Holy Place**—the bride's intimacy with Christ

Is it fair?

In the widespread culture of entitlement and egalitarianism,[307] it doesn't seem fair that God would place us in categories. Why can't we all be on equal footing in the outcome of our place in God's kingdom? Why can't we all wind up in the wilderness—like the bride—protected by God, in the last days? Is God more partial to some Christians than others? Doesn't the Bible say he is an impartial God, a respecter of no persons? The answer is "yes" and "no."

God doesn't promise the same outcome for everyone. Just read the account of God's faithful in Hebrews 11:32-39 and you'll see this is true. Some escaped death and suffering while others did not, though all walked in faith! In Acts, he delivered the apostle Peter from death row in prison, but not the apostle James.[308] God has his reasons, and so often his ways are beyond finding out. We just have to trust him in what he allows.

God rewards productivity

God made everything to *reproduce* and *bear fruit*. He rewards those who do. The parables of Jesus clearly demonstrate this, and it will also play out in the rewards we receive in the millennium. Yes, God is no respecter of persons, but in a way where he gives everyone the *same opportunity* to invest what he's given them, and then bring him back a return on his investment.

---

[307] *Egalitarianism*—the affirmation and promotion of all things equal in politics, economics, social status, and civil rights for all people.
[308] Acts 12:1-11

In God's economy, he doesn't reward laziness or indifference. His Word says that we will reap what we've sown. If we sow into fleshly things, we'll reap fleshly things. But if we sow into spiritual things, then we will reap spiritual things.[309] In other words, we'll become the most, what we behold the most. We'll reflect the most, what we watch the most. We'll become like the company we keep—if it's with fools, we'll become like fools; if it's with the wise, then we'll become as the wise.[310] It's that simple. It's called the law of sowing and reaping.

God is a wise creator, builder, entrepreneur, and investor who expects a return on his investment from his creation. Every living thing God has made—*gives*. Every living thing God has made *bears fruit*. Every living thing God has made— *reproduces*. He rewards producers. And the Christian who faithfully reproduces what they are capable of will be promoted, elevated, and placed in a greater position of honor and responsibility than those who don't. That's what is fair.

Matthew 25:19-30

After a long time the master of those servants returned and settled accounts with them. The man who had received the five talents brought the other five. "Master," he said, "you entrusted me with five talents. See, I have gained five more."

His master replied, "Well done, good and faithful servant! You have been faithful with a few things; I will put you in charge of many things. Come and share your master's happiness!"

The man with the two talents also came. "Master," he said, "you entrusted me with two talents; see, I have gained two more."

---

309 Galatians 6:7-8
310 Proverbs 13:20

His master replied, "Well done, good and faithful servant! You have been faithful with a few things; I will put you in charge of many things. Come and share your master's happiness!"

Then the man who had received the one talent came. "Master," he said, "I knew that you are a hard man, harvesting where you have not sown and gathering where you have not scattered seed. So I was afraid and went out and hid your talent in the ground. See, here is what belongs to you."

His master replied, "You wicked, lazy servant! So you knew that I harvest where I have not sown and gather where I have not scattered seed? Well then, you should have put my money on deposit with the bankers, so that when I returned I would have received it back with interest.

"'Take the talent from him and give it to the one who has the ten talents. For everyone who has will be given more, and he will have an abundance. Whoever does not have, even what he has will be taken from him. And throw that worthless servant outside, into the [outer] darkness, where there will be weeping and gnashing of teeth."

—Jesus

Various rewards—accordingly

Outer Court saints will be rewarded according to what they give back. They are the non-productive "religious" saints who live in the Outer Court and rarely, if at all, approach the tent of the Holy Place to commune, fellowship, or pray to God. They are content to let the blood sacrifice do the work, but unwilling to go to the level of becoming a living sacrifice themselves, holy and pleasing to God.[311] They've conformed to the world and give nothing back; and because they give nothing back, they get nothing more than the gift they

---

[311] Romans 12:1-2

received for *free*—that is, a salvation by faith in the sacrificed blood of the Lamb (unless they walk away from that gift and go after the Antichrist).

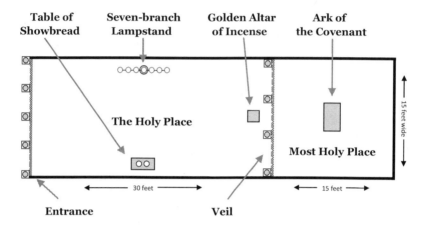

| Table of Showbread | Seven-branch Lampstand | Golden Altar of Incense | Ark of the Covenant |

The Holy Place

Most Holy Place

15 feet wide

← 30 feet → ← 15 feet →

Entrance   Veil

The Holy Place saints will be rewarded according to what they give back. They move from the Outer Court and enter the tent into The Holy Place. There they bask in the light of the seven-branched lamp stand, commune at the table of showbread, and pray at the altar of incense. They are anointed saints who fellowship daily with their Maker, unwilling to settle for an outer-court experience alone.

Most Holy Place saints go even further. They have learned the secret of *intimacy*. They aren't content with staying in the Holy Place with the light of the seven-branched lamp stand, or the bread of communion on the table of showbread, or praying *to* God at the golden altar of incense. They have tasted that the Lord *himself* is good. They've been smitten and want more than just The Holy Place (as good and virtuous as its activities are). They *want to* go behind the veil of the Most Holy Place, before the tangible Presence of God, and experience his shekinah Glory, brighter than the noonday sun. They aren't content to know *about* God, they want to feel him *about* them, to feel his breath upon them, to feel his burning passion radiating from the Ark of the Covenant, and to be undone before his unconquerable love. They want nothing less than to give back *everything* to him, to become *living* sacrifices, wholly and pleasing to God—not for themselves, but for him.

I could easily see these Most Holy Place saints in the company of the five wise virgins who will be prime candidates for the bride, ready and prepared with extra oil for their lamps, to go out and meet the Bridegroom when he comes.

> At that time the kingdom of heaven will be like ten virgins who took their lamps and went out to meet the bridegroom. Five of them were foolish and five were wise. The foolish ones took their lamps but did not take any oil with them. The wise, however, took oil in jars along with their lamps. The bridegroom was a long time in coming, and they all became drowsy and fell asleep.
>
> At midnight the cry rang out: "Here's the bridegroom! Come out to meet him!"
>
> Then all the virgins woke up and trimmed their lamps. The foolish ones said to the wise, "Give us some of your oil; our lamps are going out."
>
> "No," they replied, "there may not be enough for both us and you. Instead, go to those who sell oil and buy some for yourselves."
>
> But while they were on their way to buy the oil, the bridegroom arrived. The virgins who were ready went in with him to the wedding banquet. And *the door was shut.*
>
> Later the others also came. "Sir! Sir!" they said. "Open the door for us!"
>
> But he replied, "I tell you the truth, I don't know you."
>
> Therefore keep watch, because you do not know the day or the hour.[312]

---

[312] Matthew 25:1-13

Chapter 26

The Two Witnesses

And I will give power to my two witnesses, and they will prophesy for **1,260 days**, clothed in sackcloth.

—Revelation 11:3

THE CHURCH HAS NOW been measured to determine the place and/or plight of the saints during the last three-and-one-half years. So what's next?

Before the seventh angel blows the seventh trumpet, Revelation 11 introduces *two men* who are eyewitnesses of Jesus and will testify about him to the Jews. Their assignment is to prophesy for 1,260 days during the Antichrist's reign. Though their names aren't given, their actions align with the two most prominent prophets in the Old Testament—Moses and Elijah. Let's consider the clues.

Two happens to be the symbolic number of "witness and testimony,"[313] and Moses and Elijah were eyewitnesses of the transfiguration, resurrection, and ascension of Christ.

They were on the Mount of Transfiguration when they conferred with Jesus about his death;[314] they are believed to be the "two men" in white who were at the tomb,[315] and at the ascension of Jesus on the Mount of Olives.[316]

---

[313] 2 Corinthians 13:1 with Matthew 10:18; Luke 21:13; Acts 1:8; 3:15; 5:32
[314] Matthew 17:1-3; Luke 9:28-36; 2 Peter 1:16-18; Mark 9:4
[315] Luke 24:4
[316] Acts 1:9-10

What better witnesses to bring the gospel story to the Jews than two of the most respected prophets in Israel's history. The one (Moses) represents the law, the other (Elijah) the prophets.

Moses and Elijah will declare they saw Jesus in those three scenarios and affirm him as the true Messiah of the Jews. This is why they're called the two olive trees and two lampstands that stand before the Lord of the Earth.[317] The olive tree represents the Jews of national Israel,[318] and the lampstand symbolizes the role these witnesses will play as the last remaining "light-bearers" of God's people.

They are unassailable until the end of the 1,260 days. If anyone tries to harm them, fire will come from their mouths like flamethrowers to destroy their enemies.[319] Such displays of power will authenticate their identities to the Jews, who always demand a "sign" to verify their prophets.[320]

Performing the same displays of power as in the Old Testament will undeniably confirm their identity and claims to being Moses and Elijah. First, they'll have the power to stop the rain during the 1,260 days of their prophesying, just as Elijah did in the days of King Ahab.[321] Second, they'll have the power to turn water to blood, just as Moses did in the days of Pharaoh.[322] Third, they'll have the ability to strike the Earth as often as they want with every kind of plague.[323]

Prophets of judgment, too

It's difficult to visualize the condition of the Earth at this time after the continuing effects of the second, third, and

---

[317] Revelation 11:4
[318] Romans 11:17-27
[319] Revelation 11:1-5
[320] 1 Corinthians 1:22
[321] 1 Kings 17:1 and 18:1; Revelation 11:6
[322] Exodus 7:19-21; Revelation 11:6
[323] Revelation 11:6

fourth *seals* are intensified by the additional judgments of the seven *trumpets.*

War, famine, death, and a pandemic of plagues are ravaging the Earth and its inhabitants. But now these two witnesses have appeared, not only to carry the torch of the gospel, but also to exercise power to bring *more* judgment upon the ungodly, just as the prophets in the Old Testament brought judgment upon ungodly kings and people.

Even though Wormwood has already poisoned one-third of the planet's water, Moses and Elijah will stop the rain for the entire period of the Antichrist, in addition to turning more water into blood, which will destroy more fish and other living creatures of the waters.

Imagine how sparse food will be as famine spreads more quickly, due to the drought. The wicked that are thirsty for the blood of the martyrs will be given blood to drink. And the prophets will add to these plagues at any place, and any time they deem necessary to strike the Earth. It's possible that God will strategically direct them to where and when to bring judgment.

The fact that Moses and Elijah can't be harmed by the Antichrist or his false church will be a reminder to the inhabitants of the Earth that God's judgments are certain and his message will prevail. His two witnesses will continue to testify that Jesus Christ is their risen Lord and Savior.

And—as John the Baptist did with Herod—they'll denounce the Antichrist, his regime, and what it stands for. Their message will directly oppose his claims that *he* is the world's messiah and savior, risen from the dead.[324] The signs and wonders demonstrated by the two prophets will be their response to the *counterfeit* signs and wonders of the Antichrist and his partner, the False Prophet.[325] Moses and

---

[324] Ezekiel 28:2-9; Daniel 8:9-12; 11:36; Matthew 24:23-25; 2 Thessalonians 2:4
[325] 2 Timothy 3:8 with 2 Thessalonians 2:9-12; Revelation 13:11-14

Elijah will be a constant source of agitation to them and the followers of his regime[326]—just as Moses was to Pharaoh and Egypt; just as Elijah was to King Ahab and his wicked wife, Jezebel.

Jerusalem and the Messianic awakening

As light-bearers, these two witnesses will ignite a great awakening among the Jews converting to Christianity. Moses and Elijah will concentrate their testimony in Israel and Jerusalem, where Jesus was crucified. They'll call the city, figuratively, "Sodom and Egypt"[327] because it is no longer the "holy city" or "city of peace."[328] It will become the religious capital of the Antichrist and his counterfeit church called "Babylon."[329]

Since the time of King David, more than 3,000 years ago, Jerusalem has become the center of the nations surrounding it. The city touches three continents,[330] both religiously and geopolitically. The three most influential and monotheistic religions in the world—Jews, Christians and Muslims—have a stake within its walls. That's why Jerusalem has always been a hotspot of attention on the world stage. God will never allow for its destruction, or the Jewish people, until all Israel is saved[331]—that is, those who are "born again" under the ministry of the two witnesses.

As mentioned earlier, before Moses and Elijah come, every Gentile who can be saved will have been saved when the bride's ministry comes to a close and she's taken into the

---

[326] Revelation 11:10
[327] Revelation 11:8
[328] Some etymologists claim that Jerusalem means: "City of Peace."
[329] Revelation 17:1-6; 18:1-3
[330] Ezekiel 5:5
[331] Romans 11:26

wilderness. Paul refers to it in Romans as "the time when the full number of the Gentiles has come in."[332]

At this time, the only ones left to be converted to Christ aren't the remaining Gentiles, who all now follow the Antichrist, but the god-fearing Jews who won't follow him and, therefore, are grafted back into the natural olive tree[333] through the ministry of Moses and Elijah. These men are the icons of their heritage and faith, and they'll listen to them because their message will be authenticated with *signs* and *wonders*. These are the eyewitnesses of the true Messiah, the Lord Jesus Christ from Nazareth in Galilee.

The final days of the two witnesses

By the time Moses and Elijah finish their 1,260 days of prophesying, every last saint, both Jew and Gentile, will have been martyred by the Antichrist and the Harlot, Babylon. Only the ungodly are left—whatever is left of them. Once the ministry of the two witnesses is complete, God will withdraw his protection over them, which they had for 1,260 days (three-and-one-half years). Once that protection is gone, the Antichrist will overpower and kill them in Jerusalem, leaving their bodies lying in the street for all to see for the next three-and-one-half days.[334] The whole world will celebrate their death by sending gifts to each other[335] until something stops them cold. Here's what Revelation says will happen:

> ... after the three and a half days a breath of life from God entered them, and they stood on their feet, and terror struck those who saw them. Then they heard a loud voice from heaven saying to them, "Come up here." And they

---

[332] Luke 21:24; Romans 11:25—"Gentile" is the biblical term used to define all non-Jewish nations.
[333] Romans 11:11-32
[334] Revelation 11:7-8
[335] Revelation 11:9-10

went up to heaven in a cloud, while their enemies looked on.

At that very hour there was a severe earthquake and a tenth of the city collapsed. Seven thousand people were killed in the earthquake, and the survivors were terrified and gave glory to the God of heaven.

–Revelation 11:11-13

Imagine the look on the faces of those who will be there to see Moses and Elijah take a gasp of air, open their eyes, and stand up. Then a loud booming voice from heaven calls them up and they ascend into the clouds, just like Jesus did before his disciples. Then the clincher—a great earthquake rattles the Earth, resulting in massive deaths and destruction. Yes, the people will be extremely terrified, but without one ounce of remorse or conviction. Their hearts will be that hardened, too, when you see how they respond to the seven bowls of wrath happening on the heels of this supernatural occurrence.

With such a demonstration of God's power, I'm intrigued by the last sentence—the terrified survivors will actually give *glory* to God. In their demon-possessed state of mind, that didn't make sense to me at first. The word "glory" used in the original language can also be translated "to honor" or "to recognize;" by implication someone's skills, talents, abilities, or position. This helped me to understand that their response isn't an act of glorious praise, but rather "acknowledging" that God raised the two witnesses from the dead and sent the earthquake. Instead of a hallelujah chorus, these are demon-possessed people who still know the God of heaven is real, just as the demons in the demoniac acknowledged Jesus as the Son of God and begged him not to throw them into the Abyss.[336]

---

[336] Luke 8:27-32

Chapter 27

The United States in the Last Days

BEFORE I ADDRESS the next events in Revelation 12, it's necessary to consider the questions some have had about the United States of America. Where will America stand in the midst of this last-day chaos? Will it rise to the beacon of hope it once held for the world? Where will it be when Russia and the alliance of Middle East invaders attack Israel? And why is there no detailed mention of the U.S. in the Bible, especially in the last days?

Decline of the United States

By the time the Antichrist is in full power, the U.S. will have followed the direction of Europe, allowing socialism and the religious/political tolerance of Islamism to infiltrate the country and the infrastructure of government. Socialists will have reinterpreted the constitution and the growing culture of entitlements granted for political favors will increase. Of course it would be easy to blame political parties, but this isn't only a political problem, it's a spiritual one. It stems from an apathetic church, isolated from the politicians who are passing laws and making decisions on our behalf. When you leave government in the hands of socialists, political jihadists, moderates, conservative rhinos and only a "minority" of true conservatives, there is no representation for the interests of Christians.

Consider the exhortation of the apostle Paul to the church about her responsibility to society:

> I urge, then, first of all, that requests, prayers, intercession and thanksgiving be made for everyone—for kings and all those in authority, that we may live peaceful and quiet lives in all godliness and holiness. This is good, and pleases God our Savior.[337]

Paul clearly expresses in these words an interest in influencing governments in a way that will allow us to live peaceful and quiet lives. If we have the opportunity to vote for people who would promote such peace, then we should do so.

Three types of governments

The world today has three types of governments. First, there are **monarchies** where nobility or royal bloodlines are the key to succession of power, and where a prince or princess succeeds the king or queen. Over time, however, they are replaced by another form of government, while allowing the king or queen to retain *limited* power. Such is the case in England today.

Second, **dictators** and **totalitarian governments** are usually created through a violent coup or revolution. They are short-lived, however, when something similar comes along to replace them.

Third, **democracies** and **republics** constituting collaborative, representative, or parliamentarian officials and leaders who are elected by votes to represent the will of the people. This type of government is generally among the best-formed governments, but imperfect due to the human tendencies toward greed and corruption. Winston Churchill

---

[337] 1 Timothy 2:1-3

said this is "the *worst* form of government—*except for all the others.*" Why? Because democracies eventually commit suicide.

America has enjoyed the freedom of the third type of government for nearly three centuries. But according to the prophecies of the last days, the whole world will go the way of being governed by ten kings and a one-world dictator, mostly because democracies will become corrupt through greed and the survival of the fittest.

Democracy

Consider this popular quote, allegedly attributed to an 18th century Scottish history professor at the University of Edinburgh, Alexander Fraser Tytler. It's an eye-opening statement—one vaguely familiar to what we've observed happening to America in the last half century.

> A democracy cannot exist as a permanent form of government. It can only exist until the voters discover that they can vote themselves largesse [generous gifts] from the public treasury. From that moment on, the majority always votes for the candidates promising the most benefits from the public treasury with the result that a democracy always collapses over loose fiscal policy, always followed by a dictatorship.
>
> The average age of the world's greatest civilizations has been 200 years. Great nations rise and fall. The people go from bondage to spiritual faith; from spiritual faith to great courage; from courage to liberty; from liberty to abundance; from abundance to selfishness; from selfishness to complacency; from complacency to apathy; from apathy to dependency; from dependency back again to bondage.

If a democracy has any chance of surviving the average lifespan of 200 years, it won't go any further than the fundamentals its citizens permit. Political morals, values and worldviews are extremely important in the light of God's views on any issues promoted, allocated, or perpetuated by the government. In the light of all reason and common sense, you can't isolate God from government without advocating anarchy and chaos.

The statements of the following great men reveal their understanding of this, and that moral decay in any country is the greatest threat to the democratic nations of the West.

King Solomon

Righteousness exalts a nation: but sin is a reproach to any people.[338]

Billy Graham

If America is to survive, we must elect more God-centered men and women to public office—individuals who will seek Divine guidance in the affairs of state.

Noah Webster

It is alleged ... that religion and morality are not necessary or important qualifications for political stations. But the Scriptures teach a different doctrine. They direct that rulers should be men "who rule in the fear of God, able men, such as fear God, men of truth, hating covetousness.

George Washington

Of all the dispositions and habits which lead to political prosperity, religion and morality are indispensable supports.

James Madison

Is there no virtue among us? If there be not, we are in a wretched situation. No theoretical checks—no form of

---

[338] Proverbs 14:34

government can render us secure. To suppose that any form of government will secure liberty or happiness without virtue in the people is [an illusion or fabrication of the mind]. And Democracies have always been spectacles of turbulence and contention and as short in their lives as they have been violent in their deaths.

Benjamin Franklin

Only a virtuous people are capable of freedom.

John Adams

We have no government armed with powers capable of contending with human passions unbridled by morality and religion. Avarice [greed], ambition, revenge or gallantry would break the strongest cords of our constitution as a whale goes through a net.

Thomas Jefferson

Can the liberties of a nation be thought secure when we have removed their only firm basis? A conviction in the minds of the people, that these liberties are a gift of God? That they are not violated but with his wrath?

Abraham Lincoln

Men are not flattered by being shown that there has been a difference of purpose between the Almighty and them. To deny it, however, in this case, is to deny that there is a God governing the world. *(March 15, 1865, letter to Thurlow Weed one month before his assassination.)*

Hand withdrawn, mercy extended

Currently, the U.S. continues to display the most powerful military and political leverage among the nations, but not as effectively as we did two decades ago. Since the end of World War II, the decay of the religious, political and economic conditions of our country have diminished our reach. An example is our inability, alongside of Europe, to thwart Russia's progressive, territorial advances, including the annexation of Crimea and its ongoing attempts to do the same with the Ukraine. Such weakness will continue with our Western European allies as we move closer to the last days and the emergence of a ten-kingdom alliance. I believe this could be the precursor to a future and ultimate need— that is, to enter into an alliance with Canada and/or the southern neighbors of our hemisphere to protect our country during future wars.

The second *seal* of the fiery red horse is the seal that symbolizes "war" in Revelation 6, and the wars under that seal (already opened) will continue to spread and intensify to the end of the age (see *Seven Seals Chart* on page 412). This thought is confirmed by the wars happening in the world today, and what Jesus predicted about the violent landscape of the last days:

> You will hear of wars and rumors of wars, but see to it that you are not alarmed. Such things must happen, but the end is still to come. Nation will rise against nation, and kingdom against kingdom.[339]

I love our country, and served in the United States Air Force for four-and-one-half years. My dad served, too, and was a flight navigator on the transport planes in Europe, when Germany surrendered. He met my mother in Berlin, who had met Hitler and shook his hand when she was a young girl. At the time, she saw him no differently than a young person would see an American president—as the leader of the United States. But as she grew up under Hitler's totalitarian government, she watched what socialism did to her country, how it separated her family, and how the

---

[339] Matthew 24:6-7

communists came in after the war to pillage and rape her friends and Germany.

Before my mom passed away, she was upset with the direction our government was taking because she saw it heading down the same path she watched Germany and Europe take before World II.

The Old Testament is filled with warnings from God to Israel as to what would become of their nation if they turned their backs on him. The greatest warning is found in Deuteronomy 28:15-68. The sobering predictions in those verses are just as applicable to the U.S. today, as they were to Israel 3,500 years ago.

I believe with great sadness that God is withdrawing his hand of blessing and protection from America because of the direction we're going. If our nation follows God, we'll experience the blessings promised to a nation whose God is the Lord (read Deuteronomy 28:1-14). If not, then the opposite will happen. I believe this because, in my lifetime, we've become a post-Christian nation—ideologically and politically—seemingly unable to repent and return to the great nation we once were with God at the helm. Though we were founded as a nation after God, like Israel, no nation is immune from his justice when they forsake him.

I hope that God's mercy will be extended when the U.S. sees God saving Israel from the Ezekiel 38-39 invasion. I could see great spiritual revival coming to America; but as far as a sociopolitical turn, I'm not quite as optimistic. Even with conservatives winning the majority of the seats in the House and Senate, I think ignorance will continue to prevail, and socialism will win out in the end. I believe this because socialism will become the political system of the new-world order. I only pray that we can prolong God's mercy by doing our part to fight for our religious freedoms through educating the people around us.

Let me qualify this by saying God isn't a Republican, a Democrat, an Independent, or a Moderate. He is God and he's determined the set times for the nations and the exact places where they should live. He did this so that people would seek him and perhaps reach out for him to find him. This is what Paul told his audience on Mars Hill in Athens, Greece.[340]

In every nation God has his own kingdom, which will never be shaken. His kingdom is an *everlasting* kingdom and will be the *only* kingdom left on Earth after Jesus returns to judge the nations.

In that day, when Jesus governs the entire world, there will be no more wars, no more politicians, no more political parties, no more voting, no more greed, and no more government corruption or tyranny. Christ alone will be King of Kings and Lord of Lords, and everyone will serve under his rule in a perfect, sinless world.

I'll share more details on that time period in my sequel to this book—*In the Light of Eternity*.

---

[340] Acts 17:26-27

Chapter 28

The Bride and Her Male Child

> She was pregnant and cried out in pain as she was about to give birth. ... She gave birth to a son, a **male child**, who will rule all the nations with an iron scepter. And her child was snatched up to God and to his throne.
>
> —*Revelation 12:2, 5*

THE SEVENTH TRUMPET is about to sound at the start of the last 1,260 days. As already discussed, the two witnesses will arrive at this time to initiate their 1,260 days of prophesying. The trumpet's sound will complete the "*mystery*" of God at the close of the trumpet judgments. This is the mystery John heard spoken by the angel[341] in Revelation 10:

> When the seventh angel blows his trumpet, God's *mysterious* plan will be fulfilled. It will happen just as he announced it to his servants the prophets.
>
> —*Revelation 10:7 NLT*

So what is this *mysterious* plan and why is it so important at this time before the start of the last 1,260 days? Several theories surround this event, but I have one that might surprise you. To do so, however, requires a serious foundation of Scriptures, and an introduction to the essential

---

[341] Revelation 10:7—the angel is believed to be Jesus himself.

tools necessary to come up with the interpretation I will present.

In the beginning ...

When God created Adam and Eve, like every other living thing, he designed them to multiply. They were made in his image, perfectly sinless, and he wanted them to reproduce a race of "sinless" offspring like themselves.[342] This never occurred because the darkness of sin entered the picture and caused a separation between them and their Creator.

Since God foreknew this, he initiated a covenant with Adam and Eve to enable them to approach him by way of the substitute *blood* of an animal. In this covenant God promised Eve that a "seed" would come from a woman that would crush the serpent's head who had deceived her—emphasis placed on *her* seed, not a man's seed.[343] Sin's DNA comes through a man, not a woman. The apostle Paul later identifies this "seed" as Jesus,[344] who the Bible refers to as the *last* Adam—a *sinless* Adam.[345]

It was God's perfect plan for Adam and Eve to have offspring *without* sin before sin entered the world. But it didn't happen that way. So is it safe to assume that this plan is still in play and that Jesus, the *last* Adam, will have a bride *without* sin, and bear children *without* sin? I know this seems like a stretch, but have you ever pondered such a question? *Is this something that's possible?* Anything is possible if the Bible says, *with God anything is possible.*

Why else would God have a bride for his Son, if there weren't offspring somewhere in the picture? And, if so,

---

[342] Genesis 1:27-28
[343] Genesis 3:15
[344] Genesis 3:15 with Galatians 3:16
[345] 1 Corinthians 15:45 with 2 Corinthians 5:21

would they be literal, natural, or spiritual offspring? Let's lay some groundwork to examine this theory.

Hermeneutics

In the art and science of interpreting Scripture, the "tools" of hermeneutics are essential for arriving at an accurate conclusion. The term *hermeneutics* is derived from the Greek word *hermeneuō*, which means to "translate" or "interpret." When Ezra, the scribe, devoted himself to study and teach the Law of the Lord to the Jews (who had returned from Babylon), he had to correctly translate it, analyze it, accurately divide it, and then skillfully teach it with integrity.[346] He did so through the application of hermeneutics. This is the approach Paul spoke of when he encouraged Timothy:

> Do your best to present yourself to God as one approved, a workman who does not need to be ashamed and who **correctly handles** the word of truth.[347]

Every preacher and teacher of the Bible is responsible to correctly analyze and translate God's word on any topic with this supreme principle—*using Scripture to interpret Scripture.* And let's also throw in this adage: *When the literal text of Scripture makes sense, seek no other sense.*

Hermeneutics uses a variety of tools to interpret even mysterious and difficult passages in the Bible. Two of these tools are especially applicable when it comes to interpreting "prophetic" symbols. They are the *Symbolic Principle* and *Comparative Mention Principle.*

When studying the specifics of eschatology, these are prominent principles (or tools) used in tandem (for more on

---

[346] Ezra 7:10
[347] 2 Timothy 2:15

Hermeneutics, see *Hermeneutics Must Apply* on page 381 in the Appendix).

In the Old Testament, the book that most heavily demonstrates the *Comparative Mention Principle* is the book of Proverbs. King Solomon, Proverb's author, uses this principle repeatedly when he presents the contrasts between wisdom and folly, the wise and the foolish, the diligent and the lazy.

Let's take a look at how Paul used the *Comparative Mention Principle* in his letter to the Corinthian church regarding the *contrast* between Adam and Jesus:

> So it is written: "The *first* man Adam became a living being"; the *last* Adam, a life-giving spirit. The spiritual did not come first, but the natural, and after that the spiritual. The first man was of the dust of the earth, the second man from heaven. As was the earthly man, so are those who are of the earth; and as is the man from heaven, so also are those who are of heaven. And just as we have borne the likeness of the earthly man, so shall we bear the likeness of the man from heaven.[348]

The *Comparative Mention Principle* is the interpreting "tool" used to show the contrast and/or similarities between persons, places, things, or events. So let's apply this tool to the above passage with side-by-side columns of the two "Adams" using Paul's words:

Adam	**Jesus**
First Adam	Last Adam
A living being	A life-giving spirit
The natural came first	The spiritual came last
First man of earth's dust	Second man from heaven

---

[348] 1 Corinthians 15:44-49

Adam	**Jesus**
We bear the earthly man's likeness now	We will bear the heavenly man's likeness then

Let's look at another passage in **Romans 6:12-21** where Paul uses this same tool of interpretation to show the contrasts between Adam and Jesus. Here's a chart for that passage:

(First) Adam	**Jesus (Last Adam)**
Sin entered the world through this man	Righteousness came into the world through this man
Death came through sin	Life through Christ's death
Death has reigned since Adam	Eternal life reigns in Christ
The *pattern* of the "One" to come	Fulfillment of Adam as *the* One
Many died by his trespass	Many live by his grace and gift
A judgment of condemnation	A gift of justification
Through one act of disobedience many were made sinners	Through one act of obedience many are made righteous

The contrasts are striking between the first and last Adam. The part I want to bring attention to is where Adam, the first man, is regarded as the *pattern* of the "One" who was to come—that is, Jesus, the second man from heaven.

The word "pattern" in this verse comes from the Greek word *tupos*, which means a symbolic "type" or "prototype" of someone or something coming in the future to fulfill that type. I don't mean that Jesus followed Adam's pattern of sin, where Adam disobeyed God—Jesus *never* disobeyed the Father or sinned. Instead, I refer to a pattern, not of opposites, but of *similarities* in God's original intent for Adam and Eve.

For example, God gave the first Adam a wife,[349] and Jesus, the last Adam, will present a wife to himself.[350] Adam

---

[349] Genesis 2:20-22
[350] Ephesians 5:25-27

was given a wife commensurate to himself and *sinless* like him. Jesus, too, will present a wife commensurate to himself without spot, wrinkle or blemish—and *sinless* like him. I addressed this concept of a *sinless* bride in chapter 13, but let's take this a step further to include the male child (or manchild) of Revelation 12. The vision in Revelation presents the woman as pregnant and about to give birth. My question is, *when* did she get pregnant and by whom? We'll discover that answer coming up.

A "male child" son for Jesus

Adam and Eve had a son—a "male child." They became parents. God gave the couple to each other, not only for companionship, but also to have offspring. So why wouldn't this same pattern apply to Jesus and his bride? Will he marry a perfect, sinless bride for companionship alone, or is it somehow a part of God's *mysterious* plan for Christ and his bride to have children who are divinely conceived from heaven?

As we continue with this thought, let's keep reminding ourselves that *anything* is possible with God, and we don't know everything there is to know about his full and complete redemptive plan. There are always mysteries in God's eternal purposes and I believe this "mystery" of the bride and her male child could be one of them.

The bodies of Adam and Eve were natural bodies, made of earth's dust and, after their fall, received a sin nature which continued on in the DNA pattern of their children. On the contrary, Jesus had a spiritual body *without* sin, and is coming for a sinless bride to consummate the marriage on the Day of Atonement in Revelation 8:1-5. I believe at that very moment, flesh and blood fetuses are "supernaturally" conceived in the bride's womb. Let's consider a *pattern* of evolving similarities between Adam and Jesus, again using the *Comparative Mention Principle*:

(First) Adam	(Last Adam) Jesus
The *first* man, Adam	The *last* Adam
Created with no sin nature	Conceived/born with no sin
Natural—of the earth	Spiritual—from heaven
Adam has a natural body	Christ has a "church" body
Eve—taken from Adam's body	Bride—from Christ's church
Eve commensurate to Adam	Bride commensurate to Jesus
Eve has a womb	The Bride has a womb
A male child is conceived	A male child is conceived
Adam becomes a father	Jesus becomes a father[351]
Eve becomes a mother	The Bride becomes a mother[352]

My theory and best understanding about the male child in Revelation 12, is that they are a "company" of real children, in the same way that the "woman" of Revelation 12:1 is a company of real people, not just a metaphor.

In Revelation 8:1-5, the selection of the bride takes place with those who are ready to meet Jesus. The bride is taken from the "body of Christ," his church. She is the "rib section" of Christ's church body, just as Eve came from the rib of Adam's body. God didn't use the whole body of Adam to make a bride for him; he used a portion of it. It will be the same with the church body universally.

All saints are "betrothed" to Christ,[353] but not all saints will be ready for the wedding. Those who are ready will go through the door into the bridal chambers where the consummation takes place. It isn't a sexual encounter with Christ, but a supernatural act of conception implanted within the company of saints assigned to carry the "offspring" of

---

[351] Isaiah 9:6—a reference to Jesus as "everlasting father." When does Jesus become a father?
[352] Revelation 12:1-2—if the woman is with child and truly the bride of Christ, then who is the father of this manchild? When was the manchild conceived?
[353] 2 Corinthians 11:2

Christ and his bride. I see this company as the "womb" of the bride. Eve was Adam's rib taken out of his natural body; the bride is Christ's rib taken out of his spiritual body, the church. Eve's womb carried her male child and the womb of the bride will carry her male-child company born in Revelation 12:5:

> She gave birth to a son, a male child, who will rule all the nations with an iron scepter.

The "womb" of the bride company

If this theory is true, and it's a literal event, then it's safe to assume that the conception of these male children will take place at the beginning of the opening of the seventh *seal* on the Day of Atonement (Revelation 8:1-5), and they will develop in the womb of the bride during the sounding of the first six trumpets. To carry a child to full term is nine months. So it's possible that the era of the trumpet judgments will cover a nine month period before the last three-and-one-half years. In Revelation 8:1-5, the male-child company is conceived, and in Revelation 12:5, the male-child company is born and snatched immediately up to the throne room of God.

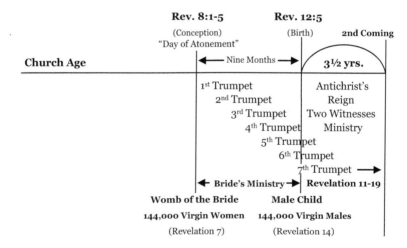

144,000 virgins—Revelation 7

So who carries the male children and how many are there? My theory is that they are the 144,000 persons chosen from the twelve tribes of Israel in Revelation 7:2-8. In that passage, gender is not mentioned, only the number of persons and where they come from. I believe the 144,000 of Revelation 7 come out of the bride company to become the "womb company" of the bride that supernaturally conceives and carries (each) a male child.

I suggest they are 144,000 virgin women from among the born again Gentiles descended from the scattered eleven tribes of Israel (12,000 each) and the 12,000 born-again Jews from the tribe of Judah.

These "sealed ones"[354] settle the question for me of whom the 144,000 male virgins might be in Revelation 14 (which follow the Lamb wherever he goes).[355] In Revelation 12:5, we see the male-child company immediately snatched into heaven from the clutches of the fallen dragon (Satan). He will seek to devour the male child as soon as he is born[356] (just as Satan attempted to kill Moses, through Pharaoh, after he was born[357] and Jesus, through Herod, after he was born[358]). Here then is a possible scenario in the three columns:

Revelation 7	Revelation 12	Revelation 14
The womb of the bride	The bride in labor	The royal offspring
144,000 virgin women	A male child is born	144,000 virgin men
chosen to carry a child	and caught up to God	before God's throne

---

[354] Revelation 7:3
[355] Revelation 14:1-5
[356] Revelation 12:2-5
[357] Exodus 1:15-2:10
[358] Matthew 2:13-18

Jesus—a father?

I know this is a difficult concept to process and it isn't easy for me to put my theory out on the table without risk. But I have asked myself again and again—*why not?* And—*what else could it be?*

No other theories I've read about the "male child" satisfy my questions more than what I've just presented to you. And I can understand where it breaks down for people when they counter my theory with questions like:

- Does this mean 144,000 demigods[359] are going to be born?
- Will Jesus have a harem like Solomon?
- Are these "literal" children, or symbolic of "spiritual" children?
- Will Jesus sexually engage with 144,000 virgin women?
- Where does the Bible show Jesus as a father?

Let me try and answer these.

First, I don't believe they're demigods, but rather the sinless offspring of the 144,000 sinless, sealed members[360] of the bride company's *womb*. They are supernaturally conceived by a "creative act" of God. They are redeemed from the Earth[361] out of the clutches of Satan in the darkest hour on a planet that had been cursed by Adam's fall.[362]

Jesus wasn't the literal son of Joseph, but Joseph was an *earthly* father to Jesus. Jesus was conceived in Mary's womb by a *supernatural* act of the Holy Spirit, but he never addressed the Holy Spirit as "Father." He spoke to God the Father as "father," however there was no sexual activity in any part of Christ's incarnation. The Holy Spirit gave Jesus a body, conceived in Mary's womb and, I believe, the Holy

---

[359] *Demigod*—half human/half deity. An inferior deity, a deified mortal.
[360] Revelation 7:3-8
[361] Revelation 12:5 with Revelation 14:3
[362] Romans 8:18-23

Spirit will give the company of 144,000 male virgins a body as well, each conceived in a womb from among 144,000 virgin women chosen out of the "rib section" of the bride company of Christ.

In heaven, and the age to come, Jesus said there will be no sexual activity,[363] and I don't believe he or the rest of us will engage sexually, simply because Jesus said we wouldn't.[364] But this doesn't exclude the possibility of God creating 144,000 sinless male virgins in a *divine act*, and Jesus becomes a "father" to this unique group of sinless men (like Joseph was to Jesus). And because he is *King* Jesus (as King of Kings and Lord of Lords), they will be the 144,000 princes of the King. After all, like Jesus, they will carry an iron scepter,[365] which suggests "royal" participation in his rule over all nations while he acts as a"father" to them.

So where in the Bible do we see mention of Jesus being a father (not Father God, the first member of the Trinity, but a father nevertheless)? It is found in **Isaiah 9:6-7**:

> For to us a child is born, to us a son is given, and the government will be on his shoulders. And he will be called Wonderful Counselor, Mighty God, **Everlasting Father**, [and] Prince of Peace.
>
> Of the increase of his government and peace there will be no end. He will reign on David's throne and over his kingdom, establishing and upholding it with justice and righteousness from that time on and forever.

Theologians and scholars agree that the context of this passage distinctly refers to Jesus, the Son of God. So if that's the case, when does Jesus become an everlasting father? I believe that answer starts with Revelation 8:1-5 when the

---

[363] Luke 20:34-36
[364] Matthew 22:30
[365] Revelation 12:5 with Psalm 2:9 and Revelation 19:15

male-child company of 144,000 is supernaturally conceived on the Day of Atonement and born in Revelation 12:5 after the period of the first six trumpets. Now this "mystery" of the bride of Christ and the male child is complete.[366] The 144,000 male infants are redeemed (snatched up) to God's throne[367] to follow Jesus, the Lamb of God, wherever he goes.[368] From this time on, Jesus will be their *everlasting* father. More on this later.

[366] Revelation 10:7
[367] Revelation 12:5 with 14:3
[368] Revelation 14:4

Chapter 29

The Bride in the Desert

The woman fled into the **desert** to a place prepared for her by God, where she might be taken care of for 1,260 days.

—Revelation 12:6

When the dragon saw that he had been hurled to the earth, he pursued the woman who had given birth to the male child. The woman was given the two wings of a great eagle, so that she might fly to the place prepared for her in the **desert**, where she would be taken care of for *a time, times and half a time*, out of the serpent's reach. Then from his mouth the serpent spewed water like a river, to overtake the woman and sweep her away with the torrent. But the earth helped the woman by opening its mouth and swallowing the river that the dragon had spewed out of his mouth.

—Revelation 12:13-16

EARLIER IN CHAPTER 25, I had mentioned that God will reward the saints according to the fruit they produce.[369] One such reward is being chosen as a member of the bride company of Christ. The Scriptures indicate that such a reward belongs to *wise* saints, *obedient* saints, *faithful* saints, *serving* saints, *reproducing* saints, *passionate* saints,

---

[369] Matthew 5:12; 10:42; 16:27; Luke 6:23; 1 Corinthians 3:14; Ephesians 6:8; Revelation 22:12

and saints who *overcome* the temptations of the flesh, the world, and Satan.

These fruitful saints, who are alive when Jesus comes for his bride, are the *only* members of the body of Christ (the "rib" section) who will be taken into the desert for preservation, provision, and protection during the 1,260 days before Christ returns. They will comprise *one-third* of the existing members of God's church from all denominations around the world (*not* including cults or non-Christian world religions).

As stated in chapter 23, statistics project 2.6 billion adherents to Christianity by the year 2025 in a world population of 8.1 billion people. If we go with that 2.6 billion figure—not including the massive harvest of souls under the bride's ministry—and remove *one-third* of that number, as indicated in chapter 25, then approximately 866 million members of the bride company will be taken into a desert place for three-and-one-half years.[370]

What happens during that time in the desert?

God will do the same thing for the bride that he did for the children of Israel when he took them out of Egypt and led them into the desert.

Let's apply the *Comparative Mention Principle* to compare the children of Israel in the Old Testament with the bride company in Revelation 12.

While Israel was in Egypt, God protected them in the land of Goshen from the plagues he had sent upon Pharaoh and the Egyptians.[371] In Revelation 12, it indicates that God will protect the bride in the desert from the seven bowls of

---

[370] Revelation 12:6, 14
[371] Exodus 8:22-23; 9:4, 26; 10:23; 11:6-7

wrath[372] he pours out on the ungodly near the end of the 1,260 days.

When Pharaoh and his army pursued Israel, after he had let them go, God delivered them out of his hands and swallowed up Pharaoh and his army in the Red Sea.[373] When the dragon (Satan cast down from heaven) pursues the bride—after she has been taken into the wilderness—he will send out an army to capture and destroy her, perhaps through the Antichrist's command to his military. But the Earth will open up and swallow this army before it can harm her.[374] Just as the Red Sea delivered Israel from Pharaoh and his army, so will the Earth deliver Christ's bride from Satan and his army.

While in the desert, God spread a cloud to shield the children of Israel from the harsh rays of the sun by day, and provided a pillar of fire for light at night.[375] I believe the same thing could happen for the bride in the desert. God fed Israel with bread from heaven and quail, and had Moses strike a rock that gushed water that flowed in the desert like a river.[376]

In Revelation 12 it says that God will feed the woman for 1,260 days in the desert[377]—perhaps in the same way he did for Israel. One thing is certain—she won't be thirsty or go hungry during the famine (and no rain) on the Earth during that time.[378]

This is what God will do for the members of the bride who are ready for the Bridegroom on the Day of Atonement. This will be their reward.

---

[372] Revelation 16
[373] Exodus 14
[374] Psalm 124 with Ezekiel 26:3; Revelation 12:16 with Numbers 16
[375] Exodus 13:21-22; Psalm 105:39
[376] Exodus 16:14 17:5-6; Psalm 105:41
[377] Revelation 12:6 (New King James Version)
[378] Psalm 107:9; Proverbs 10:3

The Enoch company

One more amazing detail needs to be mentioned here. The bride company will never experience the sword or death. She will be like Enoch, who so pleased God that God took him before he could die.[379] Enoch is the man in Genesis who *never* experienced death—ever. Elijah was taken up before he died, too, but he will return and be killed at the hand of the Antichrist.[380] There are only three companies of saints who will be taken by God and never experience death. They are the bride company, the 144,000 sealed virgin women (the womb of the bride), and the 144,000 virgin males who will be born and immediately snatched up to the throne of God.[381]

At the end of the 1,260 days, when the two witnesses are killed[382] and the Antichrist's reign comes to an end in the battle of Armageddon,[383] the only remaining *living* saints on the Earth will be the bride in the wilderness. At the last note[384] of the seventh trumpet that's been sounding throughout the last 1,260 "days,"[385] Jesus will come with an army of angels.[386] The dead in Christ will rise first from the grave, in immortal bodies,[387] and those who are alive and remain (the bride in the desert) will follow the resurrected dead to meet Jesus in the air.[388] I believe the rapture of the dead in Christ and the "living" bride of Christ occurs at the second coming—not seven years prior.

---

[379] Genesis 5:18-24; Hebrews 11:5
[380] Revelation 11:7
[381] Revelation 12:6, 14; Revelation 7:2-8; Revelation 12:5 with 14:1-5
[382] Revelation 11:7
[383] Revelation 16:16 with Revelation 19:11-12
[384] Matthew 24:30-31; 1 Corinthians 15:52; 1 Thessalonians 4:16
[385] Revelation 10:7 (New King James Version)—in the "days" of the sounding.
[386] Matthew 16:27; 24:30-32
[387] 1 Corinthians 15:52-54
[388] Daniel 12:2; John 5:25, 28-29; 1 Corinthians 15:50-57; 1 Thessalonians 4:14-18; Jude 14

By understanding Enoch's life of incredible intimacy with God, it is fitting to classify the bride of Christ as the "Enoch" company of believers. And how interesting that the only words we see spoken by Enoch had to do with his prophecy in Jude 14-16 about the resurrection of the "holy ones" at the end of the age. Interesting, too, is the fact that Enoch happens to be the "seventh" generation from Adam. See any types and symbols in that? Here are his words:

> Now Enoch, the *seventh* from Adam, prophesied about these men also, saying, "Behold, the Lord comes with ten thousands of His **saints**, to execute judgment on all, to convict all who are ungodly among them of all their ungodly deeds which they have committed in an ungodly way, and of all the harsh things which ungodly sinners have spoken against Him."[389]

A time for intercession

Once the bride company is in the desert, what will they be doing during the last three-and-one-half years? A number of things will occur that are similar to what we experience now. First, there'll be no sin nature among these 800-plus million believers. How pleasant will that be to know and relate to people with no envy or strife and who live in perfect harmony? Reunions, praise, celebration, and fellowship will be an amazing part of this experience.

Another important aspect of their time could be devoted to a season of "intercession" for those saints left behind (at the start of the Great Tribulation) when the persecution and martyrdom of all remaining saints intensifies.

These "remaining" saints include the 866-million outer-court saints.[390] The outer-court saints could be *one-third* of

---

[389] Jude 14-16 (New King James Version)
[390] Revelation 11:1-2

the total population of Christians who didn't make the bride company because they lacked oil for their lamps and missed their chance to meet the Bridegroom when he came.[391] In this hour of persecution, however, they will overcome Satan, the world, and the Antichrist by the blood of the Lamb and their testimony for Christ. Though they missed their opportunity to become members of the bride, they will have bolstered their faith to stand firmly in the face of death.[392] This is the time when the Devil is cast to the Earth and enters the scene filled with great wrath. This is the *third* woe of judgment[393] on the Earth during the *"days of the sounding"* of the *seventh* trumpet.[394]

When the Devil is cast to the Earth, a loud voice from heaven will cry, "Woe to the earth and the sea because the devil is furious and knows his time is short [1,260 days left]."[395] And when the Devil's effort to destroy the bride of Christ is thwarted (after she's taken to the desert), he will make war with the rest of her spiritual offspring,[396]i.e.—the great harvest of souls who were saved under her ministry.

Both the outer-court saints—who stay faithful to God—and the bride's offspring will become the martyrs of the Great Tribulation.[397] The Messianic Jews, also, will be slain for their conversion to Christ through the ministry of the two witnesses, Moses and Elijah.[398] At the end of the three-and-one-half years, when Jesus comes back, all martyrs for Christ from throughout church history, will rise from their graves to meet the Lord in the air.[399]

---

[391] Matthew 25:1-10
[392] Revelation 12:10-11
[393] Revelation 8:13 with 12:12
[394] Revelation 10:7 (New King James Version)
[395] Revelation 12:12
[396] Revelation 12:15-17
[397] Revelation 6:9-11; 7:9-17
[398] Revelation 15:2-4—Jews, not Gentiles, know about the song of Moses.
[399] 1 Corinthians 15:50-53; 1 Thessalonians 4:14-17; with Revelation 20:4

The remaining *one-third* out of the 2.6 billion believers will fall away (the great apostasy) and follow the Antichrist.[400] They will forfeit their salvation[401] and sell their soul to the Devil so that they may receive the mark of the beast.[402] This is what separates the *apostate* saints from the bride. The apostates include the Christians who will be more interested in their stomachs than their eternal reward. They are those who live for today's conveniences with no eternal perspective of the consequences. Their vision is limited, temporal, and carnal. Those who are chosen for the bride at that time, however, will be the saints who live with an "eternal" perspective.

Jacob and Esau

There is a scene like this in an Old Testament story of two brothers, Jacob and Esau, with different priorities. Both are of the same house with the promise of an inheritance. But Esau, the firstborn, chose to forfeit his birthright when he sold it for a pot of stew to his brother, Jacob.[403] Esau was starving—in the moment—for the *temporal*, material things. Jacob was starving for the *future*, eternal things.

Think of it—in the last-days' church one out of every three Christians will:

1) fall away and join the Antichrist
2) become martyred for their faith, or
3) become a chosen member of the bride company, preserved in the desert until Jesus comes.

---

[400] 2 Thessalonians 2:3
[401] See Mark 8:36; 2 Peter 2:17-22; 3:17; Hebrews 6:4-6; 10:26-31; see symbolism used in Jude 11-13 to describe the "fallen." *Hint:* clouds, trees, twice dead, wandering stars, wild foaming waves.
[402] Revelation 13:16-17
[403] Genesis 25:27-34

That means if you randomly select a congregation of any church and divide it into three sections, this will be the picture. A very sobering thought to ponder if true.

2.6 billion Christians (by 2025)

So here's how it will look with the projected number of Christian adherents by 2025, divided by three:

- 866 million in the *bride company* of Christians
- 866 million *outer-court* Christians martyred for their faith
- 866 million *apostate* Christians deceived by the Antichrist

Chapter 30

The Beast Who Dies and Resurrects

> And I saw a beast coming out of the sea. He had ten horns and seven heads, with ten crowns on his horns, and on each head a blasphemous name.
>
> *—Revelation 13:1-2*

ENTER THE MOST charismatic "political" figure ever to rise upon the world stage. His wisdom and intelligence will surpass the wisest leaders of his time. He'll be second to none and is depicted in John's vision with very distinct traits wrapped in iconic images.

As we saw earlier, John unseals the "little book (scroll)" in Revelation 10, and then proceeds to reveal the two witnesses of Moses and Elijah in chapter 11, and the bride of Christ in chapter 12. But now, in Revelation 13, he reveals the *Antichrist* and his role in the last three-and-one-half years before Jesus returns.

We begin Revelation 13 with the symbol of a dragon, representing Satan, standing on the shore of the sea of humanity.[404] This comes after he had been cast out of heaven by the archangel, Michael, and hurled to the Earth.[405]

Because God views man as having a beastly nature,[406] the Antichrist is seen as a "beast" coming up out of the *sea* of

---

[404] Revelation 13:1—the "sea" in the Bible is symbolic of humanity or multitudes of people (compare with Isaiah 17:12; 57:20).
[405] Revelation 12:7-12
[406] Daniel 7:17; 2 Peter 2:12

humanity. At this point in the future, the Antichrist has become the incarnation of Satan, in a similar way that Satan possessed Judas—only much more.[407] He's seen as having ten horns with a crown on each horn; an image that symbolizes the strength, power, and authority of ten global kings who, with the Antichrist, will be given full authority to rule over the Earth.[408]

Satan, who is the god of this age,[409] will give the Antichrist his power, throne, and great authority.[410] The beast in the vision resembles the *quick cunning* of a leopard, the *powerful strength* of a bear, and the *kingly roar* of a lion.[411] This could suggest that the Antichrist will be quick, crafty, cunning and strong in his ability to power through any obstacle. He will speak with such authority that he'll hold the entire world in fear and awe by his persona.

The seven heads

The seven heads John sees on this beast[412] are metaphors used to describe the ideological heads of the seven most prominent empires in history, beginning with Egypt, then Assyria, Babylon, Medo-Persia, Greece and Rome. The seventh, however, is the last empire of the ten-kingdom alliance governed and led by the Antichrist. It will be the culmination of the religious, social, and political ideologies of its predecessors, all under one umbrella.

You can look back in history and see how each empire influenced the succeeding empires in science, mathematics, agriculture, medicine, military strategies, music, the arts, technology, politics, religion, government, commerce,

---

[407] Luke 22:3; John 6:70-71
[408] Compare with Daniel 7:7, 20, 24 and Revelation 17:12
[409] 2 Corinthians 4:4
[410] Revelation 13:2
[411] Revelation 13:2
[412] Revelation 13:1; 18:9-11

astronomy, trade, urban planning, road systems, and languages—all of which have been integrated into the fabric of today's greatest nations.

The wounded head—death and resurrection

Two theories surround this mortal wound to one of the seven heads of the beast.[413] First, if the heads represent seven empires, then one empire died and was resurrected. Some believe it could be the sixth head—the empire of pagan Rome—that died, but will resurrect politically throughout Europe, before the rise of the Antichrist's empire.

The second theory is, if the fatal wound is to the *seventh* head (representing the kingdom of the Antichrist), then it could be speaking of a *literal* wound to the head of the Antichrist who will embody the last empirical kingdom on Earth

I favor the latter theory. If the Antichrist declares he is the true messiah to replace our Messiah, then his claim, backed by an actual resurrection, would greatly support the weight of his grand "lie" to the world, to apostate Christians, and to all other cults and religions, including Islam. Resurrection from a mortal wound is clearly a more tangible demonstration to astonish the world than the theory of a subtle resurrection of pagan Rome in Europe. Besides, Europe today is weaker than it's ever been as an alliance of nations and, therefore, not much a candidate for power.

Here are two Scriptures that cause me to lean toward the Antichrist experiencing a *literal* death and resurrection:

> One of the heads of the beast seemed to have had a **fatal wound**, but the fatal wound had been healed. The whole world was astonished and followed the beast.
>
> *—Revelation 13:3-4*

---

[413] Revelation 13:3

I am going to bring foreigners against you, the most ruthless of nations; they will draw their swords against your beauty and wisdom and pierce your shining splendor. They will bring you down to the pit, and **you will die** a violent death in the heart of the seas.

—*Ezekiel 28:7-8*

In the first verse, I believe the wounded head is the *seventh* head (kingdom of the antichrist) on the beast, of which he is *the* "head" of that kingdom. It is called a "fatal" wound. After his death, the wound is miraculously healed and he resurrects to astonish the world[414] in the same way that Christ's resurrection astonished his disciples (and the rest who saw him in his resurrected body).[415] Because of this, the whole world will follow the Antichrist and worship Satan who will give him his authority.

In the second verse of Ezekiel 28, the context is in reference to the *son* of the king of Tyre, a bombastic prince who declares, "I am a god; I sit on the throne of a god in the heart of the seas [of humanity]."[416] This prince's heart had grown proud through his wisdom, understanding, and the skills he possessed in trading to increase and amass great amounts of wealth.[417] But God opposes the proud, like he did King Nebuchadnezzar,[418] and pronounces judgment upon the prince of Tyre who, though he thought he was a god, would soon discover his mortality when God sent foreigners to kill him.[419]

I would like to add another thought to this idea of "foreigners" coming against this prince who, I believe, symbolizes the prophetic event of the Antichrist's death.

---

[414] Revelation 13:3
[415] Luke 24:36-41; 1 Corinthians 15:3-8
[416] Ezekiel 28:2
[417] Ezekiel 28:4-5
[418] James 4:6; Daniel 4:1-37
[419] Ezekiel 28:6-10

Who are these foreigners in Ezekiel that God calls, "the most ruthless of nations?" Which foreigners come to your mind who match this description of "the most ruthless of nations" and who will "draw their swords" against the Antichrist and kill him?

My first thought is that an extreme Islamist faction will have followers who see the Antichrist as a threat to Allah and an Islamic caliphate. They'll see him, not as the rest of the world sees him, but as a mortal, an infidel to be dispensed of, and quickly. Perhaps the Antichrist won't be able to manifest his powers, yet, and the False Prophet won't be there to protect him with his supernatural abilities.

It's possible, too, that the Antichrist won't come into full governing power and authority until *after* he resurrects from the dead and wows the entire world.[420] Then the delusion can begin, signs and wonders will manifest, and even the most extreme of the Islamist groups will bow to the beast who was slain and resurrects before the entire world.

The Law of Double Reference

Before we proceed, it's important to insert a principle of hermeneutics called, the *Law of Double Reference.* For example, God says to the prophet Hosea, "When Israel was a child, I loved him, and out of Egypt I called my son."[421] We understand in this context that God is referring to the nation of Israel and its exodus out of Egypt to the Promised Land. However, in Matthew's gospel, he pulls this passage out of the Old Testament and applies it to the infant Jesus escaping to Egypt and remaining there until after Herod's death.[422] Which application is right? Both are right, both are applicable because Hosea's words serve as a "double

---

[420] Revelation 13:3-5
[421] Hosea 11:1
[422] Matthew 2:13-15

reference" to Israel, and to Jesus. It's the same with these verses below when referring to the Antichrist in these Old and New Testament passages:

In the pride of your heart you say, "I am a god; I sit on the throne of a god in the heart of the seas."[423]

—Ezekiel's prince of Tyre

He will exalt and magnify himself above every god and will say unheard-of things against the God of gods. ... He will show no regard for the gods of his fathers or for the one desired by women, nor will he regard any god, but will exalt himself above them all.[424]

—Daniel's Antiochus Epiphanes

He will oppose and will exalt himself over everything that is called God or is worshiped, so that he sets himself up in God's temple, proclaiming himself to be God.[425]

—Paul's Antichrist, the man of lawlessness

The beast was given a mouth to utter proud words and blasphemies and to exercise his authority for forty-two months [three-and-one-half years]. He opened his mouth to blaspheme God, and to slander his name and his dwelling place and those who live in heaven. ... All inhabitants of the earth will worship the beast—all whose names have not been written in the book of life belonging to the Lamb that was slain from the creation of the world.[426]

—John's Antichrist, the beast in Revelation 13

By using the *Law of Double Reference*, the verses above all apply to the person of the Antichrist. He is seen

---

[423] Ezekiel 28:2
[424] Daniel 11:36-37
[425] 2 Thessalonians 2:4
[426] Revelation 13:5-6, 8

throughout the Scriptures under many names and titles that belonged to real characters whose lives *foreshadowed* the coming of the Antichrist in some aspect of truth. Such "double" references applied to the Antichrist are found in Scriptures like the "seed" of the serpent,[427] Judas—the son of perdition,[428] the little horn in Daniel,[429] and the fierce, vile king named, Antiochus Epiphanes.[430] New Testament verses speak directly about the Antichrist as the lawless one,[431] or the mystery of iniquity.[432]

Other types (*tupos*) of the Antichrist can be found throughout the Bible as well. These types foreshadow the opposition he'll wage against God's people. They include:

Cain—who opposed and murdered his brother Abel.

Nimrod—the 13th man from Adam; the mighty hunter and founder of Babel who oppressed the godly line of saints through Seth, including Abraham.

Ishmael—Abraham's son, who mocked his half-brother, Isaac, the promised son; and the Philistine giant.

Goliath—who mocked and opposed the shepherd-king, David.

The Antichrist will ultimately fulfill all these types mentioned when he opposes, overpowers and destroys the saints of God who refuse to receive his mark and worship him as a god. This man will sit in a *false* temple—not of brick and mortar—but one made up of the apostates who have abandoned their Christian faith, and also those who abandon

---

[427] Genesis 3:15
[428] John 17:12 (Judas); 2 Thessalonians 2:3
[429] Daniel 7:8, 20-26; 8:9, 23-25
[430] Daniel 8:9-12, 23-25; 11:21-45—happened already through the historical figure of Antiochus Epiphanes, yet certain traits of this fierce king apply to the spirit and nature of the Antichrist of the last days.
[431] 2 Thessalonians 2:8
[432] 2 Thessalonians 2:7

the faith of their father's world religions. All will worship the Antichrist's image, and Satan, who gives him his miraculous power and authority.

The antithesis of Jesus

The list is too long to present all the comparisons and contrasts, but here is a sample of just how opposite the Antichrist is to Christ.

Jesus *ministered* publically for three-and-one-half years; the Antichrist will *reign* publically for three-and-one-half years (42 months).

Jesus performed miraculous signs and wonders during his public ministry to *redeem* the world to himself; the Antichrist will perform counterfeit signs and wonders during his reign to *capture* the world to himself.

Jesus was slain and rose from the dead to *save* the world from their sins; the Antichrist will be slain and rise from the dead to *deceive* the world into greater sins.

Jesus received his authority and power from his heavenly Father, *God*; the Antichrist will receive his authority and power from his devil father, *Satan*.

Jesus *came not to destroy* but to save people's lives; the Antichrist will *come to destroy and kill* all who reject his claim to deity.

Jesus was materially *poor* with nowhere to lay his head; the Antichrist will have great material *wealth* and *riches*.

Jesus, as God, *humbled* himself and became a man; the Antichrist, a man, will *exalt* himself and claim to be a god.

Jesus did only that which the Father told him to do; the Antichrist will do what Satan tells him to do.

Jesus came meek and lowly; the Antichrist will come proud, boastful, and arrogant.

Jesus came despised and rejected by men; the Antichrist will come worshipped and admired by the entire world of lost souls.

Jesus came without external beauty; the Antichrist will come with an attractive appearance.

Jesus glorified his Father's name; the Antichrist will blaspheme God, slander his name and his dwelling place among the people, his church, and the family of saints in heaven.

Jesus recruited no earthly army; the Antichrist will establish an entire one-world, global army.

Jesus came to pave the way for his church; the Antichrist will pave the way for his harlot church— Babylon.

Jesus will conquer the Antichrist in the end; the Antichrist will be thrown alive into the lake of fire.

A leader like no other—for such a time as this

Imagine a world that has been indoctrinated and preconditioned by schools, colleges, universities, world religions, and "politically correct" governments to hate Christians, hate the Jews, and hate the God of Israel. Aren't we seeing a taste of that, today? But let's fast forward two decades from now—hypothetically—*after* the invasion of Israel, *after* the sixth seal and seventh seal have opened, and *after* the first six trumpets have sounded.

Suddenly a world leader rises out of nowhere. He is wealthy, charismatic, wise, skillful, cunning, politically savvy, and able to perform miracles, signs and wonders—like Jesus did. Here is the long-awaited solution to the world's chaos and hunger; a leader who can actually do something about the mess we're in. He is instantly embraced and branded as the international icon of hope and a brighter future in the midst of the world's desperate conditions and broken systems of government.

In January 1990, I preached that in the 90's decade and beyond, we would witness the decline of morally strong and courageous leaders in our homes, churches, schools, universities, businesses, and governments. The decline can be attributed to the lack of people who are determined and courageous enough to stand up for truth and ethical standards. I also predicted it would become increasingly difficult to find leaders who cared more for others than themselves. I could speak this confidently and with strong conviction because the Bible teaches this will be the world's condition when the Antichrist appears.

So here we stand. Look around you. Look at our governments. Look at our homes, schools and colleges. Look at the world. Where are the heroes? The world has been numbed into a state of fear. Fear of fighting for freedom, fear of offending the enemy, fear of standing up for truth in the face of popular opinion. Where are the George Washingtons, the Ronald Reagans, the Dietrich Bonhoeffers, the Corrie Ten Booms, the William Wilberforces, or the Winston Churchills? Who else do you deem worthy of being proclaimed as a great leader? People intrinsically long for such leaders who not only lead well, but believe in something more valuable than their own lives.

I say this because, as the years go by, this decline in authentic leaders will accelerate to the degree that people will be so tired of lying, incompetent politicians, they'll take anyone better than the milk toast roll-out of leaders the world's been getting. They'll want someone like the Antichrist who will be a strong voice of reason and authority generating hope and vision. He'll be so articulate on his own, without the aid of Teleprompters, that people will hang on his every word.

Because the "times" will call for a man like this, he'll easily ignite as an overnight success of stardom and popularity. The world will be dying, the six trumpet plagues will have ravaged the world, famine will be spreading, and alien-like, demonic creatures will have killed one-third of the Earth's inhabitants. Enter the man who not only *sounds* intelligent, but *is* intelligent; and to top that off, he will perform undeniable miracles that qualify his message and candidacy as the world's solution to the problems.

Never mind that the bride of Christ will have been performing "headline" miracles in the name of her Bridegroom. Those who won't have ears to hear the truth will perish in their deception. This is why John says in Revelation 13:9, "He that has an ear, let him hear," only this time without mentioning the "Holy Spirit" or the "church" as he does in Revelation 2 and 3. The Holy Spirit's influence on the deceived, who despise the truth, will be *removed* during the last three-and-one-half years, so that the same blindness found in the Pharisees at the time of Christ will be found in the ungodly when the Antichrist appears to deceive the world. Read Christ's words regarding such people:

> Though seeing, they do not see; though hearing, they do not hear or understand.
>
> In them is fulfilled the prophecy of Isaiah:[433] "You will be ever hearing but never understanding; you will be ever seeing but never perceiving.
>
> For this people's heart has become calloused; they hardly hear with their ears, and they have closed their eyes.
>
> Otherwise they might see with their eyes, hear with their ears, understand with their hearts and turn, and I would heal them."
>
> **—*Matthew 13:13-15***

---

[433] Isaiah 6:9-10

The assassination effect

In the initial honeymoon stage of world popularity, either an "alleged" right-wing wacko (spun by the media to indict Christians) or an extreme Islamist terrorist will assassinate the Antichrist—dashing the world's last hope for survival. Imagine the extreme mourning, wailing, anger, frustration and vengefulness of the inhabitants of the Earth after their beloved world leader is murdered.

Perhaps several days of despair and disbelief will pass before the shocking news settles into reality.

But wait ... what's this? Breaking news! The Antichrist has resurrected from the dead? You mean like Jesus did? Perhaps he might be dead for three days and nights before he rises, who knows? The Antichrist will have such an obsession with dethroning and replacing Jesus, why not imitate the things Jesus did, if that's possible.

Jesus left Lazarus in the grave for four days[434] so that the resurrection would be credible. It may be that the Antichrist will be dead that long, too, to ensure his death and resurrection could never be challenged as fake.

Though nothing in the Bible shows how long he'll be dead, the wound is certainly fatal. So if the Antichrist is shot and killed at the beginning of his reign—and miraculously recovers—what joy, what amazement, what astonishment will be demonstrated throughout the world over this political figure who was assassinated and then resurrects.

Even Muslims will be in awe and wonder, perhaps— because this could be their long-awaited Twelfth Imam or Isa (Jesus of the Quran), who they believe will assist the Twelfth Imam, or become the ultimate caliphate leader of the world.

When I was in seventh grade, many Americans loved the young, popular, and charismatic president, John F. Kennedy.

---

[434] John 11:1-7, 17-44

I remember everything, when the announcement came over the loudspeaker in our classroom about the attempt on his life during a motorcade in Dallas. Our nation went into shock, disbelief, and deep grief at the official report of his death. Rumors later spread that he was being kept alive by a heart-lung machine, and hidden from public view.

With this in mind, can you conceive how significant JFK's miraculous recovery would have had on the world, if he had actually resurrected from the dead and returned to office to govern America?

Multiply such an effect when this happens to the Antichrist, astonishing the world.[435] He'll use this resurrection miracle as leverage to deceive, not only the irreligious, but every religion, including Christians primed for apostasy. They'll follow and worship him as a god above all gods—believed to be the *true* messiah, capable of bringing world peace and order through establishing a one-world government, one-world army, one-world commerce, and a one-world religion—all under the umbrella of his "alleged" godhood.

"Who is like the beast?" they will say.

"Who can make war against him?" they will cry,[436] while he gathers the Earth's inhabitants into his arms and God sends a strong delusion to the perishing who will believe his lies.[437]

During the three-and-one-half years of the Antichrist's reign, the Holy Spirit restrains his influence so that the full brunt of the deceptive powers of darkness can sweep across the nations.[438]

---

[435] Revelation 13:3
[436] Revelation 13:4
[437] 2 Thessalonians 2:9-11
[438] 2 Thessalonians 2:7-8

Those who embrace the Antichrist and take the mark of the beast will perish in their deception, because they refuse to love the truth that could have saved them.[439]

---

[439] 2 Thessalonians 2:11; Revelation 14:9-11

Chapter 31

The False Prophet and the Image

Then I saw ***another*** beast, coming out of the earth. He had two horns like a lamb, but he spoke like a dragon.

—Revelation 13:11

EVERY VILLAIN HAS a right-hand henchman who implements and oversees the plans of the boss. Maybe this is why there are two beasts in Revelation 13. The Antichrist will have a partner who also has a *beastly* nature to help him carry out his strategic objective to rule the world.

Of the earth

The second beast comes out of the *earth* and not the sea like the first beast. The mention of "earth" in some Scriptures relates to God's people. For example, in the Sermon on the Mount, Jesus said, "The meek shall inherit the *earth*,"[440] and also, "you are the salt of the *earth*."[441] This leads me to believe that the second beast might have a foundational link to the church.

The second beast also has two horns like a *lamb* and speaks like a *dragon*. Lambs are meek and docile creatures, and the dragon in Scripture symbolizes Satan.[442] Outwardly, he looks like a *lamb*, but inwardly he is *satanic* and will

---

[440] Matthew 5:5
[441] Matthew 5:13
[442] Revelation 12:9; 20:2

deceive the inhabitants of the Earth through his miraculous powers while he devours the saints of the last-days' church.

Because he is referred to as the False Prophet,[443] perhaps, *as* a prophet, he'll rise within the ranks of the church through deception and fall from grace in his *prophetic* role, just as the Antichrist might fall from an *apostolic* position. Apostles and prophets were the foundation stones of the early church[444] and worked in tandem with each other.[445] In Revelation 13, I believe we see a fallen *apostle* working with a fallen *prophet* in the last-days' church. If this is true, then surely they are like the apostates who will say on the day when the Lord returns:

> "Lord, Lord, did we not prophesy in your name, and in your name drive out demons and perform many miracles?" Then [Jesus] will tell them plainly, "I never knew you. Away from me, you evildoers!"[446]

Like the others, these two apostates—the Antichrist and the False Prophet—from Revelation 13 will have prophesied in the Lord's name and cast out demons. But the Lord will not receive or recognize them in their "fallen state." They will be categorically rejected at his return.

Two horns

Just as an animal would use its horns for intimidating and fighting, the two horns on this second beast represent *strength* and *power*. This symbolism is revealed in the purpose and plans of this False Prophet. First, he will fashion an image of the Antichrist and then cause the world to worship it. Second, he'll pass a law requiring all people to be

443 Revelation 16:13; 19:20; 20:10
444 Ephesians 2:20
445 Acts 15:22, 32; Luke 11:49; 1 Corinthians 12:28; Ephesians 3:5
446 Matthew 7:21-23

marked with the number or name of the first beast (the Antichrist) in order for them to buy or sell.[447]

The words *worship, buying,* and *selling* speak to *religion* and *commerce.* The two horns represent the authority given to the False Prophet through the power and authority of the first beast. The False Prophet will manage everything that has to do with a one-world *religion* and one-world *commerce.* Like Judas Iscariot,[448] this counterfeit prophet and liar will be in charge of the purse.

The image of the beast

Throughout the Old Testament, Israel battled repeatedly with the temptation to worship her neighbors' idols. God would not allow his people to fashion an image of himself[449] or they would wind up worshiping the object instead of him. That's why they were attracted to other gods; they weren't content with an *invisible* God.

Because of this, God sent his prophets to plead with Israel to leave their idolatrous ways and repent. But they ignored his prophets, persecuted them, and killed them.

God put an end to their unfaithfulness by raising up the Assyrian and Babylonian empires to punish and remove unfaithful Israel.[450] When God restored the Jews back to their homeland, after 70 years of exile,[451] they had learned their lesson and never worshiped idols again.

The argument God continued to make through his prophets against worshiping idols can be summed up in these two passages:

---

[447] Revelation 13:14-17
[448] John 13:29
[449] Exodus 20:4
[450] See Amos 5:25-27; Acts 7:42-43, 51-53
[451] Ezra 1:1-11

Psalm 115:2, 4-8

Why do the nations say, "Where is [Israel's] God?" [when] their idols are silver and gold, made by the hands of men. They have mouths, but *cannot* speak, eyes, but they *cannot* see; they have ears, but *cannot* hear, noses, but they *cannot* smell; they have hands, but *cannot* feel, feet, but they *cannot* walk; nor can they utter a sound with their throats. Those who make them will be like them, and so will all who trust in them.

Habakkuk 2:18-19

Of what value is an idol, since a man has carved it? Or an image that teaches lies?

For he who makes it trusts in his own creation; he makes idols that *cannot* speak.

Woe to him who says to wood, "Come to life!" Or to lifeless stone, "Wake up!"

Can it give guidance? It is covered with gold and silver; [yet] there is no breath in it.

Idols cannot breathe, see, speak, hear, feel with their hands, or walk with their feet—a logical case to be made by God.

Is there any person—created by God—who is able to breathe life into an image made in his or her own likeness? They are nothing more than lifeless, inanimate objects. To take wood or clay to form an idol, cover it in gold, bow down to worship it, or ask it for guidance is a moronic thing to do. It's like the scientist who says to God:

"Lord, we don't need you anymore. Science has finally figured out a way to create life out of nothing. In other words, we can now do what you did at the beginning."

"Oh, is that so? Tell me ..." replies God.

"Well," says the scientist, "we can take dirt and form it into the likeness of You and breathe life into it, thus creating man."

"Well, that's interesting. Show me."

The scientist bends down and begins to mold the soil beneath his feet.

"Oh no, no, no ..." interrupts God, "Get your *own* dirt."

Everything that is *material* traces back to the Creator. Yet, because of pride, unregenerate man cannot acknowledge that we exist by God's grand design. So they make and worship their own gods, including themselves, at times.

Contrast this thought with Revelation 13 where we see the False Prophet ordering a statue to be made in honor of the Antichrist, who was slain by a sword and resurrected.[452] Most likely the statue will be made in the Antichrist's image.

This will be no ordinary idol; it will be beyond belief. Not only will the Antichrist be given a resurrected life, but also this idol, made in his image, will receive life—perhaps mimicking his every move. The False Prophet will cause breath to come into this inanimate object (wake up!) so that it can speak. And everyone who refuses to worship it will be executed by beheading.[453]

I have to go back to my childhood memories for a visual of such an image. I recall this gargantuan statue called, Talos, from the Isle of Bronze, in the 1963 film, *Jason and the Argonauts*. He comes to life to pursue Jason's men who had trespassed beneath him in his treasure house. Perhaps the image of the beast might be like that when it comes to life—not as a giant computer or a cinematic, digital animation, but as a metallic object with real movement. Such a wonder could astonish and deceive the world's religions into bowing down to such an enormous display of power— one of the many signs and wonders the False Prophet will accomplish.

---

[452] Revelation 13:3-4 with Ezekiel 28:7
[453] Revelation 20:4

Is such a thing possible? Yes, it is. Consider the biblical example of when Aaron threw down his wooden rod in front of Pharaoh and it became a snake. Pharaoh's sorcerers, Jannes and Jambres, followed suit and threw down their rods, which also turned into life-breathing snakes.[454] Like Jannes and Jambres, the False Prophet will possess the power to turn an inanimate image of the Antichrist into a life-breathing idol. This event could be televised for the entire world to see, that is, in the parts of the world with access to an electrical source.

The mark of the beast—666

Once the image is given life, the False Prophet will order the entire world, along with every religion, to *worship* the Antichrist and receive the number of his name on their foreheads or right hands. This could become the new world order currency to replace all other forms of monetary exchange.[455]

If technology isn't destroyed by electrical-grid blackouts caused by the great earthquake of the sixth seal, or the devastation from the first four trumpets, people might be tagged with a tiny, passive biochip implant inserted under the skin of their forehead or right hand to monitor their sales and purchases. If there is no access to technology, then it could be a literal mark of some type, like a tattoo.

The numeric value

The number of the name of the beast is 666. This is another way of saying *"the numeric value"* of the name of the beast. When a word in Greek is written out, it has a

454 Exodus 7:8-13 with 2 Timothy 3:8
455 Revelation 13:16-17

mathematical value called the gematria.[456] The Greek word for "Jesus" (IhsouV) has a mathematical equivalent of 888. The number "8" in the Bible is symbolic of "new beginnings" —a very appropriate number for those who are born again as a new creation.

The numeric value of the name of the beast is three sixes. Six is the number of "man" who was created on the sixth day. Since man is a tri-part being, 666 marked on people's bodies could imply the complete possession of a person's entire being— body, soul, and spirit—when the Antichrist's name is taken. Once that happens, like cattle branded by an owner, so will those who receive the mark be branded inside-out. They'll be completely possessed by the powers of darkness and incapable of removing that mark for all eternity.

On the other hand, "new beginnings" await those who have the mark of Jesus (888) upon them, committed to Jesus, and completely possessed by the Holy Spirit. These are the ones who will refuse to accept the mark of the beast and embrace martyrdom for their faithfulness.

But don't fear dear saints.

Just as the Son of God appeared in the fiery furnace with Shadrach, Meshach, and Abednego—when they refused to bow down to worship Nebuchadnezzar's image—so shall Jesus walk with you among the flames of persecution and martyrdom. The three Jews came out without a hint of smoke or one hair singed from the flames.[457] Every Christian martyr who refuses to take the mark of the beast will come out of the fiery furnace of the Antichrist's wrath, into the eternal arms of Jesus in heaven.

---

[456] *Gematria:* from the Greek word: *geōmetria*—1. a cryptograph in the form of a word whose letters have the numerical values of a word taken as the hidden meaning (Merriam-Webster Dictionary).

[457] Daniel 3:1-7—*Note:* the statue of King Nebuchadnezzar was **six**ty cubits high, and **six** cubits wide, with **six** instruments playing to cause the officials of Babylon's provinces to bow down and worship the image.

> I saw the souls of those who had been **beheaded** because of their testimony for Jesus and because of the word of God. They had not worshiped the beast or his image and had not received his mark on their foreheads or their hands.[458]
>
> —*John*

> Precious in the sight of the Lord is the **death** of his saints.[459]
>
> —*David*

> So we are always confident, even though we know that as long as we live in these **bodies** we are not at home with the Lord. ... Yes, we are fully confident, and we would rather be away from these earthly bodies, for then we will be at home with the Lord.[460]
>
> —*Paul*

In light of what has gone on in the Middle East, it isn't hard to believe that people could be cruel enough to behead hundreds of thousands of Christians in the last days. When we witness the perpetual slaughter of saints in Islamic-controlled territories and states, this resembles the genocide in the early church under Roman emperors like Nero in A.D. 64, and Diocletian in A.D. 303.[461] It's interesting to point out that the numerical value of Nero Caesar was 666.

---

[458] Revelation 20:4
[459] Psalm 116:15
[460] 2 Corinthians 5:6, 8 (New Living Translation)
[461] "It was the nineteenth year of Diocletian's reign [A.D. 303] and the month Dystrus, called March by the Romans, and the festival of the Savior's Passion was approaching, when an imperial decree was published everywhere, ordering the churches to be razed to the ground and the Scriptures destroyed by fire, and giving notice that those in places of honor would lose their places, and domestic staff, if they continued to profess Christianity, would be deprived of their liberty. Such was the first edict against us. Soon afterwards other decrees arrived in rapid succession, ordering that the presidents of the churches in every place should all be first committed to prison and then coerced by every possible means into offering sacrifice." —Eusebius, *History of the Church (VIII.2), The Destruction of the Churches* (http://www.newadvent.org/fathers/250108.htm)

Be on guard—don't forfeit your salvation

At the time this edict is given by the False Prophet, the bride will be in the wilderness and the manchild company in heaven with Jesus. The Holy Spirit will have removed his restraining power against the forces of darkness, and the two witnesses will be prophesying to the Jews to encourage the remaining saints to be faithful, *before* they're hunted down and beheaded.

No saint remaining will be allowed to buy or sell unless they *forfeit* their salvation[462]—by denouncing Jesus—and receive the mark of the beast. Consider these next Scriptures about the *apostate* saints who will abandon their faith.

—Those who cling to worthless idols **forfeit the grace** that could be theirs.[463]

—What good is it for a man to gain the whole world, yet **forfeit** his soul? ... If anyone is ashamed of me and my words in this adulterous and sinful generation, the Son of Man will be ashamed of him when he comes in his Father's glory with the holy angels.[464]

—Therefore, dear friends, ... be on your guard so that you may not be carried away by the error of lawless men and **fall from your secure position.**[465]

—He who **disowns** me before men will be **disowned** before the angels of God.[466]

—If we died with him, we will also live with him; if we endure, we will also reign with him. If we **disown** him, he will also **disown** us.[467]

---

[462] 1 John 2:24-25 with Romans 11:22; Colossians 1:21-22; Hebrews 6:4-6; 10:26-31; 2 Peter 2:20-22; Revelation 3:5
[463] Jonah 2:8
[464] Mark 8:36-38
[465] 2 Peter 3:17-18
[466] Luke 12:9

I humbly submit—to those who believe Christians can't lose their salvation—that it *is* possible to *forfeit* it[468] if we *disown* Jesus and take the mark to buy food and goods to survive.

Esau, a son in his father Isaac's house, forfeited his own birthright and inheritance when he sold it for a single meal.[469] He could never take it back. Here's how Paul applies Esau's action to us:

> Exercise foresight and be on the watch to look [after one another], to see that no one falls back from and fails to secure God's grace (His unmerited favor and spiritual blessing), ... That no one may become ... a profane (godless and sacrilegious) person as **Esau** did, who sold his own birthright for a single meal. [Gen 25:29-34.]
>
> For you understand that later on, when he wanted [to regain title to] his inheritance of the blessing, he was rejected (disqualified and set aside), for he could find no opportunity to repair by repentance [what he had done, no chance to recall the choice he had made], although he sought for it carefully with [bitter] tears. [Gen 27:30-40.]

> —*Hebrews 12:15-17* (Amplified Bible)

---

[467] 2 Timothy 2:11-12
[468] Look up and think about what these Scriptures mean in 1 John 2:24-25; Romans 11:22; Colossians 1:21-22; Hebrews 6:4-6; 10:26-31; 2 Peter 2:20-22; and Revelation 3:5. They imply the possibility of qualifications to keep our salvation; not by works, but by obedience and loving not our lives unto death.
[469] Genesis 25:29-34 with Hebrews 12:16-17

Chapter 32

144,000 Virgins and the Lamb

Then I looked, and behold, a Lamb standing on Mount Zion, and with Him **one hundred and forty-four thousand**, having His Father's name written on their foreheads. And I heard a voice from heaven, like the voice of many waters, and like the voice of loud thunder. And I heard the sound of harpists playing their harps. They sang as it were a new song before the throne, before the four living creatures, and the elders; and no one could learn that song except the **hundred and forty-four thousand** who were redeemed from the earth. These are the ones who were not defiled with women, for they are virgins. These are the ones who follow the Lamb wherever He goes. These were redeemed from among men, being firstfruits to God and to the Lamb. And in their mouth was found no deceit, for they are without fault before the throne of God.

—***Revelation 14:1-5*** *(NKJV)*

SEVERAL THEORIES surround this company of people. The most prominent opinion held is that they are the same 144,000 sealed ones found in Revelation 7.

Cults often claim special rights to this number, too, elevating their members as these sealed ones.

It is my belief, however, that no one can grow into *becoming* this company. Why? Because they are divinely conceived by the Holy Spirit.

Another theory

There is also the theory I presented in chapter 28; that these 144,000 virgins represent the male offspring (the "manchild company") born at the cusp of the Great Tribulation in Revelation 12:5 just before the Antichrist comes into full power.

They are conceived on the "Day of Atonement" in Revelation 8, when the bride company receives her sinless nature as the *third* work of grace. They are then carried to full term in the "womb of the bride," which is composed of the 144,000 virgin women sealed in Revelation 7. Nine months after conception they are born in Revelation 12:5. Immediately upon their birth, they're snatched up to God and to his throne.[470]

In Revelation 14 (also at the beginning of the three-and-one-half years) they're seen standing with the Lamb, not as infants just born, but as 144,000 virgin male adults who are walking in fully redeemed bodies—immortal and without a sin nature—like the glorified, adult body of Jesus.

They are undefiled by women, which could imply 1) that they were not born of an unredeemed, unclean woman who had to go through a purification process after giving birth,[471] 2) they were not "spiritually defiled" by the daughters of the harlot church, or 3) they were not defiled by women because they are virgins who have never been with a woman on earth. They simply were not on earth long enough for any touch or taint of sin, because they are immediately snatched up to God's throne and are, therefore, faultless, holy, and pure, with no deceit in their mouths. This would make them the *firstfruits* of the final harvest gathering of saints, who will also receive immortal bodies when Jesus returns to gather them at the end of the Great Tribulation.

---

[470] Revelation 12:5
[471] Leviticus 12:1-7

In contrast to those who take the mark of the beast (666) on their foreheads or right hands, these 144,000 male virgins carry the name of the Father (Lord) and the Lamb (Jesus) on their foreheads. The numerical value of Jesus is 888, indicating a *new beginning* for God's people who are fully redeemed and immortalized in body, soul and spirit. These 144,000 male virgins are the firstfruits of a *new beginning* when the Earth is restored to its original form. I will share more on that as well, in my sequel.

The "mystery" of the male-child company

The mystery surrounding this company can be witnessed in the scene where a great sound from heaven, like the rush of a roaring waterfall, is accompanied by thunder and the sound of harps. This heavenly music accompanies a song that no one else knows. Only the 144,000 male virgins will be able to learn this *new song*—perhaps about a new thing that God will do, like no other time on Earth. No words to this song are written in the Scriptures, so we won't hear its words until the next age. But they will sing it before God's throne, where the twenty-four elders and the four living creatures abide. It could be a song about the "mystery" John spoke of in Revelation 10. It is the *mystery* fulfilled and completed at the beginning of the sounding of the *seventh* trumpet.

Here is the "new thing" for us to consider with the preceding mysteries.

First, there is the *mystery* of the immaculate conception of Mary who bore the Christ child. Who can comprehend such a thing? The world scoffs at it as a fable, but it was real and never done before—a *new* thing.

Second, there is the *mystery* of the marriage between Christ and his church—a wedding that will take place between a perfect, spotless, sinless company of people and Jesus before he returns. Again, difficult to comprehend, yet the only way Jesus can be joined to the bride company is that she's commensurate to his sinless stature—another *new* thing never before done. Many in the church today scoff at such an idea—like unbelievers have over Christ's sinless birth from a virgin.

Then there's this *mystery* of an immaculate conception of an offspring within the "womb" of the bride company (Revelation 7); an offspring unlike no other—144,000 male virgins born of 144,000 virgin women without sin—a *new* thing for a *new* song.

Consider the creation of Adam, *without* sin, but then he brought corruption to the rest of the human race. The sin nature was passed on through the seed of man, not the woman, though she, too, became sin and was thereafter born into sin. But Jesus is different! He wasn't born of the seed of man, but by the "holy seed" of the Holy Spirit who overshadowed the virgin, Mary. Mary was born *with* a sin nature, but her sin nature *wasn't* passed on to Jesus, indicating that the sin nature comes through the male "seed."

Finally in Revelation 8, on the Day of Atonement, the 144,000 *sealed* virgins, out of the bride company, receive the *third* work of grace of a sinless nature. In that consummation, the holy seed of the Holy Spirit is placed within each virgin—*not in women with a sin nature*, as Mary had, but within 144,000 women who have *no* sin nature. Ponder that for a moment.

Do you realize what this means?

The 144,000 virgin males in heaven (or "manchild" company) have no connection to sin, whatsoever, and perhaps might represent a *new* thing in the age to come. I wonder what that might be. Could it be that the *new* thing is the populating of other inhabitable worlds in the *new* universe[472] with a race of sinless inhabitants throughout the

---

[472] Revelation 21:1

universe on a grander scale than what God intended for Adam and Eve *before* sin entered the world?

Is it possible that God's *new* universe made up of an innumerable span of galaxies with solar systems like ours, will be there for more purposes other than lights in the sky for Earth? Let that sink in for a moment. Reread this paragraph and ask yourself, *"Is it possible for God to do something like this?"*

You see, we tend to be so attached to this planet and this life that we give little thought to the *afterlife*. Our time on Earth is merely the "womb of eternity," and the fallen human race is on *probation* until our time is up. In this time now, we are afforded the opportunity to make a decision to either reject or accept God's invitation. If we accept it, then we'll be contributing somehow to God's eternal plan once we've become part of his family.

Where will you stand in the end days, if you are alive? You have the potential to be a candidate for the bride of Christ, and if you, as a Christian, are a young, single, virgin woman, you could be part of the 144,000 sealed ones (though I don't recommend you maintain your celibacy for that, if God wants you to marry).

Our lives today, and the choices we make, can have an *eternal* outcome. But because we live so attached to this world, and its present day attractions, we're distracted from developing spiritual eyes to see God's eternal plan. Don't forget that Jacob saw God's bigger plan, but Esau didn't.

God designed marriage to *procreate* and *multiply*. He made men and women to bring that about. Adam was given Eve as his wife. They were commanded by God to procreate and multiply *immortal* children "before" they fell into sin and became sinners.

Now follow this thought ... God declared that by woman (Eve), sin entered the world through her deception and disobedience, but by her "seed," the human race could be redeemed by *another* woman with the same corrupt and sinful nature—Mary, a virgin. Mary conceived Jesus by the overshadowing of the Holy Spirit. Jesus is the righteous, *sinless* Son of God who, by his death, would produce a *new* creation—his redeemed church. And out of Christ's church— his body—will come his bride company (the rib section), *perfected* and made *sinless* on the Day of At-**one**-ment.

Now, through the 144,000 sinless virgins (the womb-company), Jesus will become "father" to 144,000 immortalized, incorruptible male virgins who *never* need to be redeemed from sin, because they are born of 144,000 *sinless* virgins by divine conception. Wow!

To help you get a clearer picture, take a look at these two comparison charts. The second and third charts are modified adaptations of Kevin Conner's charts in his book, *The Book of Revelation—An Exposition*.

Three Primary Mothers in the Bible

Eve	Mary	The Bride
Created w/o sin	Born with sin	Receives sinless nature
Loses immortality	Born a mortal	Born a mortal
Created a virgin	Virgin mother	144,000 virgin mothers
Mother of all living	Mother of Jesus	Mother of 144,000 sons
Cain slays Abel	Jesus destroys sin/death	144,000 sons never die

Three "Manchild" Figures in the Bible[473]

Moses	Jesus	144,000 in Rev. 14
Amran and Jochebed	Mary and Joseph	Christ and his Bride
Jochebed—wife/bride	Mary—virgin mother	Bride—virgin
Jochebed was the father	Father God became father	Jesus becomes father
Firstfruit seen in the Law	Firstfruit of a new creation	Firstfruit of a new race

473 Kevin J. Conner, *The Book of Revelation: An Exposition* (Vermont, Victoria: K.J.C. Publications, 2001), 397-398.

Moses—*cont'd*	Jesus	144,000 in Rev. 14
Pharaoh—slays children	Herod—slays children	Dragon—slays offspring
Born in sin	Born w/o sin nature	Born w/o sin nature
Moses in Tabernacle	Jesus in Herod's Temple	Manchild at God's throne
Translated to Heaven	Ascended to Heaven	Snatched to Heaven
Mortal from mortal	Immortal from mortal	Immortalized
Born of imperfect	Perfect born of imperfect	Perfect born of perfect
Sinful from sin nature	Sinless from sin nature	Sinless from sinless
Unclean from unclean	Clean from unclean	Clean out of clean
Old creation from old	New creation from old	New creation from new
Human born of human	Human-Divine of human	Human-Divine of perfect
Needed redemption	Needed no redemption	Needs no redemption

The Two "Virgins" in the Bible[474]

The Virgin Mary	The Virgin Church
Mary—the Virgin of Israel	The Virgin Church—Spiritual Israel
Espoused to Joseph—her husband	Espoused to Jesus—her Husband
Overshadowed by the Holy Spirit, before Joseph completes marriage	Overshadowed by the Holy Spirit, before Jesus completes marriage
Incorruptible Seed planted in her	Incorruptible Seed/Word planted in her
The Word to be made flesh	The Word to be made flesh
Mary found with child while Joseph was away	The Church found with child while Jesus is in heaven
A virgin to conceive and bear a son	Zion shall conceive and bear a manchild
Joseph marries Mary knowing she was with Child by the Holy Spirit	Jesus marries his bride, knowing the manchild is of the Holy Spirit
Sorrow, travail and reproach	Sorrow, travail and reproach
The virgin birth—a sign spoken against	The virgin church—Great Sign (Rv. 12:1)
The manchild—Jesus Christ	The manchild company—Isaiah 53:10
Perfect, sinless, immortal and new Creation	Perfect, sinless, immortal and new Creation
Firstborn and firstfruit of all New Creations	Firstfruits of the New Creations of God
Only Begotten of God, the Firstfruit	Begotten of God as the Firstfruits
Reproach of the Virgin Birth on Mary	Reproach of the 144,000 virgins
Many to rise and fall over the truth of the Manchild—Jesus Christ	Many will rise and fall over the truths of the Manchild (144,000)

Before us is an amazing and marvelous *mystery*. God's eternal plan has always been to have a race of *sinless* people,

---

474 Ibid., 473-474.

born *without* sin and immortal, which would come out of a people—the bride of Christ—redeemed through the cross of Christ and made perfect.

After, the millennium ends, the ungodly will be judged at the Great White Throne Judgment, and a new universe and new Earth will be created. It's possible that this *new* creation of the 144,000 male virgins, the firstfruits—which *never* needed to be redeemed from sin, but redeemed out of a sin-stained world—might be sent forth to populate the new galaxies and Earth to multiply and have dominion as God had intended for Adam and Eve. Only *this* time, it's not for one planet, but perhaps for many with the *new* Earth at the center of the *new* heavens.

Death to the manchild

I know it's inevitable to be ridiculed or mocked for such an idea, maybe even be labeled a heretic, or a closet Mormon (of which I am neither). But if Pharaoh attempted to execute the "manchild," Moses, by slaying all Hebrew male infants; or if Herod attempted to execute the "manchild," Jesus, by having all the male children under the age of two, slaughtered in Bethlehem; and if the dragon will stand before the bride of Christ in an attempt to devour the "manchild" infants as soon as they are born; then it wouldn't be a surprise if some wanted to silence this great "mystery" of a manchild company in Revelation 12 and 14.

Perhaps there might be a clue as to why this concept is "silent" when you see the pattern of what happens after each manchild's birth. Notice that a great victory and deliverance occurred on the heels of each incident.

First, Moses' birth brought about the downfall of Pharaoh and he became the shepherd-deliverer of the children of Israel who brought them out of the bondage of slavery to Egypt.

Second, Christ's birth brought about the downfall of Satan, sin, and death and he became our Shepherd-deliverer who, by his death on the cross, brought us out of the bondage of slavery to sin.

Finally, the birth of the manchild company in Revelation 12 will bring about the casting of Satan out of the heavens to Earth. As the adult offspring of Jesus and his bride, each manchild will carry a rod of iron to shepherd the nations that will live in a world free from contamination, free from temptation, and free from sin. The new race of sinless offspring nations will have been delivered completely from ever experiencing sin, Satan, death, or the grave throughout eternity as God populates the universe. Perhaps he will use us, his redeemed from this life, to tell those of the new race about all that Christ had redeemed us from, and why they have what they now have after the first Earth's baptism of fire.

If what I believe is true, then it makes sense why Satan would dislike this teaching. He'll want to devour the *firstfruits* of a new sinless race that might inhabit both the new Earth and the new heavens as a race of people who have never experienced or been touched by sin—and never will!

Something like this would be the greatest victory and triumph over the fallen, sinful state of human history brought on by Adam's disobedience. A new-creation race, brought on by Christ's obedience, the Son of Man who is the "firstfruit" of the 144,000 *firstfruits* to come.

Revelation 7	*Revelation 8*	*Revelation 12*	*Revelation 14*
144,000 Virgins	Day of Atonement	Bride in labor	144,000 Virgin Males
Womb of the Bride	Wedding of the Bride	Gives birth	Follow the Lamb
Spirit Overshadows	Marriage Complete	Dragon ready to devour	Bears Father/Son's name
Sealed to carry the	Womb of the Bride is	Manchild is born	Redeemed from the Earth
Manchild until birth	now with child	Snatched up to God	Before the Throne of God

Chapter 33

Three Warnings

Then I saw another angel flying in midair, and he had the eternal gospel to proclaim to those who live on the earth—to every nation, tribe, language and people. He said in a loud voice, "Fear God and give him glory, because the hour of his judgment has come. Worship him who made the heavens, the earth, the sea and the springs of water."

—Revelation 14:6-7

THE EVENT OF this first messenger-angel occurs at the beginning of the three-and-one-half-year period of the Great Tribulation. The bride has finished her ministry, the manchild has been safely snatched up to God's throne, and she has been carried into an unspecified place in a desert somewhere, protected from the Antichrist and the seven bowls of wrath to come. The two witnesses, Moses and Elijah, have begun their ministry of testimony to the Jews, Satan has been cast down, and the Antichrist and False Prophet deceive the world into taking the mark (666) to buy and sell goods.

The remaining saints who are encouraged by these words from the sky comprise three categories: 1) the five foolish virgins company who missed their window of opportunity when Christ came for those who were ready, 2) the millions of souls saved during the bride's ministry, and 3) the Jews being converted to Christ through the testimony of the two witnesses. These are all the saints who will refuse to take the mark and are beheaded for their steadfast devotion to Jesus.

Though we may think of this as a brutal thing (which it is), God delights in the death of these *overcomers* because they are immediately brought into his presence. The veil of flesh that stands between the temporal and the eternal will be lifted to come into the "eternal realm" of fellowship with God. This is why it is written in the Psalms:

> Precious in the sight of the Lord is the death of his saints.[475]

The eternal gospel

Given the hostile environment at that time, only the two witnesses, Moses and Elijah, will be free to preach the gospel without harm. The messenger-angel, however, remains in midair to speak without obstruction to all nations, tribes, languages, and people of the Earth, and to encourage the saints during their suffering.

When Jesus began his ministry, he entered the synagogue of his hometown, Nazareth. When they handed him the scroll of Isaiah, he read this to his audience:

> The Spirit of the Lord is on me, because he has anointed me to preach good news to the poor. He has sent me to proclaim freedom for the prisoners and recovery of sight for the blind, to release the oppressed, to proclaim the year of the Lord's favor.[476]

This was good news—Jesus announcing the mission and ministry he came to do. But the gospel is not all good news, as we understand good news; there's another side. Jesus

---

[475] Psalm 116:15
[476] Luke 4:18-19

stopped before reading the last sentence of that passage, which said, *"and the day of vengeance* of our God."[477]

The gospel age of the Lord's favor will come to a close at the beginning of the Great Tribulation period, when the Antichrist starts his reign. The dispensation of grace will be over and *the day of vengeance* will come upon the world through the judgments of the seven bowls of wrath. I would write that the eternal gospel of this messenger-angel boils down to this:

> It's time to fear God all you inhabitants of the earth, and not the Antichrist. God is the creator of the *heavens* where he will display judgment. He created the planet *earth,* which will travail under his judgment. He created the *seas* and the *springs of water,* which will be destroyed by the plagues of the seven bowls of wrath. Worship God, fear him, and give him glory, because his **favor** is over, and the day of **vengeance** has come to complete Isaiah's prophecy.

	2nd Coming
The Year of the Lord's Favor	*Day of Vengeance*
The Dispensation of Grace	Great Tribulation

It's good news for the righteous when the wicked are punished and justice prevails. God's vengeance is coming. The Lion of Judah is coming. That's part of the eternal gospel because there can be no good news without judgment; and there can be no good news without a message of reconciliation that redeems us from judgment.

---

[477] Isaiah 61:1-2

It is good news to know that the wicked will receive judgment according to their deeds. That's why Paul says to Timothy:

> The sins of some men are conspicuous (openly evident to all eyes), going before them to the judgment [seat] and proclaiming their sentence in advance; but the sins of others appear later [following the offender to the bar of judgment and coming into view there].[478]

A second messenger-angel

> Fallen! Fallen is Babylon the Great, which made all the nations drink the maddening wine of her adulteries.
>
> —*Revelation 14:8*

Immediately after the first messenger-angel, a second announces that Babylon is fallen. Babylon is pictured as a woman in Revelation chapter 17. Her name means *confusion* and for a short time, she is supported by the Antichrist and his ten kings.[479] All the nations will drink from the wine of her spiritual adultery and fornication. She will mix religion with politics just as the Roman Catholic Church did in the Middle Ages.

The fact that "fallen" is mentioned twice suggests close attention should be given to this announcement, similar to when Jesus would say, "Truly, truly I tell you." This false church is filled with *apostate* Christians and members from other world religions. The time of Babylon's judgment (as the false church) has come and the fusion of her religious/political union will end. The Antichrist and ten kings will have no more use for her, because once all the

---

[478] 1 Timothy 5:24 (Amplified Bible)
[479] Revelation 17:1-6

remaining saints are martyred, she becomes obsolete. More
on this later in chapters 38 and 39.

A third messenger-angel

A third angel followed them and said in a loud voice: "If
anyone worships the beast and his image and receives his
mark on the forehead or on the hand, he, too, will drink of
the wine of God's fury, which has been poured full strength
into the cup of his wrath. He will be tormented with
burning sulfur in the presence of the holy angels and of the
Lamb. And the smoke of their torment rises for ever and
ever. There is no rest day or night for those who worship
the beast and his image, or for anyone who receives the
mark of his name."

—Revelation 14:9-11

All the inhabitants of the Earth are being pressured at
this time to receive the mark of the beast. A "loud" angelic
warning goes forth, describing the consequences of this
action. Once the mark is received on the right hand or the
forehead, there's no turning back. This angelic warning isn't
for those who have already been deceived and accepted the
lie, but for the remnant of the redeemed saints who remain:

This calls for patient endurance on the part of the saints
who obey God's commandments and remain faithful to
Jesus.

Then I heard a voice from heaven say, "Write: Blessed
are the dead who die in the Lord *from now on.*"

"Yes," says the Spirit, "they will rest from their labor, for
their deeds will follow them."

—Revelation 14:12-13

Jesus warned his disciples that they would be treated the
same way as their master.[480] The world hated him, so it will

---

[480] John 15:18-21

hate them. The world persecuted him, so it will persecute them. The world beat and crucified him, and so it will kill them, too. This messenger-angel implies to the saints—who have not, *yet*, been martyred—what Jesus said to his disciples:

> I tell you, my friends, do not be afraid of those who kill the body and after that can do no more. But I will show you whom you should fear: Fear him who, after the killing of the body, has power to throw you into hell. Yes, I tell you, fear him.
>
> —*Luke 12:4-6*

Between the first two messenger-angels in Revelation 14, the saints are reminded that it is better to be killed by the beast, than to burn with the beast. Don't fear him, and what he and his cohorts can do to your body; fear God who can cast both soul and body into hell and, ultimately, into the lake of fire.

The message is clear to the remnant. Have *patient endurance* during your final days on Earth until you join the honored company of the beheaded martyrs who have gone before you. It'll be a quick death, with God's grace upon you to endure it. For that moment in time, obey God's commands, don't worship the image or take the mark, remain faithful to him, and you will be blessed when you die for him. You will rest from your labors, and your deeds will follow you into eternity. That's his promise to his faithful ones who do not love their lives, but love *him*—to their death.

The alternative—eternal torment

The angel describes the alternative in graphic detail. If any Christians become *apostates* during this time, they forfeit their salvation and subject themselves to the same punishment the rest will receive who take the mark.

In the context of this warning, the messenger-angel calls on the saints to hold fast to their devotion to Jesus—or else. The "or else" can be noted in what the author of Hebrews wrote to the persecuted Christians of his time. They were tested to stay with God, or throw away their confidence:

> If we deliberately keep on sinning after we have received the knowledge of the truth, no sacrifice for sins is left, **but only a fearful expectation of judgment and of raging fire that will consume the enemies of God**. Anyone who rejected the law of Moses died without mercy on the testimony of two or three witnesses. **How much more severely** do you think a man deserves to be punished who has trampled the Son of God under foot, who has treated as an unholy thing the blood of the covenant that sanctified him, and who has insulted the Spirit of grace? For we know him who said, "It is mine to avenge; I will repay," and again, "**The Lord will judge his people**." It is a dreadful thing to fall into the hands of the living God.
>
> Remember those earlier days after you had received the light, when you stood your ground in a great contest in the face of suffering. Sometimes you were publicly exposed to insult and persecution; at other times you stood side by side with those who were so treated. You sympathized with those in prison and joyfully accepted the confiscation of your property, because you knew that you yourselves had better and lasting possessions.
>
> **So do not throw away your confidence**; it will be richly rewarded. You need to persevere so that when you have done the will of God, you will receive what he has promised. For in just a very little while,
>
> "He who is coming will come and will not delay. But my righteous one will live by faith. And **if he shrinks back**, I will not be pleased with him."
>
> —*Hebrews 10:26-38*

Read carefully again through these verses above and note the author's words and phrases that clearly describe a person who *had been* redeemed by the blood of the covenant; but willfully chooses to keep on sinning and reject Christ who had saved them.

The author (Paul) reminds them of their experiences and what they saw their brothers and sisters endure. According to this passage in Hebrews, it's possible for someone to succumb to the pressure of public hostility in order to avoid death. The passage also warns us of *our* potential to throw away God's promise and become subject to his wrath. Why? Because we would step on the Son of God by regarding his shed blood, that had sanctified us, as nothing; and we would insult the Holy Spirit of grace.

The punishment for apostasy is far worse than for the person who had never been saved. The *apostate* will experience the full measure of God's fiery indignation, just as the third messenger-angel had warned those who might be tempted to take the mark.

I've read the testimonies in books by people who have died and gone to hell,[481] and there are detailed descriptions from Scriptures about hell.[482] Despite how horrible those images and stories are, I'm exposing you to what could happen to us, *if* we are alive at that time and become apostates in the great falling away.

First, we could die from one of the plagues of the seven bowls poured out on the planet and then be sent to hell where the worm does not die nor the fire is quenched. If we survive the plagues, then we'll end up in the battle of Armageddon in the Antichrist's army to fight against Jesus when he returns. In that army we'll be consumed by the

---

[481] *23 Minutes in Hell* by Bill Weise; *A Day in Hell* by Nancy Bosford; *A Divine Revelation of Hell* by Mary K. Baxter; *My Descent into Death* by Howard Storm.
[482] Mark 9:43, 48; Luke 16:22-24; 2 Peter 2:4

brightness of Christ's coming in flaming fire. We'll then be held for a thousand years in the fiery, gloomy dungeons of hell, where the worm does not die nor the fire is quenched, until our resurrection at the end of the millennial reign of Christ. At that time we'll follow Satan again, when he's released from the chains that had bound him for 1,000 years. We'll march across the breadth of the Earth with the resurrected billions of other deceived souls to come against God's people—once again.

But then we'll meet our "second death," the fiery wrath of God from heaven that will devour and destroy our bodies—again.[483] Heaven and Earth will flee and we'll be standing before God in the final judgment of the Great White Throne. After that judgment, our names will not be found in the Lamb's Book of Life because they'll have been "blotted out," and not found.[484]

We'll then be thrown headlong into a boiling stew of sulfurous, liquid fire, where the Antichrist and the False Prophet are tormented. When our heads return to the fiery, boiling surface, we'll thrash about in insufferable pain, tiring from the strain of trying to stay afloat without something solid under our feet.

Though in our former life we were told the lie that death would deliver us from the sorrows and pains of life, we'll discover our souls imprisoned in immortalized flesh, bobbing about in a lake of fire.

Based on testimonies I've heard, it isn't beyond the realm of possibility that we'll receive immortal flesh, with immortal skin that will burn perpetually by peeling off and being replaced with new flesh to burn and peel again.

Our burning, blistering lips and swollen tongues will perpetually thirst for water that doesn't exist. Our lungs will

---

[483] Revelation 20:5, 7-10
[484] Psalm 69:28; Exodus 32:32, 33; Revelation 3:5

never inhale another gulp of fresh air. Our noses will be eternally assaulted by the eye-watering smell of stench from our burning flesh and the putrid, sulfurous smoke of the lake of fire—a smell that reeks like spoiled, rotten eggs.

There'll be no rest, day or night, in our torment for us who became *apostates*; and for all of our groaning, cursing and swearing in the lake of liquid fire, no one will heed our cries. Not even the Holy Spirit who you stopped listening to and no longer now listens to you.

There's no one around you to care anymore.

No one! For eternity.

With a picture like this, I believe it's infinitely better to *die* by the sword of the world who will hate you, than to *join* the world who will hate you in the fires of hell and eternal damnation.

Chapter 34

The Death of a Saint

BEFORE WE FINISH with the rest of Revelation 14, I am inserting this excerpt from my novel, *The Unveiling* (1997). I want you to experience this scene, because we tend to focus more on the brutality of martyrdom, instead of exploring what happens *after* you die and go to heaven. Bear with me, if you will, in reading about the experience of my primary character, Bob Jansen; a believer who missed the bride company and goes into the period of the Great Tribulation.

————————————

"Move it, Jansen!" the guard said, pushing Bob through the wooden-carved doors of the foyer and into the cold, night air.

Outside, the nauseating stench of a bloated road kill, made him gag. He followed the source of the smell to a pile of cadavers stacked eight feet high to the left of the church building. A cold chill ran up his spine when he saw they were headless.

"Quit dragging your feet!" the guard snarled, with his gun in Bob's back, poking him toward the rowdy, seated crowd in the stands.

As Bob stumbled into the spotlight of the arena, he felt their stares lock on him like starve-crazed beasts. Before him stood a raised, wooden platform, twelve feet high, lit up by spotlights from the steeple of the church.

At the top of the platform on its floor sat a bloodstained block. Beside the block stood a tall, burly man who stared at him without expression. His hands rested on the hilt of what appeared to be a samurai-type sword. A long, blood-soaked rag hung down the side of his leg from his belt, apparently used to wipe the blade clean between each victim. When Bob saw him, he became queasy as he fought to control his fear.

"Death to the rebel!" someone shouted. "Kill the dog!" another yelled.

The crowd erupted with screams of profanities to the rhythm of stomping feet, rattling the metal stands.

With a poke of his gun the guard shouted above the clamor, "Climb!"

Bob ached so much from his beatings, he barely felt the abusive jab. He stepped up to the platform, wiped the sweat off his brow, and grabbed the railing of the stairs. Exhausted from the day's events, his trembling feet could barely take the first step.

When he reached the fifth step, his head became dizzy, forcing him to pause and cling to the rails. As he closed his eyes, the image of the little girl in the prison cell came to mind. He remembered the note from her mother she handed him when the guard came to get him.

Supporting his weight with one hand, he reached into his pocket with the other for the crumpled piece of paper that read:

> They overcame Satan by the blood of the Lamb and by their bold witness. Because they loved Jesus more than their own lives, they were willing to die for him.

Bob clutched the note to his chest and looked up at the dark sky. "Lord," he whispered, "help me ..."

Suddenly, a tingling sensation rippled across his skin until a numb, intoxicating feeling cloaked his body like a blanket.

"Move it, Jansen!" the guard screamed below. The crowd stomped their feet faster and shouted louder.

Bob stared at the last seven steps above him and with a renewed hope from God's presence, completed his climb.

The executioner waited for him on top beside the blood-stained block. He pointed impatiently to a white-painted X in front of it. "Kneel here!" he shouted above the roar of the rumbling stands.

Bob stared at the X and prayed, *not my will, but yours, Lord.*

The chants and stomps of the crowd were now deafening, as Bob walked to the block and knelt down.

The executioner raised his sword and shouted, "Any last words, heretic?"

"Yes," Bob shouted back, "I forgive you."

Bob hovered above his headless body, laying on the platform, and gazed at the lifeless form, which only seconds ago had housed his soul and spirit.

How strange it was to watch the executioner display Bob's head to the crowd and pitch it over the side of the platform. His headless body was then dragged to the edge and shoved over.

The crowd roared with delight, even more so, when the next Christian emerged from the same doors Bob came through only moments ago. It was Cliff Malloy.

The crowd went wild again in a crazed frenzy as Malloy entered the arena. When the guard pushed him up the steps toward the top of the platform, Bob shouted, "Cliff!"

"He can't hear you," said a voice beside him.

Startled, Bob turned and discovered a nine-foot angel in a glowing white garment. A golden sash wrapped tightly around his waist.

"Who are you?" Bob asked, shaken by the sudden encounter.

The divine creature flashed a warm smile and said, "Don't be afraid, I'm Gamliel, your escort. I'm here to take you home."

Speechless, Bob tried to process everything happening so quickly. As he looked back on the scene below for a reality check, he found himself higher off the ground than before, but felt conspicuous floating above the crowd in midair.

"Don't worry," Gamliel said, "they can't see you."

Bob stared at this celestial chauffeur. "How'd you know what I was thinking?"

"I know how you think, Bob Jansen," he said with a smile. "I've been your watcher."

Bob realized they were continuing to ascend from the ground, but forgot about it when he realized the hunger pangs he had were gone. He then remembered the severe beating he suffered and checked his eyes and face. Not a trace of swelling from the cuts and blows he had received to the head. Actually, he still had his head. He felt strong again, too, healthier than at any time in his life.

"There's no sickness or disability on this side," Gamliel said.

Before Bob could respond, not yet used to his discerning observer, he felt his body rotate toward the black, starlit sky as though a giant hand had cradled him, turning him in that direction.

"You ready?" Gamliel asked.

"Yeah," Bob said, glancing back one more time to see Malloy kneeling at the X before the block.

As Gamliel grabbed Bob's hand, a flash of light burst before them and everything went blurry. Bob felt the sensation of hurtling dizzily through a winding, translucent funnel.

In lightning-speed, he watched images of his past flash by—scenes going back to the earliest days of his childhood and up to the time when Malloy and Cap' prayed to receive Christ. There were scenes of every occasion where he did something good, no matter how great or small. Though it screamed past like a fast-forwarded epic, everything he saw in a blur was clear in his mind. Nothing ugly or sinful showed up during this playback. His sins had been erased by the blood of Jesus.

The trip was over quickly and Bob felt himself slowing down and descending. Gamliel still held his hand as they touched ground and stepped onto the breathtaking landscape of another world.

Bob couldn't believe what he saw. No sun was visible, yet light appeared just as brightly everywhere, illuminating the flowers and trees, and vast fields of grass. Everything seemed slightly transparent with the light shining in and through it all from every direction. It was bright, yes, but not blinding—and there were no shadows anywhere. Everything was enhanced and defined by a rainbow of brilliant, pastel-like colors.

"Look," Gamliel said, pointing to a multitude of people on the horizon, all dressed in white robes.

Bob wanted to go to them and, surprisingly, found himself with them the moment he thought about it. He was among a sea of faces, all heading in the same direction, and there were so many, no one could count their number. Every ethnic race he knew of was represented, and some he never knew existed.

Bob looked at Gamliel, "Who are all these people?"

Gamliel motioned with a wave of his hand and replied, "These are the saints who came out of the Great Tribulation you left behind. Others are yet to join them, like your friend Malloy. Their clothes—like yours—have been washed and their robes made white by the blood of the Lamb."

Suddenly a voice could be heard from the city ahead saying, "Blessed are the dead who die in the Lord after this."

Then a soft breeze blew across Bob's face and the Holy Spirit whispered into his spirit:

> *"They will rest from their labor, because their deeds will follow them here."*

Chapter 35

Two Harvests

Then I looked, and behold, a white cloud, and on the cloud sat One like the Son of Man, having on His head a golden crown, and in His hand a sharp sickle. And another angel came out of the [heavenly] temple, crying with a loud voice to Him who sat on the cloud, "Thrust in Your sickle and reap, for the time has come for You to reap, for the **harvest of the earth is ripe**." So He who sat on the cloud thrust in His sickle on the earth, and the earth was reaped.[485]

—*Revelation 14:14-16*

THE HARVEST IN the above Scripture is that of a *grain* harvest[486] and complements the parable of Jesus in Matthew 13 about the end-time harvest of wheat and tares.[487] The wheat in that parable represents the saints of God, and the tares represent the wicked separated from the wheat in the last days.[488]

I believe this *first* harvest of the two is for the Great Tribulation saints who, through martyrdom, are taken out of the world before the wrath of God is poured out upon the ungodly inhabitants of the Earth. The martyrdom of the

---

[485] New King James Version
[486] John 4:35—"I tell you, open your eyes and look at the fields! They are ripe to harvest."
[487] *Tare:* a noxious weed called a "darnel" that looks identical to the heads of wheat.
[488] Matthew 13:24-20

saints at this time is actually an act of God's mercy, and the Son of Man, who was beaten and martyred himself, will be intimately involved in this harvest, just as he was when Stephen, the first martyr of the church, was stoned.[489]

This isn't the second coming of Jesus, as some believe. Not yet. This *grain* harvest will occur at the beginning of the three-and-one-half years when the mark of the beast (666) is implemented and millions of saints will be slain for refusing to worship the Antichrist and take his mark.[490]

The second harvest

> Then another angel came out of the temple which is in heaven, he also having a sharp sickle.
>
> And another angel came out from the altar, who had power over fire, and he cried with a loud cry to him who had the sharp sickle, saying, "Thrust in your sharp sickle and gather the clusters of the vine of the earth, for her grapes are fully ripe." So the angel thrust his sickle into the earth and **gathered the vine of the earth**, and threw it into the great winepress of the wrath of God. And the winepress was trampled outside the city, and blood came out of the winepress, up to the horses' bridles, for one thousand six hundred furlongs.[491]

—Revelation 14:17-20

The *grain* harvest of the tribulation saints was completed early on in the three-and-one-half years; now the *final* harvest comes at the end of the three-and-one-half years. It is a harvest of *grapes*, like the tares that were separated from the wheat.

---

[489] Acts 7:55-56—Stephen, full of the Holy Spirit, looked up to heaven and saw the glory of God, and Jesus standing at the right hand of God. "Look," he said, "I see heaven open and the Son of Man standing at the right hand of God."
[490] Psalm 116:15—"Precious in the sight of the Lord is the death of his saints."
[491] Revelation 14:17-20 (New King James Version)

Jesus had said, "I am the vine and you are the branches."[492] The Antichrist actually "infers" this claim by replacing Christ with himself. Apostates and all world religions will be grafted into the *false* vine of the Antichrist, and at the end of his reign, they'll be gathered like grapes at harvest and thrown into the winepress of God's wrath at the battle of Armageddon.

Their lifeblood will be crushed and trampled underfoot by the Son of God, fulfilling what Isaiah said about the second coming of Christ, "The Spirit of the Sovereign Lord is on me [Jesus] ... to proclaim ... *the day of vengeance* of our God."[493] Later in the chapter, Isaiah says of Christ's return:

> Who is this, robed in splendor, striding forward in the greatness of his strength?
>
> "It is I [Jesus], speaking in righteousness, mighty to save."
>
> Why are your garments red, like those of one treading the **winepress**?
>
> "I [Jesus] have trodden the **winepress** alone; from the nations no one was with me. I trampled them in my anger and trod them down in my wrath; their blood spattered my garments, and I stained all my clothing.
>
> For *the day of vengeance* was in my heart, and the year of my redemption has come."
>
> —*Isaiah 63:1-4*

When Jesus came the first time, he came as a Lamb, proclaiming the year of the Lord's favor, which extends to the last, converted Jew and Gentile on the Earth.

By God's mercy, the *overcomers* will be martyred and taken to heaven until Christ returns.

---

492 John 15:5
493 Isaiah 61:1-2

At the second coming, however, Jesus will arrive with *vengeance*, as the Lion of the tribe of Judah—completing the rest of Isaiah's quote.[494]

Grain Harvest of...
- Believers
- Wheat
- The Overcomers
- At the beginning

Grape Harvest of...
- Unbelievers
- Tares
- The Overcome
- At the end

---

494 Ibid.

Chapter 36

Heaven's Opened Temple

WE NOW ENTER into Revelation chapter 15. Those remaining are the Antichrist, the False Prophet, the ungodly masses, and the fallen apostates. The bride is still in the wilderness and the two witnesses are still untouched as they continue to strike the Earth with plagues as often as they wish, including keeping the sky void of rain.[495]

The scene in heaven

> I saw in heaven another great and marvelous sign: seven angels with the seven last plagues—last, because with them God's wrath is completed.
>
> *—Revelation 15:1*

Revelation 15 is the shortest chapter in the book and sets the stage for the seven bowls of wrath yet to come. Remember that the *seventh* trumpet continues to sound through the entire three-and-one-half years with the events in that period overlapping progressively as revealed in chapters 11-18, and ending in chapter 19 when the *seventh* trumpet sounds its last trumpet blast at the second coming.[496]

Out of the seventh seal comes the seven trumpets, and from the seventh trumpet comes the seven bowls of God's

---

[495] Revelation 11:6
[496] Matthew 24:30-31; 1 Corinthians 15:52; 1 Thessalonians 4:16

wrath upon the ungodly. They are called the *last* plagues because they will *complete* God's wrath.

"Seven" is the number of completion and these plagues arrive at the end because the atoning work of the cross has been completed. That means there is no one left on Earth to be saved, who *can* be saved—and since the atoning blood of the new covenant is the only way to avoid God's wrath upon sin, nothing remains that can turn these seven plagues away from the remaining wicked people who have rejected the true Messiah, and the blood he shed to save them.

Sea of glass and fire

> And I saw what looked like a **sea of glass mixed with fire** and, standing beside the sea, those who had been victorious over the beast and his image and over the number of his name. They held harps given them by God and sang the song of **Moses** the servant of God and the song of the **Lamb**.
>
> —*Revelation 15:2-3a*

As the stage is being set for the seven coming plagues, this scene above is presented first, but why? The answer comes from another place in Revelation 4 where this same sea of glass appears—before the throne of God. There we find no mention of martyrs or fire in the sea of glass at that time, whereas in chapter 15, we now see the tribulation saints who died under the reign of the Antichrist. Though the Antichrist took their earthly lives from them, they overcame him by the word of their testimony and entered eternity through the portal of their death. So with harps we now see them singing a song of *victory*: the song of Moses (Law) and the song of the Lamb (Grace).

> Great and marvelous are your deeds, Lord God Almighty. Just and true are your ways, King of the ages.

Who will not fear you, O Lord, and bring glory to your name? For you alone are holy.

All nations will come and worship before you, for your righteous acts have been revealed.[497]

How interesting this song is since Moses sang the very first song of redemption in praise and worship to God who had delivered him and Israel from the armies of Pharaoh.[498] Now we see the *overcomers* in Revelation 15, combining an Old Testament song of redemption with the New Testament song of the Lamb who redeemed and delivered them from the Antichrist through martyrdom.

These tribulation saints sing from a glorious, eternal perspective, not bemoaning their death, but glorifying God's name in celebration of the justice of his wrath to come that will avenge their deaths. So with harps they sing this prophetic song,[499] about God's Law (Moses) and God's Mercy (Jesus) now kissing each other[500] to *complete* their redemption.

The curtain closes on heaven, but the next scene is back on Earth where the plagues will wrap up God's redemptive purposes for the ages.

Heaven's temple—seven angels

After this I looked and in heaven the temple, that is, the tabernacle of the Testimony, was opened. Out of the temple came the seven angels with the seven plagues. They were dressed in clean, shining linen and wore golden sashes around their chests. Then one of the four living creatures gave to the seven angels seven golden bowls filled with the wrath of God, who lives for ever and ever. And the temple was filled with smoke from the glory of

---

[497] Revelation 15:3-4
[498] Exodus 14:1-18
[499] See 1 Chronicles 25:3 with 2 Kings 3:14-16
[500] Psalm 85:10

God and from his power, and no one could enter the temple until the seven plagues of the seven angels were completed.

—Revelation 15:5-8

For various reasons, it's my opinion that a literal temple of God will never be rebuilt in Jerusalem in the last days. The temple that the Antichrist inhabits[501] is more likely a reference to the *false* temple made up of apostate Christians who were once living stones in the temple of the Holy Spirit, but are now mixed in with the world religion of the *false* church, the harlot Babylon.[502]

When Jesus left the temple in Jerusalem for the last time, God's glory went with him but returned in the book of Acts in the *new* temple, a *spiritual* temple—which was and now is the body and church of the Lord Jesus Christ.

Since the passing of the Old Testament era, God no longer lives in temples made with hands, but in each of us, his believers, and in the universal body of Christ.[503] The Tabernacle of Moses and Solomon's temple were mere copies of the pattern of the tabernacle/temple in heaven.[504] But they no longer exist and are obsolete. Now, in Revelation 15, heaven's temple is opened, not to *save* the world by atonement, but to *judge* the remaining ungodly inhabitants who are *without* atonement.

The seven angels who serve at this heavenly temple come out with seven bowls filled with plagues. They've been given their instructions—mercy is no more, only judgment remains. The smoke of God's glory filling the temple is no longer from the incense and prayers of the saints as it was in

---

[501] 2 Thessalonians 2:4
[502] John 2:19-22 with 1 Corinthians 3:16-17; 6:19-20; 2 Corinthians 6:16; and Ephesians 2:21
[503] John 2:19-21; 1 Corinthians 3:16-17; 6:19; 2 Corinthians 6:16; Ephesians 2:21
[504] Hebrews 8:5 with 9:24-24

Revelation 8 at the time of the bride's atonement.[505] Now the smoke represents judgment,[506] and no one can enter this heavenly temple until the seven plagues of God's wrath are executed.

In Egypt, God judged the gods of that land with ten plagues—each plague attacking a specific Egyptian god, including Pharaoh, himself, who was worshiped as a god. Now, at the end of the Antichrist's reign, *his* self-proclaimed deity is about to be judged—completely!

---

[505] Revelation 8:3-4
[506] See Genesis 19:23-28; Exodus 19:16-19; Psalm 18:7-8

Chapter 37

Seven Bowls of Wrath

> If you remain hostile toward me and refuse to listen to me, I will multiply your afflictions **seven times** over, as your sins deserve.
>
> *—Leviticus 26:21*

> Then I heard a loud voice from the temple saying to the seven angels, "Go, pour out the **seven bowls** of God's wrath on the earth."
>
> *—Revelation 16:1*

THINK OF THE most wicked individuals, organizations and religious extremists in the world today. Bring their names to mind and ask: *Are they evil enough to deserve punishment for their crimes against God and humanity?*

What books, what movies, or what TV shows are there—with heroes and villains—where you don't feel good about seeing the good guys win and the bad guys get their just desserts?

It is an inherent quality of human nature to desire triumph over evil and see justice prevail. Why? Because we were made in God's image. God is good, he is love, he is righteous, but he is also just; and because he is righteous and just, he rewards everyone according to his or her deeds.[507]

Evil was never meant to prevail or exist for all eternity. It is confined to "time," which is the age of *probation* for

---

[507]Psalm 28:4; Jeremiah 17:10; 21:14; 25:14; 32:19; 50:29; Hosea 4:9; Obadiah 15; Revelation 2:23

humanity. God allotted to every one of us a temporary probation period called, "life." From beginning to end, our life on Earth is time that God has allotted to us to choose between good and evil. Once our time is over, our choice will determine our eternal destiny.

God is good; the Devil is bad. God is uncreated and eternal; the Devil is created and is confined to the temporal period of human history, and then it's over. God will judge the Devil and his fallen angels, along with every human being.

God had established *before* time, a predetermined point when it all wraps up. Satan and the defiant wicked will get what they deserve, which is an eternal separation from God and eternal damnation.

Don't believe the lie that God is happy about this. God isn't willing for anybody to perish; he wants everyone to repent and join his family.[508] But this isn't always the case since he gave his angels and us a free will. Because of this, not all will choose him and his plan of redemption; therefore, they'll receive the eternal consequences of their choice.

At this time of the unfolding story in Revelation, we'll witness the final act, the last scene of human history. Sin must be dealt a final blow to complete what Jesus accomplished on the cross—he judged sin.

Wicked humanity will be removed from the Earth and Satan locked up and shut away for a thousand years. Because their cups of iniquity are running over, God's cup of wrath will be poured out to the fullest extent through the seven plagues.

These plagues will touch no one who belongs to God, but *everyone* who belongs to Satan, including the Antichrist and the False Prophet. These plagues aren't spiritual metaphors,

---

[508] 2 Peter 3:9

either; they're as literal as the ten plagues God had sent upon Pharaoh and all Egypt.

Plague one—malignant cancer[509]

The *first* bowl touches the godless masses with malignant and ulcerous sores—possibly a form of skin cancer. Anyone who has experienced advanced skin cancer knows the stabbing, aching and burning pain that goes with it. Ulcerous tumors can press on the nerves and create significant pain, not to mention the foul smell that occurs when they break through the skin and become ugly, open sores in visible areas such as the face and the neck.

Imagine everyone, still alive at this time, being struck by this pandemic. Cancer is the result of bad blood and in the case of these ungodly recipients, a clear reflection of their spiritual condition. They chose ugly, sinful living and the mass genocide of saints over Jesus who died for them. Now they are struck with the slow painful death of cancer—but this is only the beginning.

Plague two—dead man's blood in the sea[510]

The *second* bowl touches the sea, this time on the entire planet, rather than a third, as in the second trumpet.[511] It turns the waters into blood like that of a dead man, and every living thing in the sea will die and float to the surface.

Whatever ship remains at sea or is docked at a port will be stranded and dead in the bloody ocean from the floating carcasses of sea creatures. No more commerce, no more fishing industry, no more seafood—just red oceanic bodies of blood throughout the world.

---

[509] Revelation 16:1-2
[510] Revelation 16:3
[511] Revelation 8:8-9

Plague three—blood in the water[512]

The *third* bowl touches all the rivers and springs of water, not just a third, as in the third trumpet,[513] but the entire planet. Go to the kitchen or bathroom faucets and blood will pour out. Go to the spring-fed lakes, ponds, reservoirs and rivers, and nothing but blood will be seen. This is a very serious problem—just as it was in the first plague on Egypt[514] —no fresh water to drink.

At least sixty percent of the adult body is made up of water and our body cells need water to function. Water lubricates our joints, regulates our body temperature through sweating and respiration, and helps to flush waste. Even the healthiest person can't last longer than a week without water; the average length is three to five days, and even less if the body is sick or heat conditions are extreme.

In his vision of this plague, John hears the angel in charge of the waters say:

> You [God] are just in these judgments, you who are and who were, the Holy One, because you have so judged; for they have shed the blood of your saints and prophets, and you have given them blood to drink as they deserve.
>
> *—Revelation 16:5-6*

Then John hears the martyrs under the altar[515] respond:

> Yes, Lord God Almighty, true and just are your judgments.
>
> *—Revelation 16:7*

Why the intermittent vision?

---

[512] Revelation 16:4
[513] Revelation 8:10-11
[514] Exodus 7:19-21
[515] Revelation 6:9

Remember your response when the bad guys got their just desserts at the end of a movie or a book? We all think (or say), "Yes!!! They got what they deserved." Isn't that what we wait for and expect at the end of a show? We all know it's going to happen. We know it intrinsically. We celebrate truth and justice. That's why we love the make-believe world of superheroes.

My favorite was Superman who was faster than a speeding bullet, more powerful than a locomotive, able to leap tall buildings in a single bound ... and my favorite line— *fighting the never-ending battle for truth, justice, and the American way.* In his stories, justice prevailed and the bad guys were dealt with.

So here we have an angel, essentially saying, "You wicked were so bloodthirsty in your hunt for the saints, well then, here you go—nothing but blood for the bloodthirsty."

And a voice from the altar says, "Yes! Lord God Almighty." That's the same voice that comes from the altar in the *fifth* seal. This is the justice they had been waiting for, just as you and I wait for justice when wicked people seem to get away with murder.[516]

> [Fifth Seal]—I saw under the **altar** the souls of those who had been slain because of the word of God and the testimony they had maintained. They called out in a loud voice, *"How long, Sovereign Lord, holy and true, until you judge the inhabitants of the earth and avenge our blood?"* Then each of them was given a white robe, and they were told to wait a little longer, until the number of their fellow servants and brothers **who were to be killed as they had been** was completed.
>
> —***Revelation 6:9-11***

---

[516] See Psalm 73:1-20, 27; 94:3; 119:84; Habakkuk 1:2-4

Plague four—a scorched Earth[517]

The *fourth* bowl is now poured out on the sun. From it comes the *fourth* plague—the sun, scorching the godless masses with fire. Such an image has sparked the theory that this could be describing an X-class[518] solar flare erupting from the sun's surface shooting toward Earth.

This made perfect sense to me at first, but upon examining scientific articles, it appears that solar flares don't actually alter climate change as significantly as the scorching described in the fourth plague. It would seem so, but the magnetic field around Earth has been designed by God to protect us, and the Earth's atmosphere actually reflects the strong radiation back into space.

But as far as this plague's affect on the godless— dehydration, sunstrokes, heat exhaustion, radiation poisoning, and first-degree burns from the UV rays—will occur and be added to the pain of the malignant, cancerous sores on their skin. Perhaps the "global warming" folks will have their day of vindication—though it's safe to assume by then, no one will care.

What I find amazing is that despite yet another plague, the godless masses still curse the name of God and still refuse to repent and glorify him.[519] This isn't a surprise given that they are fully controlled by the Antichrist, essentially demon-possessed, when they take his mark.

Plague five—a dark Earth[520]

The *fifth* bowl deals with the "throne" of the Antichrist in Jerusalem. In the very end, his kingdom will be plunged into

---

[517] Revelation 16:3
[518] One of three categories used to measure the largest solar flares.
[519] Revelation 16:9
[520] Revelation 16:3

complete, utter darkness, similar to the judgment of the ninth plague in Exodus upon Pharaoh's Egypt.[521]

Looking back at the *fourth* trumpet, a third of the day and night became dark. In this bowl, however, it's *complete* darkness. The geomagnetic fields from the solar flare will damage any electronic devices and what's left of the electrical grid (if any has survived the judgments of the trumpets).

God will now judge the heart of the Antichrist's political and religious campaigns, and Jerusalem, not as a holy city, but as "Sodom and Egypt"[522] where the Lord was crucified.

For their cursing, blasphemous tongues against God, and their refusal to repent of their wicked deeds, it says they will bite and gnaw on their swelling tongues from the lack of water. The extreme pain from the cancer and burns continue as all are shrouded in darkness, blanketing the kingdom of the Antichrist.

Remember, the Antichrist and the False Prophet are experiencing these plagues like everyone else—but not the bride or the two witnesses. God is protecting his two prophets for now, and the bride is safe at her wilderness location. She'll receive food, water, and shelter from God directly,[523] just as he took care of the children of Israel during their 40 years in the desert.

This plunge into darkness reflects the hearts and spiritual condition of the ungodly darkened by following the Antichrist.

Plague six—the great Euphrates[524]

The *sixth* bowl of wrath will dry up the Euphrates River to prepare the way for the kings from the East. The

---

[521] Exodus 11:21-29
[522] Revelation 11:8
[523] Revelation 12:6, 14
[524] Revelation 16:12-16

Euphrates covers approximately 1,740 miles, beginning in the Armenian mountains of Turkey, and courses through Syria and the land of Iraq to the Persian Gulf.

It is considered by some expositors that the "kings of the East" might symbolize resurrected saints—the kings and priests[525] in Christ's army—when they return with him at the second coming.

However, Jesus said his coming would be as lightning flashes from the "east" to the west.[526] So, this concept is possible, but harder for me to reconcile with the appearing of Christ above the Earth *with* his resurrected saints when the sky rolls back like a scroll.

The Euphrates River has always been a barrier to conventional ground war, and will be especially so this time with the world thrown back to the Dark Ages because of the devastation caused by the plagues. The "kings from the East" could very well be kings from one or more nations under the umbrella of the ten-kingdom alliance found in Iran, the "stan" nations,[527] and possibly India and China.

To entice the kings, three unclean spirits—like frogs—will go forth from the mouths of the unholy trinity: Satan, the Beast, and the False Prophet. These three spirits will go out to the world, performing miraculous signs to rally the kings to the plains of Megiddo,[528] east of the coastal city of Haifa, on the northeast side of Mount Carmel.

Because of its strategic location, Megiddo has been the site of thirty-plus historical battles. Its ground is 20 miles long by 14 miles wide, covering 280 square miles.

Napoleon Bonaparte once said of this plain, "There is no place in the whole world more suited for war than this." It is

---

[525] Revelation 5:10 with 1 Peter 2:9
[526] Matthew 24:27
[527] Afghanistan, Pakistan, etc.
[528] Armageddon in Hebrew (Revelation 16:16). Today it is called the valley of Jezreel and is Israel's breadbasket.

here, where the Antichrist and his ten kings will wage war against the King of Kings in the battle of Armageddon. This is the war of all wars and will be the culmination of the second seal of "war" in Revelation 6:2.[529] It is the same point in time described at the closing of the sixth seal at the return of Christ described in Revelation 16:12-14.

Inserted within the context of the three spirit-messengers of the sixth bowl, is this statement made by Jesus himself:

> Behold, I come like a thief! Blessed is he who stays awake and keeps his clothes with him, so that he may not go naked and be shamefully exposed.
> —*Revelation 16:15*

This is an interesting exhortation at this time, perhaps making reference to a small remnant of saints, not in the bride, but of her spiritual offspring[530] who might have managed to stay hidden and need encouragement.

I tend to lean more to it *not* being a remnant of saints, because they've all been martyred by now—before the seven bowls of wrath are poured upon the Earth.

The point to be made here, however, is clear—if we stay alert, hang on to our clothes of righteous, and not forfeit our salvation by taking the mark of the beast, then we won't find ourselves on that day, walking in naked shame and exposed in our sin when Jesus returns.

He will come like a thief—unexpected as a lightning strike. This reminds us to stay alert and be as ready for his arrival, as if it were today.

---

[529] The second seal is the fiery red horse of "war." Once a seal is opened it remains open and intensifies with whatever the seal represents. This is a seal of war, which culminates at the return of Christ in the battle of Armageddon, the war of all wars.

[530] Revelation 12:17

Plague seven—the great Earthquake[531]

The *seventh* bowl is opened with a loud voice from heaven's throne, "It is finished!" This is followed with flashes of lightning, rolling thunder, and the severest global earthquake of all time, rocking the world. It is so severe that every city, mountain and island on the planet will be leveled and disappears while tsunamis ravage the coastlines of every continent. Based on Scriptures about the millennium, I believe this quake could cause a global shift of the Earth's tectonic plates, pulling the continents together.

 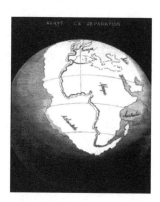

And if the earthquake isn't enough, God will bombard the ungodly masses with huge hailstones—about a hundred pounds each—crushing anyone in their path. Imagine one ball of ice that size falling from the sky, multiplied by tens of thousands, devastating and deadly. Yet, with all that, those who received the mark of the beast will still curse God's name because of the hail.[532]

The timing of these plagues will occur in rapid succession near the close of the last three-and-one-half years of human history and the Antichrist's rule. When you think of everything that has happened up to now, imagine how

---

[531] Revelation 16:17-21
[532] Revelation 16:21

diminished the population will be from all the devastating plagues. God's spokesman and prophet, Isaiah, foresaw the conditions of this time when he declared:

> I will punish the world for its evil, the wicked for their sins. I will put an end to the arrogance of the haughty and will humble the pride of the ruthless. I will **make man scarcer than pure gold**, more rare than the gold of Ophir.
>
> Therefore I will make the heavens tremble; and the earth will shake from its place at the wrath of the Lord Almighty, in the day of his burning anger.
>
> *—Isaiah 13:11-13*

The sounding of the seventh trumpet during this time releases the seven bowls of wrath and then blasts its last note on the day of Christ's return. None of these plagues, however, will touch Christ's protected bride, alive in the wilderness, or his two witnesses—Moses and Elijah.

Examine the chart below to see the timing of these plagues.

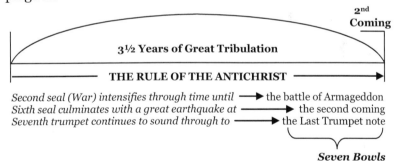

Chapter 38

The Harlot Church

I saw **a woman** sitting on a **scarlet beast** that was covered with blasphemous names and had seven heads and ten horns. The woman was dressed in purple and scarlet, and was glittering with gold, precious stones and pearls. She held a golden cup in her hand, **filled with abominable things** and the filth of her adulteries. This title was written on her forehead:

MYSTERY

BABYLON THE GREAT

THE MOTHER OF PROSTITUTES

AND OF THE ABOMINATIONS OF THE EARTH.

—Revelation 17:3-5

THE ONE-WORLD CHURCH in the future will play a key role in supporting the Antichrist and his ten-kingdom alliance. This will be a repeat, in part, of the time when Pagan Rome became Papal Rome during the Middle Ages.[533]

In those days, the church became headquartered in Rome, and controlled kingdoms, governing officials, and the economy. Corruption prevailed and the saints, who denounced the church's corruption while attempting to break free of its grip, were persecuted and martyred.

---

[533] A.D. 606 to A.D. 1517—from the rise of the Papacy to the time of the Reformation.

Both church officials and kings of that era exploited each other to benefit their political and religious agendas in the most abominable acts before God. I believe the church at that time foreshadows the collaboration that will be seen between the world religions and world governments of the coming new world order.

Who will be in the harlot church?

I don't believe the Catholic Church *is* the harlot described in Revelation 17. I can understand why many believe this, but I lean more toward a conglomeration of all the "isms" of the world. This harlot is called the "mother of harlots" (plural) for a reason.

Babylon means, "confusion," and confusion abounds when ecumenical alliances of diverse faiths and competing cults join forces. Such will characterize the global ecumenical movement of this harlot woman who rides on the back of the scarlet beast, typifying the Antichrist.

Joining the movement will be all world religions such as Hinduism, Shintoism, Taoism, Buddhism, Islamism, Mormonism, Animism, Demonism, eastern and orthodox churches, *apostate* Catholicism, *apostate* Protestantism, and *apostate* Pentecostalism. All the deceived religious will join the ecumenical movement of the harlot church in order to survive the catastrophic events of the seven trumpets.

The harlot church will use her influence and wealth to back the establishment of a one-world government with the ten kings of the ten-kingdom alliance. Together, religion and government will support the Antichrist and assist him in eradicating every Jew and nonconforming Christian who refuses to join the ecumenical movement. This consolidation of religion and government will happen *prior* to the dedication of the image of the Antichrist and the edict for all to receive his mark or die.

This is what the picture in Revelation 17 is about—the rise of an outwardly adorned woman whose beauty is skin deep. Inside she's bloated with corruption. She's a harlot, full of confusion and the mother of all spiritual prostitutes who serve and worship other gods. She's in bed with kings and the scarlet beast (Antichrist), who will combine the ideologies of all former empires into his one-world empire with ten horns, that is, ten kings in allegiance with him and his Babylonian mistress—a murderess, drunk with the blood of the saints. But Babylon's days are certainly numbered, as was the last Babylonian king, Belshazzar, who received the writing on the wall,[534] and which the prophet Daniel interpreted the first sentence as saying:

> God has numbered the days of your reign and brought it to an end.

The Roman Empire, with all its gods, hailed Caesar as a *god*, and so shall this one-world ecclesiastical religion, with all its gods, hail the Antichrist as a god. *Antichrist* means "in the place of Christ" and in the beginning of his reign, he will set himself up as a *god* over all gods and all religions. The world today and even segments of the church see Jesus as an *option* among religions. This is called "universalism."[535] A position common with the characteristics of the Millennial generation rising to experience those days.

For now, the world accepts the "option" alternative—which is a lie—while tolerance for all other religious persuasions is progressing rapidly in society's culture in the name of "getting along." This provides free reign to more aggressive religions like Islam, exploiting the world's

---

[534] Daniel 5:26-28—"*Mene:* God has numbered the days of your reign and brought it to an end. *Tekel:* You have been weighed on the scales and found wanting. *Peres:* Your kingdom is divided and given to the Medes and Persians."
[535] *Universalism*—the doctrine that teaches that all religions lead to God and, therefore, one cannot judge the other.

tolerance toward all religions, while tolerance for Christianity is diminishing.

This "optional" thinking feeds into the rise of the ecumenical movement throughout the world, and eventually the rising harlot church. Tolerance is and will become the global, cultural mind-set, but once it serves its purpose, the Antichrist and his ten-kingdom alliance will trample tolerance into the ground. For in his kingdom, there'll only be one God, himself—and tolerance for no other.

Consider how Rome allowed the conquered countries to keep their gods and religious practices—*as long as they paid homage* to Caesar as a god. So shall the Antichrist and the False Prophet—his official "mouth-piece"[536]—who will govern two departments under the Antichrist's regime: *world religion* and *commerce*.

The two "horns"[537] on the second beast (the False Prophet) in Revelation 13 symbolize the two functioning roles of the harlot church. In Revelation 17, she is seen as the *first* horn in the early days of her glory (see the left side of the column below). And in Revelation 18, she is seen as the *second* horn of the False Prophet and what remains of her glory after her destruction as a one-world church (the right side column).

Revelation 17 — 1st horn	*Revelation 18* — 2nd horn
• Babylon the *false* Church	• Babylon the City
• World Religious Umbrella	• One-World Government
• Ecclesiastical	• Commercial
• Religious Spiritual Leaders	• Political Leaders—10 Kings

The harlot's inquisition

It is important to remember that chapters 17 and 18 of Revelation happen *during* the three-and-one-half years of

---

536 Revelation 13:11—"He spoke like a dragon ..."
537 Revelation 13:11—"He had two horns like a lamb ..."

the Antichrist's reign. At the beginning of the three-and-one-half years, the *apostate* leaders among the Catholics and Protestants will join the ecumenical/political movement in order to gather every world religion under one umbrella to survive the devastation of the trumpet judgments. Through the harlot church, the Antichrist and False Prophet will turn the new world order from being a "democracy" into a "theocracy"—a global *state* religion. Much like Islam wants to establish a theocratic, global caliphate.

Given the chaotic climate in that day coming, attention to differences between religions will be shelved to focus on the greater enemies of famine, starvation, anarchy, rampant plagues, and targeting of Christians and Jews who are faithful to God and refuse to join the ecumenical movement of the new world order.

Anyone not joining will make themselves enemies of the state and its "sanctioned" religious practices, which will include persecuting and hunting down Christians for sport.

This is what ISIS and other extremist movements are doing in the Middle East. They execute all who refuse to denounce their faith and join the ranks of the Islamists under Sharia law. What's happening today, among the radical, extreme factions of Islam, is merely a foreshadowing of what's to come in the new world order.

Let the games begin

At the beginning of the Antichrist's regime, he'll give the world church and coalition of armies an enemy to fight and destroy—the Christians and Jews. But the annihilation of Christians and Jews won't be his only goal; their destruction is merely the smoke and mirrors of his ultimate plan, that is, to have no other gods before him—period.

The martyrdom of Christians and Jews will be phase one—sending a shot across the bow for *anyone* who might oppose him or worship any other god than him. He will be the ultimate narcissist, refusing to share his proclaimed godhood. *"Who is like the beast? Who can make war against him?"* This will become the mantra of the world's religious and political leaders. They'll back his authority to wage war against the saints and conquer them. The deaths of the saints will replace our modern-day sports and become like the games of the coliseums in the Roman Empire, particularly during the reigns of the ruthless emperors from A.D. 54 to A.D. 313.

Emperor *Nero* blamed Christians for the fire he started that burned down more than half of Rome. They were persecuted and killed for it. *Domitian* demanded to be worshipped as god and called himself "Jupiter." Jews and Christians who refused were martyred. *Trajan* passed a law making it illegal to be a Christian. *Marcus Aurelius* opposed Christians as imposters and beheaded thousands. *Septimius Severus* issued an edict, which waged fierce persecution against the saints. *Maximinus I and II, Decius, Valerian,* and *Aurelian* all persecuted, tortured and slaughtered Christians.

The most horrendous of these emperors, however, was *Diocletian* who ruled for ten years. He ordered every Bible to be burned, every church building torn down, and all who refused to renounce their faith in Christ lost their citizenship and the protection of the law.

You don't have to look any further than *Foxe's Book of Martyrs* to see the details of atrocities committed against the church during that time. Is it any wonder that God looks upon sinful man as beasts?[538]

I believe people today are being numbed to such a time as this through Hollywood's blockbuster movies like "The Hunger Games" and "Divergent" and others waiting in the queue to dull our sensitivities to the point of accepting such

---

[538] Psalm 49:12, 20; 73:22; Daniel 7; 2 Peter 2:12; Revelation 11:7; 13:1-18

atrocities as the new "norm." It isn't coincidental, either, that a generation has grown up on cyber games of war and mayhem in virtual realities that desensitize young minds to think nothing of walking into campus buildings, theaters, or schools to gun down innocent people. Under the deception of the Antichrist, people will become heartless, brutal beasts toward humanity.

How many more gruesome acts by ISIS do you think it will it take before we become calloused to the beheading of people, like the martyrs who are beheaded in the book of Revelation? The more of it we see, the less shocked and disgusted we are by it. It becomes the "norm" in our violence-saturated world. Media images of violence can create the same cold-heartedness that Nazi Germany had toward the Jews. Hitler deceived people into regarding the Jews as dogs to be slaughtered and wiped out.

My mother lived through WWII as a young adult. She told me that smart, sophisticated, civilized, intelligent people were able to be deceived in serious economic times by a charismatic leader. He hammered them with the same type of deceitful propaganda the world has embraced today about the aborted unborn. "They're only fetuses, not humans," says the deceived. In Nazi Germany, people came to believe, "They're only Jews, not humans." They were told that Jews had no value; they were the problem with the world. They were told they needed to be discarded in favor of a *master* race!

As in the time of the ten oppressive emperors of Rome, Hitler, and ISIS (or IS) today—a Jew or Christian (whether adult or child) will be hunted down and sentenced to death by the members of the harlot church—all in favor, not of a master race, but of a master *faith*. The lives of god-fearing Christians and Jews will be no more valuable than a pesky mosquito. Can this be possible? History shows it is, and it's happening today. The slaying of Christians in other countries receives little media attention and mostly goes unnoticed by the world.

One day, this'll find its way onto American soil—and the rest of the world—under the rule and reign of a man who will call himself "God." The global genocide of Christians and Jews will happen in the earliest days of the last three-and-one-half years in a quick fashion.

The harlot church will whip up extreme factions into a murderous frenzy. She'll be wealthy enough to offer members of this universal following a *bounty* for the head of every Jew and Christian. In a time of no jobs and economic collapse, this will be attractive and very lucrative, as long as there are Christians and Jews to be found. The harlot church will provide a job for mercenaries—very much like ISIS (or IS) adherents, who recruit and employ thousands of soldiers to their cause. This is portrayed in Revelation 17 and 18:

> With her the kings of the earth committed adultery and the inhabitants of the earth were intoxicated with the wine of her adulteries.
>
> —*Revelation 17:2*

> I saw that the woman was drunk with the **blood** of the saints, the **blood** of those who bore testimony to Jesus.
>
> —*Revelation 17:6*

> In her was found the **blood** of prophets and of the saints, and of all who have been killed on the earth.
>
> —*Revelation 18:24*

A change of plans — no other "gods" allowed

Many today believe that annihilating Israel is the primary goal of Islamist extremists. But though Israel is in their sights for destruction and occupation, that nation is not the grand prize, and neither is America—though both are coveted.

No, the goal of Islam is to conquer *every* nation and god on Earth and to make all people servants of Allah and the caliphate. They're not content to be *a* religion *among* other world religions. They're not content to share the world with infidels of other faiths. In the minds of Islamist extremists, *jihad* will never stop until the last infidel on Earth is converted, subdued, or slain. Then and only then do they believe the world can have peace under an Islamic, *theocratic* rule, because when they reach that point, no other opposition will exist to conquer.

The Antichrist will have the same goal. He won't be content with being *a* god among other gods, like the Caesars. He'll want to be rid of the God of the Jews and Christians. He'll want to be rid of Allah, the god of the Muslims. He'll want no other god to be worshipped among any other religions, other than himself as the one and only true god. So once the Jews and Christians are destroyed, the only religious entity left to obstruct his objective for supreme godhood is the harlot church herself—Babylon.[539]

During the initial days of the Antichrist's rule, he'll allow himself to be in competition with other religious gods as a necessary compromise to achieve victory in his war against the saints. The grand prize, however, won't be the Jews or the church; the ultimate prize will be to strip *all* world religions of allegiance to their gods. It can no longer be their god, plus the Antichrist. It can *only* be the Antichrist as their messiah and god. So how will he pull this off? Enter the ingenious and brilliant strategy of the *image* and *mark* of the beast.

---

[539] Babylon means *confusion*, and confusion abounds when a collaboration of opposing faiths—with competing gods—joins forces in a cause.

The first horn destroyed

The *first* horn of the two horns[540] seen on the False Prophet (the second beast) represents the religious union of religious leaders in a one-world religious body to serve the initial agenda of the Antichrist—to annihilate Jews and Christians. As mentioned before, this will happen in the early days of the Antichrist's reign, and then the *religious* side of Babylon—the harlot church—will be destroyed. Here's how Revelation 17 ends regarding her religious destruction:

> Then the angel said to me, "The waters you saw, where the [harlot] sits, are peoples, multitudes, nations and languages. The beast [Antichrist] and the ten horns you saw will hate the [harlot]. They will bring her to ruin and leave her naked; they will eat her flesh and burn her with fire. For **God has put it into their hearts** to accomplish his purpose by agreeing to give the beast their power to rule, until God's words are fulfilled. The woman you saw is the great city [Babylon] that rules over the kings of the earth."

The False Prophet will have an image (or statue) of the Antichrist designed and created to stand as a symbol of his supreme divinity. All must bow to the image, all must receive the mark, and all must denounce and reject their *own* gods and submit to the full allegiance and worship of none other than the Antichrist. Anyone who refuses, strays from the fold, or denounces the Antichrist's self-proclaimed deity, will be hunted down and beheaded, just like the Jews and the saints will be.

By this time, the *queen*[541] of the Antichrist becomes obsolete. Her purpose is accomplished and, therefore, she's tossed aside and discarded because there's no need for an

---

[540] Revelation 13:11—"He had two horns like a lamb ..."
[541] Revelation 18:7—"I sit as a queen ..."

ecumenical entity, and no remaining need for a unification of world religions and the ecclesiastical role of spiritual leaders each representing their religious brand. All priests, shamans, imams, caliphs, bishops, the papacy, cardinals, witch doctors, and any other type of religious spiritual leaders must go, leaving no other god to worship than Satan and his incarnate son, the Antichrist.

What irony. The Antichrist and the ten kings, who initially helped Babylon's religious crusade of genocide against her own people and prodigals, will destroy the entity of *her* religious sect.

Like the secular Jews who denounce God and the saints who will fall away from the faith and their allegiance to Christ, every world religious faith will be faced with the same decision to denounce their gods and religious practices. It'll be the law of the land to worship the image of the beast and receive his mark. This is how every world religion will be conquered. Once they receive the mark and the number 666, they'll be demonized in spirit, soul, and body, completely possessed by Satan to do his bidding, and will abandon their beliefs once held by their forefathers for generations.

The only piece of Babylon remaining will be the *second* horn of a one-world government, one-world commerce, and a one-world political alliance of ten kings. Note chart below:

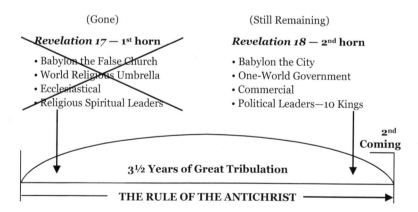

Chapter 39

The Fall of Babylon

After this I saw another angel coming down from heaven. He had great authority, and the earth was illuminated by his splendor. With a mighty voice he shouted:

"Fallen! Fallen is Babylon the Great! She has become a home for demons and a haunt for every evil spirit, a haunt for every unclean and detestable bird. For all the nations have drunk the maddening wine of her adulteries. The kings of the earth committed adultery with her, and the merchants of the earth grew rich from her excessive luxuries."

—Revelation 18:1-3

AT THE BEGINNING of the Great Tribulation period all world religions in Babylon are abolished once the mark of the beast is implemented and worshipping the Antichrist as "God," is the only religious activity accepted. However, by the end of the three-and-one-half years, God's judgments have destroyed everything political and commercial in Babylon. The prophets Jeremiah[542] and Isaiah both predicted the extent of this future judgment in their time. [543]

Babylon traces all the way back to Genesis when Nimrod built the tower of Babel.[544] It then treks progressively

---

[542] Jeremiah 50-51
[543] Isaiah 13-14; 47
[544] Genesis 10:8-10; 11:1-8

through the Bible,[545] emerging along the way in various manifestations consistent to its nature—primarily that of "religious confusion."

Babylon begins as a seedling in Genesis and ends in the book of Revelation as a full tree, rooted in all world trade and commerce, many luxuries, many types of sorceries ("sorcery" means enchanters and makers of drugs), demonic worship and idolatry, merchandising in drugs and human trafficking, and the enterprising death-sport of slaughtering everyone who refuses to take the mark of the beast.[546] All of this is described in detail in Revelation 18. So here is how the chart will look at the end:

The theme of two women

Read any good fiction and you'll find the author placing an object or *mystery* person into a scene to momentarily engage your attention. Something such as a rifle hanging above the fireplace, will be used later in the scene of another chapter. This is called *foreshadowing*.

---

[545] 2 Kings 17-25; 2 Chronicles 32, 33, 36; Ezra; Nehemiah; Esther 2; Psalm 137; Isaiah 13, 14, 21, 39, 43, 48; Jeremiah 20, 21, 22, 24, 25, 27-29, 32, 34-35, 37-44, 46, 49, 50-52; Ezekiel 17, 19, 21, 24, 26, 29-30, 32; Daniel 1-5, 7, Micah 4:10; Zechariah 2:7; 6:10; Matthew 1:12, 17; Acts 7:43; 1 Peter 5:13
[546] Revelation 18:24

The Bible is filled with "foreshadows," first mentioned in Genesis. They appear throughout the next 64 books and culminate in the 66th book of the Bible—Revelation. All *foreshadowing* in Genesis grows in progressive points of revelation throughout the Bible. In fact, every book in the Bible will find some portion of its contents in the pages of the book of Revelation.

Throughout the Bible, a particularly intriguing "foreshadow" emerges: a theme of *two women* in conflict.

A woman in the Bible is typically symbolic of the "church," whether true or false. We discover the first mention of two women in a conflict with their counterparts in Genesis. They are Sarah, who is Abraham's wife and, Rachel, who is Jacob's wife. Both husbands love their wives, however each husband is attached in some way to *another* woman who creates conflict in the house. In Sarah's case, the "other" woman is Hagar, her Egyptian handmaid. In Rachel's case, it's her older sister, Leah.

The contrasts are illuminating as you follow the pattern of this theme of *two* women in the Bible. The message that emerges is one of two religious paths that people will take in the last days—the *true* path, which is the narrow road leading to eternal life; or the *false* path (composed of a universal religious body)—which is the broad road that leads to eternal destruction.

As you will see in the examples on the next two pages, some are in the same house with the same husband. Some are out of the same house, such as sisters. Some who begin their journey in the *same house* of the *true* church will become deceived and wind up on the wide and broad road that embraces *any* religion as an option to God.

This gross deception will escalate in the last days and is becoming increasingly evident among many of our young people, who are taught this in school today. Many, even those who have grown up in church, have also eaten from the forbidden fruit of *universalism*—the doctrine that teaches *all* religions lead to God and, therefore, one religion can't judge another.

This doesn't apply, however, to Islam. The world ignores the fact that Islam persecutes other religions as if that's okay, because political correctness requires that we don't offend or incite the anger of any religion.

Political correctness was not the approach that Jesus took when he called out the hypocrisy of the Pharisees. Jesus didn't come to appease, or make everyone like him. He came to bring truth that would offend the religious sensitivities of the "establishment" of that day because they were leading everyone away *from* God, and not *to* God, by their traditions.

As you examine the contrasting columns below, you'll readily see that the women depicted in the column for the *false church* symbolizes the harassers, hecklers, and opposers of the *true* church, loyal to Christ (the *only* way, the truth, and the life).

Consider the contrasting accounts of two women below— which begin in Genesis and culminate in the final hour of Revelation.

True Church—Bride of Christ	False Church—Harlot of Antichrist
Sarah (Genesis 16, 21)	**Hagar**
Mother	Mother
Pure line	Egyptian line (mixture with pure)
Isaac (fruit of promise & faith)	Ishmael (fruit of unbelief)
In the same house	In the same house
Barren womb	Fruitful womb
Conflict	Conflict
Rachel (Genesis 29)	**Leah**
Mother	Mother
Beautiful (glory)	Weak or dull-eyed
In the same house	In the same house
Barren womb	Fruitful womb
Conflict	Conflict

True Church—Bride of Christ	False Church—Harlot of Antichrist
Hannah (1 Samuel 1:16)	**Peninnah**
Mother to be	Mother
In the same house	In the same house
Barren womb	Fruitful womb
Loved	Adversary & heckler
1ˢᵗ Harlot (1 Kings 3:16-18)	**2ⁿᵈ Harlot**
Mother	Mother
True mother (compassion)	False mother
Let the child live (pro-life)	Kill the child (pro-choice)
Same house	Same house
Conflict	Conflict
Proverbs 31 Woman	**Proverbs 7 Woman**
A bride (traits of the Bride)	A harlot (traits of the Harlot)
Oholibah (Ezekiel 23:14)	**Oholah**
Sister	Sister
My tent is in her	Her "own" tent (her own religion)
Jerusalem	Samaria
Capital of Judah	Capital of Israel
From the same house	From the same house
Conflict	Conflict
Woman & the Lost Coin (Lk. 15:8)	**Woman & the Leaven** (Mt. 13:33)
Heart for the lost	Mixture of leaven in doctrine
Woman Taken (Mt. 24:41)	**Woman Left**
Together	Together
Grinding out her grain (doctrine)	Grinding out her grain (false doctrine)
Revelation 12 (this woman taken)	Revelation 17 (this woman left)
Revelation 12	**Revelation 17-18**
In the Wilderness (God provides)	In the Wilderness (God-forsaken)
The Beast — against the Bride	The Beast — supporting his queen
Standing on the Moon (Christ)	Sitting on the beast (Antichrist)
Clothed with Heavenly Glory	Clothed with Earthly Glory
A Bride	A Harlot
Mother (of 144,000 princes)	Mother (of daughter harlots)
Blood Atonement	Rejects Blood Atonement
On eagle's wings to protection	On scarlet-colored beast to destruction
This one is taken (to keep alive)	This one is left (deceived to die)
True to the King of Kings	Seductress to earthly kings
Cup of Blessing (the Lord's Table)	Cup of Abominations & Corruption
Pure	Mixture

Revelation 12—*cont'd.*	***Revelation 17-18***—*cont'd.*
Freedom in Christ	Religious Bondage
No compromise	Compromise
True doctrine	False doctrine
The Overcomers	The Overcome
Great Mystery (of Godliness)	Mystery (of iniquity)
New Jerusalem (a spiritual city)	Babylon (a city of demonic spirits)

Babylon—a literal city?

Many scholars in eschatology believe that the Babylon of Revelation 18 is a *literal* city in a specific location, and is destroyed before the second coming of Christ. Some believe it is Rome, others believe it will be the ancient site of Babylon in Iraq. I run into difficulty supporting these theories, but we can't really know for sure until it all plays out.

In the meantime, I lean more toward Babylon *not* being a brick-and-mortar city, but rather a symbolic name for a global composite of business oligarchs[547] in bed with the *ecclesiastical* side of the harlot church. They could be headquartered in a strategic location for commerce and trade; but their demise will be the result of a global economic meltdown, due to the last and greatest earthquake. The Babylon oligarchies will receive a double portion of judgment for what they have done.

Another reason I lean more toward a symbolic commercial system, rather than a literal city, is that the *true* church is likened to the "city" of Jerusalem, but isn't a literal, brick-and-mortar Jerusalem.

In the Sermon on the Mount, Jesus refers to God's kingdom people as a "city" set on a hill.[548] In Galatians, Paul says that the free woman, Sarah, represents the people of the new covenant, which, *figuratively*, is the "city" of Jerusalem

---

[547] Oligarchy—a small group of people having control of a country, organization, or institution.
[548] Matthew 5:14

on Mount Zion.[549] In the book of Hebrews, God's new covenant people are characterized as the heavenly Jerusalem, the "city" of the living God.[550] Finally—to complete this pattern—the woman in Revelation 12 is the truest representation of the *heavenly* city of Jerusalem, not the *literal* city.

Consistent with the woman in Revelation 12, representing the company of the bride, Babylon is her antithesis in Revelation 17-18. The woman, Babylon, symbolizes the characteristics and traits of the godless masses in the one-world commerce system. The harlot riding on the beast is in bed with kings, oligarchs, and government officials who, in the end, will control every aspect of world trade and commerce. So instead of a literal city, I believe Babylon symbolizes the commerce and trade exploited by kings, merchants, and sea captains who had benefitted as the recipients of her treasuries. Read the following passages with this in mind:

> The kings of the earth committed adultery with her, and the merchants of the earth grew rich from her excessive luxuries.
> —***Revelation 18:3***

> Therefore in one day her plagues will overtake her: death, mourning and famine. She will be consumed by fire, for mighty is the Lord God who judges her.
> When the kings of the earth who committed adultery with her and shared her luxury see the smoke of her burning, they will weep and mourn over her. Terrified at her torment, they will stand far off and cry:
>> "Woe! Woe, O great city, O Babylon, city of power! In one hour your doom has come!

---

[549] Galatians 4:21-26
[550] Hebrews 12:22-24

The merchants of the earth will weep and mourn over her because no one buys their cargoes anymore—cargoes of gold, silver, precious stones and pearls; fine linen, purple, silk and scarlet cloth; every sort of citron wood, and articles of every kind made of ivory, costly wood, bronze, iron and marble; cargoes of cinnamon and spice, of incense, myrrh and frankincense, of wine and olive oil, of fine flour and wheat; cattle and sheep; horses and carriages; and bodies and souls of men [enslavement or human trafficking].

They will say, "The fruit you longed for is gone from you. All your riches and splendor have vanished, never to be recovered." The merchants who sold these things and gained their wealth from her will stand far off, terrified at her torment. They will weep and mourn and cry out:

> "Woe! Woe, O great city, dressed in fine linen, purple and scarlet, and glittering with gold, precious stones and pearls! In one hour such great wealth has been brought to ruin!"

Every sea captain, and all who travel by ship, the sailors, and all who earn their living from the sea, will stand far off. When they see the smoke of her burning, they will exclaim, "Was there ever a city like this great city?" They will throw dust on their heads, and with weeping and mourning cry out:

> "Woe! Woe, O great city, where all who had ships on the sea became rich through her wealth! In one hour she has been brought to ruin! Rejoice over her, O heaven! Rejoice, saints and apostles and prophets! God has judged her for the way she treated you."

—Revelation 18:8-19

God's judgment against the Babylonian system of a one-world commerce will happen at the culmination of the *sixth* seal, the culmination of the sounding of the *seventh* trumpet, and the culmination of the *seventh* bowl of wrath; all ending with the same giant earthquake that will level every island, mountain and city on the Earth.

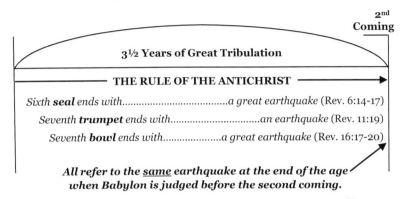

2nd Coming

3½ Years of Great Tribulation

THE RULE OF THE ANTICHRIST

*Sixth **seal** ends with*.....................................*a great earthquake* (Rev. 6:14-17)

*Seventh **trumpet** ends with*...............................*an earthquake* (Rev. 11:19)

*Seventh **bowl** ends with*.....................*a great earthquake* (Rev. 16:17-20)

All refer to the <u>same</u> earthquake at the end of the age when Babylon is judged before the second coming.

Then a mighty angel picked up a boulder the size of a large millstone and threw it into the sea, and said:

> "With such violence the great city of Babylon will be thrown down, never to be found again. The music of harpists and musicians, flute players and trumpeters, will never be heard in you again.
>
> No workman of any trade will ever be found in you again. The sound of a millstone will never be heard in you again.
>
> The light of a lamp will never shine in you again. The voice of bridegroom and bride will never be heard in you again.
>
> Your merchants were the world's great men. By your magic spell all the nations were led astray.
>
> In her was found the blood of prophets and of the saints, and of all who have been killed on the earth."
>
> **—Revelation 18:21-24**

Not only is the theme of two women seen throughout the Bible, these same women each represent a city.

Note the contrast on the next page between Revelation 12 and Revelation 17-18:

Revelation 21-22	Revelation 17-18
Woman represents new **Jerusalem**	Woman represents **Babylon**
A heavenly city	A worldly city
A Holy and pure city	An unholy and vile city
Inhabited by God's Spirit	Inhabited by demonic spirits
Nations walk in the light of her glory	Nations are drunk by her wine
God's eternal city	Satan's temporal city

Do you see it? Amazing isn't it, how you can find material to compare and contrast, woven throughout the entire Bible. What you've observed me using to arrive at these conclusions are the hermeneutic tools of 1) the *First Mention Principle*, 2) the *Comparative Mention Principle*, 3) the *Complete Mention Principle*, 4) the *Progressive Mention Principle*, 5) the *Symbolic Principle*, and 6) the *Typical Principle*.

Here's what we've covered so far in Revelation chapters 11-19, and how they overlap each other *during* the Great Tribulation period:

Revelation Chapters 11-19

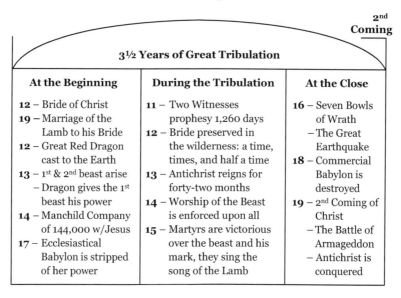

Chapter 40

The Wedding Supper of the Lamb

After this I heard what sounded like the roar of a great multitude in heaven shouting:

> "Hallelujah! Salvation and glory and power belong to our God, for true and just are his judgments. He has condemned the great prostitute who corrupted the earth by her adulteries. He has avenged on her the blood of his servants."

And again they shouted:

> "Hallelujah! The smoke from her goes up for ever and ever."

The twenty-four elders and the four living creatures fell down and worshiped God, who was seated on the throne. And they cried:

> "Amen, Hallelujah!"

Then a voice came from the throne, saying:

> "Praise our God, all you his servants, you who fear him, both small and great!"
>
> —***Revelation 19:1-5***

THIS IS HOW Revelation 19 begins, after the destruction of Babylon and every vestige of her existence. This takes place at *the end* of the Great Tribulation period when all heaven rejoices over the judgment of God upon Babylon, bringing her corrupt deeds and genocide of the saints to justice. The great earthquake has destroyed everything commercially around the world. And to top it off, God follows up with a downpour of 100-pound hailstones upon the godless masses.[551]

The announcement of the wedding supper

The moment that heaven and Earth has been waiting for has finally come. The creation itself has been groaning and travailing under the weight and bondage of sin, ever since it entered the world and corrupted the planet. [552]

Not only has the creation been longing eagerly for the manifestation of the bride's glorious freedom and complete redemption, the angels and saints in heaven have also been waiting. They now have the joy of announcing that the wedding supper of the Lamb is about to commence:

> Then I heard what sounded like a great multitude, like the roar of rushing waters and like loud peals of thunder, shouting:
>
> > "Hallelujah! For our Lord God Almighty reigns. Let us rejoice and be glad and give him glory! For the wedding of the Lamb *has* come, and his bride has made herself ready. Fine linen, bright and clean, was given her to wear."
>
> Then the angel said to me, "Write: 'Blessed are those who are invited to the wedding supper of the Lamb!'" And he added, "These are the true words of God."
>
> *—Revelation 19:6-10*

First, the angels state that the marriage of the Lamb *"has"* come (past tense). "Has" because the marriage of the Lamb took place in Revelation 8:1-4 when the bride came into the full measure and stature of Christ, and her marriage to her Bridegroom was consummated.

---

[551] Revelation 16:20-21
[552] Romans 8:18-25

In Revelation 8, I believe she conceives and, nine months later, gives birth to the male-child company (in Revelation 12:5). These are the 144,000 male babies who were carried in the womb of the 144,000 sealed virgins in Revelation 7.

Upon birth, the male-child company is immediately caught up to the throne of God, triggering the war in heaven, where Satan and his angels are permanently cast out of heaven.[553]

The bride is then carried off into the wilderness for protection *and* preparation. In the wilderness she'll *make herself ready* for the wedding supper of the Lamb *after* the arrival of Christ at his second coming. Three-and-one-half years she'll be hidden in the desert, patiently waiting for her enemies to be trampled underfoot by her Bridegroom-Husband.[554]

Isaiah saw this "hiddenness" when he said:

> Go, my people, enter your rooms and shut the doors behind you; hide yourselves for *a little while* until his wrath has passed by.
>
> See, the Lord is coming out of his dwelling to punish the people of the earth for their sins. The earth will disclose the blood shed upon her; she will conceal her slain no longer.
>
> **—*Isaiah 26:20-21***

When Christ returns for his bride, the wedding supper will be celebrated with all the friends of the bride and her Bridegroom. After that, they will enjoy their honeymoon together—one that will last 1,000 years.

The contrast of Jewish weddings

---

[553] Ephesians 4:13; Revelation 12:5; 14:1-5
[554] Revelation 14:20

In the Bible there is a principle, simply stated: "first the *natural*, then the *spiritual*."[555] By using this principle it is fascinating to observe the similarities in the customs of the Jewish wedding, and how they correlate to the wedding of Christ and his bride, the church. Ponder carefully this list adapted by Kevin Conner's exposition on the Book of Revelation:[556]

Jewish Wedding—*Natural*	**Christ's Wedding—*Spiritual***
The son leaves his father's house to go to the home of his future bride.	Jesus leaves his Father's heaven to come to Earth, the home of his future bride.
The son pays the price for the betrothal; a dowry to secure the covenant.	Jesus pays the price for the betrothal, his own blood to secure the covenant.
Legally betrothed, but not married.	Legally betrothed, but not married.
Separated indefinitely while the bridegroom returns to his father's house to prepare a place for his betrothed bride.	Separated in the Church Age while our Bridegroom returns to heaven to prepare a place for his betrothed bride.
During the absence of the Bridegroom the bride prepares her wedding gown.	During the absence of the Bridegroom the bride makes herself ready.
She keeps herself pure and exclusively committed to her Bridegroom.	She keeps herself pure and exclusively committed to her Bridegroom.
The bride keeps her lamp filled with oil, she doesn't know the day or hour that her Bridegroom will return.	The bride keeps her lamp filled with the oil of the Holy Spirit, she doesn't know the day or hour of Christ's return.
The Bridegroom returns in his best robes, with friends and a great procession.	Jesus returns in a robe dipped in his blood, and with his angels and saints.
Approaching the house, the Bridegroom gives a shout for his bride to hear and prepare herself to meet and receive him with her lamp burning.	Jesus comes on the Day of Atonement, preceded by the sound of The Feast of Trumpets, to alert the bride to prepare to meet him.
The bride trims her lamp and goes out to meet the Bridegroom at night.	The bride's lamp is trimmed and filled with oil to meet Jesus at midnight.

---

[555] 1 Corinthians 15:46
[556] Kevin J. Conner, *The Book of Revelation: An Exposition* (Vermont, Victoria: K.J.C. Publications, 2001), 569.

Jewish Wedding—*Natural*	Christ's Wedding—*Spiritual*
The marriage takes place and is consummated behind closed doors, which are guarded by the friend of the groom.	The marriage takes place and is consummated behind closed doors. No one else can enter the chamber.
The wedding supper follows with all the guests clothed in wedding garments.	The wedding supper comes at the end of the 3½ years, when Christ returns.
Only those dressed in wedding garments can attend, or be thrown out.	Only those dressed in the fine, bright linen of righteousness can attend.
After the wedding supper—honeymoon and a life together as husband and wife.	After the wedding supper—1,000 years' honeymoon and eternity together.

The romance foreshadowed

As stated earlier, the book of Revelation is the culmination of all the romance stories of the Bible. Christ comes to receive his bride, and they are married happily ever after, throughout eternity.

Many stories and Scriptures in the Bible *foreshadow* this ultimate goal—for God the Father to have a bride for his Son, so they can become parents of a *new* creation.

Following are some of the most obvious romance stories that typify Christ and his bride. Check them out and look for the similarities. Perhaps you can make your own comparison chart, using the tool of the *Comparative Mention Principle*. Try it—you'll have fun doing it.

- A Bride for Isaac — *Genesis 24*
- Boaz and Ruth — *the book of Ruth*
- The King and his Royal Bride — *Psalm 45*
- Solomon and the Shepherdess — *Song of Songs*

Chapter 41

The Rider on the White Horse

I saw heaven standing open and there before me was a white horse, whose rider is called Faithful and True. With justice he judges and makes war. His eyes are like blazing fire, and on his head are many crowns. He has a name written on him that no one knows but he himself. He is dressed in a robe dipped in blood, and his name is the Word of God. The armies of heaven were following him, riding on white horses and dressed in fine linen, white and clean. Out of his mouth comes a sharp sword with which to strike down the nations. "He will rule them with an iron scepter." He treads the winepress of the fury of the wrath of God Almighty. On his robe and on his thigh he has this name written:

KING OF KINGS AND LORD OF LORDS.

—Revelation 19:11-16

THE TIME HAS FINALLY arrived for the second coming of Christ in full, visible glory. He returns to resurrect the dead, retrieve his bride from the wilderness, and completely destroy the Antichrist and the False Prophet, along with the ten kings.

The great earthquake has happened, the two witnesses are back in heaven, commercial Babylon is destroyed, and the kings of the east have gathered together with the rest of the world in the valley of Megiddo to fight against Christ.

Now I could just "tell" you what happens, but I think it would be more fun to "show" you this scene from my novel, *The Unveiling*. I will throw in most of the Scriptures used in Revelation—and other passages—that describe this very significant and famous point in time.

In this scene, you'll see Reuben Aster, the man who plays the role of the Antichrist, and John Drakon, the man who plays the role of the False Prophet. They are with their armies at Megiddo, prepared to face Jesus. Let's take a look.

———————

ASTER AND DRAKON SAT on their horses in the plain of Jezreel where Mount Tabor and the site of the image had once towered over the valley. Beside them were the ten kings of the world alliance, also on horses.

The plain spread miles before them, this time without Mount Tabor, Carmel or Ebal. The great earthquake had swallowed every mountain in Israel with the exception of Mount Zion, eighty miles south of Jezreel.

Aster surveyed the sizeable remnant of troops that had arrived on horseback or by foot. No one drove vehicles because they had either been destroyed by the hundred-pound hailstones, swallowed up in open crevices during the earthquake, or blocked by barriers of stone, rubble, and wide fissures.

As the armies stood ready for battle, an endless sea of glittering helmets, rattling swords, and flashing guns could be seen stretched across the vast plain—an impressive and encouraging sight to behold for Aster. But a sinking feeling came over him for the first time since he began his forty-two-month reign over the world. His cities were gone, his resources depleted, and his communication systems were all but destroyed. To envision a future beyond this day seemed futile.

"Reuben!" Drakon shouted, motioning toward the sky. Aster looked up and groaned. A cloud of birds, from every direction, was approaching miles away across the surrounding horizon. The massive shadow of their flight crept across the plains while the noise of their screeches increased. God had invited every species of winged scavengers to dinner, outnumbering the armies—fifty birds to one soldier. Aster couldn't imagine things getting any worse. It was an unnerving omen of imminent death.

Their mass completely blocked out the sun's rays, while they flew in elevated layers of circling patterns, until only one gaping hole was left to be seen of the sky, directly above the mounted horsemen on the field.

Then an angel appeared, standing in the sun's path in the middle of the gaping hole. He shouted to the birds:

> *"Gather yourselves to the great supper of God. Eat the flesh of kings, generals, champions, horses and their riders. Gorge yourselves on them all—free and slave, small and great."*

When the angel disappeared, a shout from the armies rippled across the plain. The eyes of every soldier were fixed on the hole in the middle of the circling birds.

What now? Aster thought, straining to see through the blinding rays of light. The birds expanded their circling pattern until the hole exposed the sky, peeling away like the opening curtain in a play.

Where the blue sky rolled back, the dark, starlit space above Earth's atmosphere served as a backdrop to frame a majestic rider—radiant, glistening, and sitting on a white horse pawing in space. Aster wiped the pouring sweat from his brow with his trembling hands as he stared at the sight of the innumerable host of angels surrounding Jesus.

Chapter 42

The Battle of Armageddon

Then I saw the beast and the kings of the earth and their armies gathered together to make war against the rider on the horse and his army. But the beast was captured, and with him the false prophet who had performed the miraculous signs on his behalf. With these signs he had deluded those who had received the mark of the beast and worshiped his image. The two of them were thrown alive into the fiery lake of burning sulfur. The rest of them were killed with the sword that came out of the mouth of the rider on the horse, and all the birds gorged themselves on their flesh.

—Revelation 19:19-21

THAT'S IT? That's all there is to describe the final, great and ultimate battle? Where's your creative edge, John? With all the buildup in Revelation, couldn't you have provided us with a little more narrative than this, about *how* Jesus captures the Antichrist and the False Prophet? Where's the struggle? Why couldn't you throw in a scene or two of angels wielding their swords against the swords of the Antichrist's armies; or Jesus riding majestically through the masses, barreling through their ranks like a bowling ball as it strikes the pins?

Why isn't there anything more to this, than, "they gathered together to make war—BUT—the beast was captured, and with him the False Prophet?" As for the rest of the battle it says nothing more than they were killed with the sword that came from the mouth of Jesus. Boom! End of story. It's over, just like that.

Many years ago, someone sent me a YouTube video of a marine and a kung-fu martial artist ready to fight inside a ring of onlookers. The fight begins with the kung-fu fighter jumping around like a monkey to display his virility and prowess in a series of acrobatic moves. I'm assuming to intimidate the marine. As the kung fu exhibitionist does one last flip to catapult out of a rotation toward his opponent, the marine takes one step forward and clocks him with one blow—boom! The kung-fu fighter is out cold, lying on the ground. End of story. It was the fight that never happened.

While the kung-fu clown was engaged in his pre-fight exhibition, full of himself and his pride, the marine was assessing his opponent's moves, waiting for an opening to take him out. This is the kind of fight the Antichrist and his armies will experience with Jesus. He's already assessed the Antichrist's exhibition of arrogance, boasting, and blasphemy that's been taking place for three-and-one-half years. So as we, the onlookers arrive for the event—BOOM—the fight's over in one blow. End of story.

The sword coming out of the mouth of Jesus is the Word of God, sharper than any double-edge sword. And with one shout, Christ will smite the nations.[557] No struggle and no round one, two or three for him to win—not like the end of the 40-day wilderness test with the devil before his ministry began. This time it's going to be one big foot stepping on a small ant pile in Megiddo.

> And then the lawless one will be revealed, whom the Lord Jesus will overthrow with the ***breath of his mouth*** and destroy by the splendor of his coming.
>
> —*2 Thessalonians 2:8*

---

[557] Hebrews 4:12; Revelation 19:15

This will happen when the Lord Jesus is revealed from heaven **in blazing fire** with his powerful angels. He will punish those who do not know God and do not obey the gospel of our Lord Jesus. They will be punished with everlasting destruction and shut out from the presence of the Lord and from the majesty of his power **on the day he comes** to be glorified in his holy people and to be marveled at among all those who have believed.

—*2 Thessalonians 1:6-10*

For the Lord himself will come down from heaven, with **a loud command**, with the voice of the archangel and with the trumpet call of God ...

—*1 Thessalonians 4:16*

He **treads the winepress** of the fury of the wrath of God Almighty.

—*Revelation 19:15*

These passages from Paul's letters to the church in Thessalonica clearly demonstrate a one-punch knockout. The Antichrist and the False Prophet won't know what hit them. One moment they're watching the receding sky revealing the armies in heaven with Jesus, the next minute they find themselves snatched up like rag dolls and thrown into the lake of fiery sulfur. It's over that quick and justice can't be served more swiftly than that. That's why John has nothing more to narrate about this battle except that it isn't going to be much of a battle at all.

Other passages in the Bible expand somewhat on the details of this day of the Lord. They include the Earth being lit up by his glory,[558] his coming will be as swift as lightning flashes from the east to the west,[559] all the Earth (every eye)

---

[558] Zechariah 14:12-15

[559] Matthew 24:23-27 — lightning travels as a fast as 3,700 miles per second, but the light coming from lightning is traveling at 186,000 miles per second. That would put Jesus going around the planet's circumference 7.4 times within a

will be terrified and mourn when they see him coming,[560] and he will return as visibly in bodily form as when he ascended in a cloud from the Mount of Olives.[561]

Will anyone survive this battle?

The quick and simple answer to that question is—no. Paul was very clear on this point when he said:

> He will punish those **who do not know God and do not obey the gospel of our Lord Jesus**. They will be punished with everlasting destruction and shut out from the presence of the Lord.[562]

The Antichrist and False Prophet are captured and thrown *alive* (with bodies of flesh) into the lake of fire. The remaining army of the Antichrist *and* the decimated population in the rest of the world will all be destroyed.

I bring this question up because many teach there'll be *unbelievers* who survive the seven trumpets, the seven bowls of wrath, *and* the second coming of Christ. Some assume these people—possibly "doomsday preppers"—will hole up in the mountains or other hidden areas, avoiding all the deception, mayhem and destruction. Somehow they'll manage to make it through and come out of hiding for the 1,000-year reign of Christ. One problem with this thought—if it's true—they'll still be mortal.

I believe those who teach this concept sincerely think it's necessary due to some difficult Old Testament passages they can't reconcile with the millennial era. Granted there are

---

second. That means he could he could travel around the Earth 444 times in one minute, easy enough for every living soul left on the planet to see him. How many times, I don't know, but God will somehow make it happen.

[560] Revelation 1:7; 11:15-19; James 5:7-8; Matthew 24:27-30; 1 Corinthians 1:7; Revelation 22:10

[561] Acts 1:10-11

[562] 2 Thessalonians 1:9-10

obscure passages that leave questions in our minds, but the safer approach to knowing how an Old Testament prophecy fits into the New Testament narratives of the last days, is to go with the obvious, clearer passages that speak without contradicting other end-time passages.

Though Old Testament prophecies can provide additional insight to future events and eternity, when it comes to details leading up to the second coming, the safest way to proceed is with the New Testament.

In the New Testament, the apostles were, and still are, the infallible interpreters of the Old Testament. The apostle Paul clearly states—confirming John's vision in Revelation— that every unbeliever and wicked person will die at the second coming of Christ.

This means that the 1,000-year reign of Christ and his people will be a "Christian Millennium" where no ungodly people exist. I'll speak more about this in my sequel to interpret those difficult Old Testament passages and share why some believe sinners will survive in the millennium.

In the meantime, review these Scriptures, which seem to confirm what Paul says will happen to unbelievers at the point of Christ's return. See if they speak the same thing to you as they do to me.

Psalm 21:8-10

Your hand will lay hold on **all** your enemies; your right hand will seize your foes.

At the time of your appearing you will make them like a fiery furnace.

In his wrath the Lord will swallow them up, and his fire will consume them.

You will destroy their descendants **from the earth,** their **posterity**[563] from mankind.

Psalm 37:10-11

A little while, and the wicked will **be no more**; though you look for them, they will not be found.

But the meek will inherit the land and enjoy great peace [in the millennium[564]].

Isaiah 13:9

See, the day of the Lord is coming—a cruel day, with wrath and fierce anger—to make the land desolate and destroy the **sinners** within it.

Isaiah 66:15-16

See, the Lord is coming with fire, and his chariots are like a whirlwind; he will bring down his anger with fury, and his rebuke with flames of fire.

For with fire and with his sword the Lord will execute judgment upon **all men**, and many will be those slain by the Lord.

Malachi 4:1-2

"Surely the day is coming; it will burn like a furnace. **All the arrogant and every evildoer will be stubble**, and that day that is coming will set them on fire," says the Lord Almighty. "**Not a root or a branch will be left to them.**"

---

[563] *Posterity*—the offspring of one progenitor to the furthest generation; all future generations. (DICTIONARY CITATION NEEDED?)

[564] Hebrews 4:8-11—the "day" spoken of here is the 1,000 year day of rest, the millennial rest, the Sabbath-Day rest of all God's people who inherit the Earth and the wicked are no more.

Zephaniah 1:14-16

"The great day of the Lord is near—near and coming quickly.

Listen! The cry on the day of the Lord will be bitter, the shouting of the warrior there.

That day will be a day of wrath,

a day of distress and anguish,

a day of trouble and ruin,

a day of darkness and gloom,

a day of clouds and blackness,

a day of trumpet and battle cry against the fortified cities and against the corner towers.

I will bring distress on the people and they will walk like blind men, because they have sinned against the Lord.

Their blood will be poured out like dust and their entrails like filth.

Neither their silver nor their gold will be able to save them on the day of the Lord's wrath.

In the fire of his jealousy **the whole world** will be consumed, **for he will make a sudden end of all who live in the earth**."

2 Peter 3:7

By the same word the present heavens and earth are reserved for fire, being kept for **the day of judgment** and **destruction of ungodly men**.

Jude 14-16

See, the Lord is coming with thousands upon thousands of his holy ones to **judge everyone**, and to **[punish]**[565] **all the ungodly** of all the ungodly acts they

---

[565] The word used in the NIV is "convict" and in the KJV its "convince." The Greek word used for this is *exelegcho* (ex-el-eng'-kho), which means to convict fully, i.e., (by implication) to punish.

have done in the ungodly way, and of all the harsh words ungodly sinners have spoken against him.

These Scriptures lead me to believe that *no* unbeliever, *no* ungodly person, and *no* hiding prepper will be able to survive the burning punishment of God's consuming fire on planet Earth.

Do I delight in this fact? For justice to prevail, yes. But, for the souls who are lost and refuse to repent, my answer is, no—because I'm saddened they threw away their opportunity to be with God for eternity, choosing rather to embrace eternal separation from him.

This message of eternal damnation and punishment is a sobering reality, one that provokes me to do whatever I can, to win as many souls as possible to the Lord—thus, snatching them out of the fire.

> Be merciful to those who doubt; snatch others from the fire and save them.
>
> *—Jude 22-23*

No wrath or fiery judgment?

Many teachers of eschatology hold a view that there will be no wrath, no judgments, no plagues, and no fiery destruction of the planet in the last days. They believe these images are merely symbolic of events that have happened already in church history. They don't believe Revelation should be taken literally—at least not all of it. They do believe in a visible return of Christ, but not in the frightening way Revelation presents it to us at first glance.

Oh, how I wish that were true. Who in their right mind would want to experience the things I've been describing to you throughout this book? But what if their view is not true and these things really will happen on Earth? Of course, I'm not going to live in abject fear, but when these events do begin to happen in the way it seems Revelation describes them (in a literal sense), then I will have a map to navigate through it all and will be able to exploit the events to win others to Christ.

Jesus came as a *Lamb* and will return as *Lion*. By his crucifixion, death and resurrection at the first coming, he disarmed principalities and authorities and triumphed over them by the cross.[566] He conquered Satan, sin, death and the grave.[567] He did it judicially on the cross and then began to conquer men's hearts and souls[568] to establish his kingdom on Earth within the hearts of men and women.

His kingdom has been advancing ever since, from one believer (Mary Magdalene), to the 12 disciples, to the 120 in the upper room, to the 3,000 saved on the day of Pentecost, to the additional 5,000 saved the day after, and all within the first few days of the birth of the church.

His kingdom then spread to the uttermost parts of the Earth, becoming the fastest growing religion in the world, numbering more than 2 billion adherents of the Christian faith today. And it isn't over, yet. Wait until the bride manifests in all her glory for the great harvest of souls.

Jesus—with eyes blazing like fire and dressed in a robe dipped in the blood of his enemies—now returns as the Lion of the tribe of Judah to dispense justice through war, treading on his adversaries like grapes in a winepress.[569] He comes to *complete* his kingdom era on Earth and lead it to the next kingdom level in the millennium. There it will be a kingdom minus the tares,[570] minus the bad fish,[571] minus the goats,[572] minus the leaven,[573] and minus Satan, whom he will

---

[566] Colossians 2:15
[567] 1 Corinthians 15:26; 2 Timothy 1:10; Hebrews 2:14
[568] Revelation 6:2—the rider on the white horse (Rev. 19:11).
[569] Revelation 19:11-15
[570] Weeds that look like wheat—Matthew 13:24-30.
[571] The wicked caught in the fisher's net and thrown away—Matthew 13:47-52.
[572] The cursed goats (ungodly) separated from the sheep—Matthew 25:31-45.

remove from the face of the Earth and bind with a great chain in the Abyss for 1,000 years during Christ's millennial reign.[574]

Sin is defeated.

Death is defeated.

The grave is defeated. And Satan is defeated.

Boom! End of story.

His-story.

---

[573] False teachings in the church—Matthew 13:33-35.
[574] Revelation 20:1-3

Chapter 43

The Resurrection of the Saints

Brothers, we do not want you to be ignorant about those who fall asleep, or to grieve like the rest of men, <u>who have no hope</u>. We believe that Jesus died and rose again and so we believe that **God will bring with Jesus those who have fallen asleep in him.**

—1 Thessalonians 4:13-14

For the Lord himself will come down from heaven, with a loud command, with the voice of the archangel and with the trumpet call of God, **and the dead in Christ will rise first**.

—1 Thessalonians 4:16

Listen, I tell you a mystery: We will not all sleep, but we will all be changed—in a flash, in the twinkling of an eye, at the last trumpet. For the trumpet will sound, **the dead will be raised imperishable**, and we will be changed. For the perishable must clothe itself with the imperishable, and the mortal with immortality.

—1 Corinthians 15:51-53

IMMEDIATELY BEFORE Jesus deals with the massive army of the Antichrist at Jezreel, he must retrieve his bride before he torches the plain. The heat will be so intense that it will consume all living things. Preceding this judgment, he'll resurrect the bodies of every saint from the Old and New

Testament eras of history. They will rise ahead of the bride who is still "alive and left" in the desert.[575]

The prophet Daniel spoke of this resurrection when he said:

> Multitudes who sleep in the dust of the earth **will awake**: some to everlasting life.[576]

Jesus said the same:

> Do not be amazed at this, for a time is coming when all who are in their graves will hear his voice and come out— those who have done good **will rise** to live.[577]

And so did Enoch, when quoted by Jude:

> See, the Lord is coming with thousands upon thousands of his **holy ones**.[578]

When Jesus arrives in triumphant glory, as King of Kings and Lord of Lords, he'll gather his "holy ones" to himself, both in heaven and on Earth. Those presently in heaven, in soul and spirit, will return to the place they were buried, enter their bodies—turned to dust—and break through the ground with new, resurrected bodies—imperishable and immortal.

These young, youthful, bodies will be clothed in fine, white linen. They'll immediately ascend into the sky to meet Christ in the air, where space meets Earth's atmosphere and be placed on white horses to join the King. And if, by chance, you have any fear of horses, don't worry, your fear of heights will distract you enough to not care about it. You'll be glad to have a horse under you, instead of floating in midair.

---

[575] 1 Thessalonians 4:16-18—The dead in Christ will rise first. After that, **we who are still alive and are left** will be caught up together with them in the clouds to meet the Lord in the air. And so we will be with the Lord forever.
[576] Daniel 12:2
[577] John 5:28-29
[578] Jude 14

The rapture of the bride

Next to join the heavenly host is the bride being raptured up from the desert where God kept her safe and fed. Those who have been part of this bride company will also receive imperishable, immortal bodies clothed in fine, white linen as well as a horse waiting for them to mount. I think it would be safe to assume the bride will be positioned closest to her Bridegroom, along with the 144,000 male, virgin princes who follow the Lamb wherever he goes.

In addition to those already mentioned are the powerful angels who arrive with Jesus. Of course, he won't need them to battle at this event, but if he did employ them, it might be good to mention that one angel is capable of taking out 185,000 soldiers (which is what happened against the Assyrian army of Sennacherib in the Old Testament).[579]

So accompanying Jesus at his return are his angels, his bride, his 144,000 male, virgin princes (with their rod scepters), and the host of resurrected saints. What a grand sight this will be.

Now that everyone is safely out of harm's way—away from the battle zone—Jesus swiftly punishes the wicked, and the Earth is burned with fire so intense, all the elements and evidence of human existence will disappear.

> But the day of the Lord will come like a thief. The heavens will disappear with a roar; the elements will be destroyed **by fire**, and the earth and everything in it will be laid bare.
>
> Since everything will be destroyed **in this way**, what kind of people ought you to be? You ought to live holy and godly lives as you look forward to the day of God and speed its coming.
>
> —*2 Peter 3:10*

---

[579] Isaiah 37:33-37

Rapture or first resurrection or both the same?

This momentous event is the first resurrection that takes place at the *beginning* of the millennial reign of Christ. From examining the Scriptures, it appears to me that the rapture and resurrection are one and the same event occurring at the visible return of the King of Kings and Lord of Lords in Revelation 19. This is when the loud command, the shout, and the last note of the seventh trumpet sounds; and all the seals, the trumpets, and the bowls of wrath have concluded their purpose of judgment.

Here's my interpretation of the events occurring when Jesus returns:

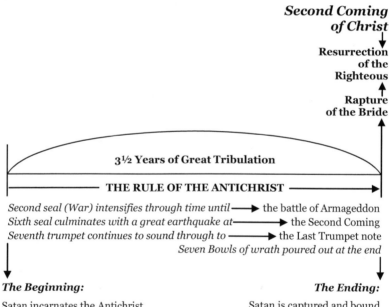

Second Coming of Christ

Resurrection of the Righteous

Rapture of the Bride

3½ Years of Great Tribulation

THE RULE OF THE ANTICHRIST

Second seal (War) intensifies through time until ──▶ the battle of Armageddon
Sixth seal culminates with a great earthquake at ──▶ the Second Coming
Seventh trumpet continues to sound through to ──▶ the Last Trumpet note
Seven Bowls of wrath poured out at the end

The Beginning:

Satan incarnates the Antichrist
The Antichrist begins his reign
The False Prophet erects the image
The godly are martyred
The bride taken/protected in the desert
Remaining saints are martyred
Grain Harvest of martyred believers

The Ending:

Satan is captured and bound
The Antichrist is captured
The False Prophet is captured
The armies are destroyed
The bride is raptured
Remaining wicked are destroyed
Grape Harvest (winepress)—unbelievers

Chapter 44

The Millennial Controversy

I saw thrones on which were seated those who had been given authority to judge. And I saw the souls of those who had been beheaded because of their testimony for Jesus and because of the word of God. They had not worshiped the beast or his image and had not received his mark on their foreheads or their hands. They **came to life** and reigned with Christ **a thousand years**. (The rest of the dead did not come to life *until* ***the thousand years*** *were ended*.) This is the first resurrection. Blessed and holy are those who have part in the first resurrection. The second death has no power over them, but they will be priests of God and of Christ and will reign with him for **a thousand years**.

—*Revelation 20:4-6*

THE MOST THRILLING part of the Revelation to me is the 1,000-year reign of Christ, otherwise known as the *millennium*. So much is going on during this time, I'll have to wait to address the details of it in my sequel for this book.

Much controversy surrounds the interpretation of the millennium events and where it falls in the order of end times. It is here that the distinctions become much clearer about the "why" different views are held about the events leading up to the second coming. This chapter is devoted to examining the five major interpretations of the "millennium" in the church. Please don't ignore this one. You'll find it to be very informative and eye-opening. Here they are:

Dispensational (Futurist) Premillennialism

This view is the most widely held interpretation today, and is actually an extension of *Futurist* Premillennialism. The only difference is in the added element of dividing human history into seven distinct periods.

These dispensations are:

- Dispensation of *Innocence*—Adam and Eve before sin
- Dispensation of *Conscience*—from Adam's fall to the Flood
- Dispensation of *Human Government*—from the Flood to Abraham
- Dispensation of *Promise*—from Abraham to the Law at Mt. Sinai
- Dispensation of *Law*—from the Law to the ministry of Christ
- Dispensation of *Grace*—from the Cross to the rapture of the Church
- Dispensation of the *Kingdom*—from Christ's return to the New Heavens and New Earth

Dispensations in Time

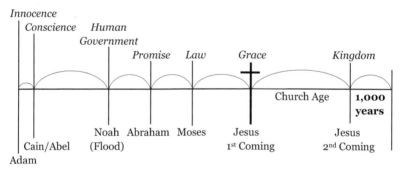

Proponents of this view believe that the kingdom of God is a Jewish, material and political kingdom (not a spiritual kingdom) and, therefore, hasn't happened, yet. To them, the kingdom of God is postponed until the end of the age because the Jews rejected and killed their Messiah. Had they accepted him as the Son of David at his first coming, they would have embraced his kingship, instead of crucifying him.

They see the church as mostly a Gentile church and, therefore, "parenthetical" or plan B. It is secondary to God's ultimate plan for Jews to awaken and accept Jesus as the rightful heir to David's throne in the last days. This is also the reason why they believe the New Covenant hasn't been established, yet (also postponed), but will be established upon Christ's return when he sets up his Davidic Kingdom in the land of Israel. Literal, nationalistic, political, and headquartered in Jerusalem, it will be a theocratic kingdom where the Jews are "the head and not the tail,"[580] exalted above all Gentile nations, which will be in submission to the throne of David.

In their Jewish millennium, the practices of animal sacrifices, feasts, and ritual ceremonies found in the Mosaic Covenant will be reinstated. Ezekiel's temple (in chapters 40-48) will be rebuilt to carry out the practices of the Mosaic economy. The Gentile nations will be required to submit to this economy. They believe at this time that every unfulfilled prophecy in the Old Testament about Israel will be fulfilled in the Jewish millennium.

The second coming unfolds in "two stages:" the secret rapture and the visible return of Christ seven years later. Concerning the 70-week prophecy of Daniel, they believe a gap exists. The first sixty-nine weeks are fulfilled at the inauguration of Jesus as Messiah, and the last week (the 70th week) is fulfilled at the end of the age as the seven-year tribulation (includes all of the events transpiring from Revelation 4 through 19).

In that seven-year period, the Antichrist will be on the world stage as a dictator, setting himself up as "God" in the rebuilt temple of Jerusalem.

Here's how their chart looks:

----

[580] Deuteronomy 28:13

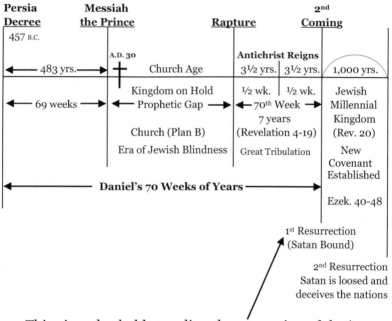

This view also holds to a literal resurrection of the just at the beginning of the 1,000 years, and the wicked at the end.

During this millennial period, mortals (the unsaved) and immortals (the saved) will mingle together. Life for mortals will be greatly extended under the paradise conditions of the Earth. The unconverted Gentile nations, who pretend submission to Jesus, will be deceived by Satan at the end of the millennium and rebel against God and his Jewish people.

Historic Premillennialism

This view has significant differences from the futurist and dispensational view. To the Historic Premillennialist, the kingdom of God was *not* postponed until the end of the age. His kingdom is "now" and he rules from heaven over his church—made up of both Jews and Gentiles. The church is *not* seen as secondary to God's ultimate plan, but has always been *the* plan to bring both Jew and Gentile together into one new creation.[581]

The New Covenant has not been postponed but was established at the cross when Christ made animal sacrifices obsolete. According to the book of Hebrews, he replaced that system with his own blood that was shed—once and for all.[582]

Though Christ's Davidic throne is established spiritually in this age, they see the fullest extent of his kingdom being manifested in the future millennium of Revelation 20. At some time in the last days, the Jews will experience an awakening and the Holy Spirit will be poured out upon their nation. Those who embrace Jesus as their Messiah will be grafted back into the good olive tree, along with the Gentiles, who were grafted into the "cultivated" olive tree by faith.[583] The restoration of the Jews is a *spiritual* restoration to God, rather than a natural restoration back to Mosaic Covenant rituals. Again, according to the book of Hebrews, the Old Covenant was fulfilled and abolished at the cross through the redemptive work of Christ.[584]

The millennium in this view will *not* be a dominant, nationalistic, political, or theocratic Jewish era; nor will there be a reinstatement of Old Testament practices of animal sacrifices, feasts, and ritual ceremonies found in the Mosaic Covenant.

Historic Premillennialists do not believe in "two stages" of the second coming; they only see "one" coming. The rapture happens at the second visible return of Christ.

The 70-week prophecy of Daniel is interpreted as having *no* gap between the first sixty-nine weeks and the last week. They believe that Daniel's prophecy in chapter 9 was

---

[581] Ephesians 2:11-19
[582] Hebrews 9; 10:1-18
[583] Romans 11:11-24
[584] Hebrews 8:13

completely fulfilled at the stoning of the first church martyr, Stephen, in Acts 7.[585]

As for the Great Tribulation, they believe it took place in A.D. 70 when Rome ransacked Jerusalem, tore down the temple, and crucified a million-plus Jews. They don't believe the images of Revelation 4 through 18 are future events, but were rather fulfilled in the first century (with the exception of the "future" second coming of Christ and the millennium).

The Antichrist is not seen as a literal person, but as an *anti*-Christ "spirit" of evil forces and forms of government systems that have persecuted the church over the centuries. This Satanic spirit will continue to oppress Christians until the second coming, which is followed by a 1,000 years of righteousness, peace, and joy. Satan will be bound and chained during these 1,000 years until he's released for a short time at the end.[586]

Historic Premillennialists believe in two resurrections— the just at the beginning and the ungodly at the end. During the millennium, *mortals* (unbelievers who come into the millennial period from the previous age) will mingle with *immortals* (the dead saints who are resurrected into immortal bodies).

The mortal unbelievers will reproduce unregenerate offspring who will grow exponentially into the nations that Satan eventually deceives when he's released from the Abyss. They will rebel against Jesus and attack God's redeemed (the resurrected mortals), but God will send down fire on them and bring them before the Great White Throne Judgment to receive their eternal sentence in the lake of fire.

Here's how their chart looks:

---

[585] Acts 7:54-60
[586] Revelation 20:1-3

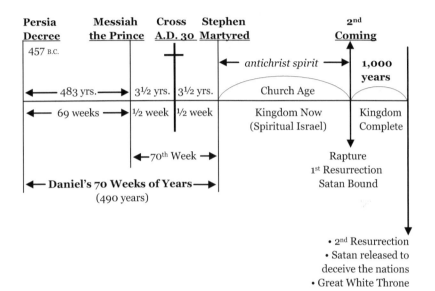

Postmillennialism

Proponents of this view believe that the 1,000 years is not literal but spiritual, i.e., it is an indefinite number that could also mean "forever." This period is more of a figure of speech, referring to all the years between the first and second coming of Jesus.

Like Historic Premillennialists, Postmillennialists also don't see the church as secondary to God's ultimate plan, but instead it has always been *the* plan to bring both Jew and Gentile together into one new creation. The New Covenant has *not* been postponed, but was established at the cross when Christ made animal sacrifices obsolete and replaced that system with his own shed blood—a once and for all sacrifice.

At some time in the last days, the Jews will embrace Jesus as their Messiah and be grafted back into the good olive tree.[587] The millennium in their view will not be a dominant, nationalistic, political, theocratic Jewish era, nor involve the Old Testament practices found in the Mosaic Covenant.

Postmillennialists also do not believe in "two stages" of the second coming; they only see "one" coming and the rapture is one and the same with the second visible return of Christ at the end of the undefined millennium period.

The 70-week prophecy of Daniel in chapter 9 was fulfilled completely at the stoning of the first church martyr, Stephen, in Acts 7.[588]

As for the Great Tribulation, they do not believe the images of Revelation 4 through 18 are future events. Instead, the church has always suffered tribulation and it will not stop until Christ returns *at the end* of the "undefined" millennium period when the church is sovereign over a "Christianized" world and Christ can come back to take his rightful place.

The Antichrist is not seen in this view as a literal person, but as an *anti*-Christ "spirit" of evil forces and forms of government systems that have persecuted the church over the centuries. Also, they don't see Satan released at the end to deceive the nations; instead he'll be "progressively" bound through the church.

Postmillennials believe in a general resurrection (not two) at the second coming of Christ. Both the just and the unjust will resurrect simultaneously in immortal bodies to go before the last court of judgment. There it will be determined who remains with God and who is cast into the lake of fire.

Here's how their chart looks:

---

[587] Romans 11:11-24
[588] Acts 7:54-60

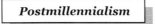

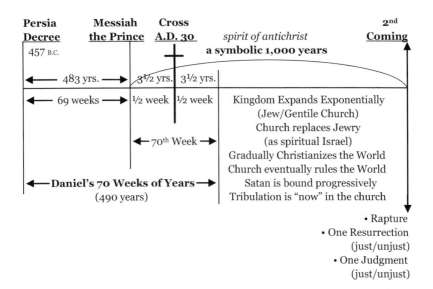

Persia	Messiah	Cross		2nd
Decree	the Prince	A.D. 30	*spirit of antichrist*	Coming
457 B.C.			**a symbolic 1,000 years**	

◄——— 483 yrs. ———► | 3½ yrs. | 3½ yrs.

◄——— 69 weeks ———► | ½ week | ½ week | Kingdom Expands Exponentially
(Jew/Gentile Church)
Church replaces Jewry
(as spiritual Israel)
Gradually Christianizes the World
Church eventually rules the World
Satan is bound progressively
Tribulation is "now" in the church

◄—70th Week—►

◄——Daniel's 70 Weeks of Years——►
(490 years)

• Rapture
• One Resurrection
(just/unjust)
• One Judgment
(just/unjust)

A-millennialism

Proponents of this view reject the idea of Revelation 20 being a literal 1,000-year period before or after the return of Christ—they believe this period is figurative. Their undefined, figurative millennium was ushered in at Christ's first coming and remains in place until the second coming of Christ where the just and the unjust are judged simultaneously.

They see Satan bound at the *first* coming of Christ until the second coming where he'll be thrown into the lake of fire.

Satan is unable to keep the nations deceived anymore from receiving the gospel throughout this time. Along with his angels, his release at the end is only for final judgment.

To the A-millennialist, there is no longer a place for Israel, only a spiritual Israel (Jew/Gentile)—the church, which is Christ's body and kingdom. No nationalistic, political, or material Jewish kingdom will exist as distinct from Gentiles. Both Jew and Gentile believers are seen as one new man, a new creation in Christ.

They believe that Daniel's 70-week prophecy was completed and fulfilled by the time of Stephen's stoning, so there is no secret rapture. The rapture and the general resurrection at Christ's second coming are one and the same event.

They also see the Great Tribulation fulfilled in A.D. 70 when Rome destroyed Jerusalem. Tribulation continues to this day, throughout the church age, until it culminates in the last days under the persecution of the Antichrist, the devil incarnate. The Antichrist is also seen as an "anti-Christ" spiritual system.

When Christ returns, the general resurrection occurs, the last judgment is complete, and eternity is set in place with a new heaven and a new Earth.

Here's how their chart looks:

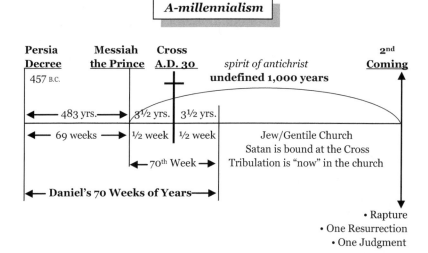

Partial Preterism

Proponents of this view often align their beliefs with Postmillennialism, while other Preterists align themselves with Historic Premillennialism. All three of these views believe that the majority of the prophecies in Revelation and Matthew 24 were already fulfilled by the time Jerusalem fell in A.D. 70; and they don't see the church as secondary to God's ultimate plan or the New Covenant being postponed.

They all believe at some time in the last days, the Jews will experience an awakening and embrace Jesus as their Messiah. The Jews will not become a distinct, dominant, nationalistic, political or theocratic Jewish kingdom, as the Dispensational Futurists believe. To the Partial Preterist, that opportunity for the Jews was lost when they rejected their Messiah at his first coming.

Partial Preterists do not believe in "two stages" of the second coming; they only see "one" coming, and the rapture is one and the same with the second visible return of Christ at the end of the age.

They all see the 70-week prophecy of Daniel in chapter 9 fulfilled completely at the stoning of the first church martyr, Stephen, in Acts 7. The Great Tribulation was fulfilled in the A.D. 70 destruction of Jerusalem by the Roman Empire during which a million-plus Jews were nailed to crosses that surrounded the city.

As for a last-day Great Tribulation, Partial Preterists don't believe the images of Revelation 4-18 are future events (most of Revelation to them is already fulfilled in church history). Instead of a Great Tribulation period, they believe the church has always suffered tribulation and it won't stop until the church is victorious over a Christianized world and Christ takes his rightful place.

Partial Preterists do not see the Antichrist as a literal person, but as an *anti*-Christ "spirit" of evil forces and forms of government systems that have persecuted the church throughout the centuries.

As for the millennial era, Partial Preterists go the way of the *Historic Premillennialist* or *Postmillennialist*. Consider the charts below of both these views regarding Christ's return, the millennium, the resurrections, Satan's release, and the Great White Throne Judgment:

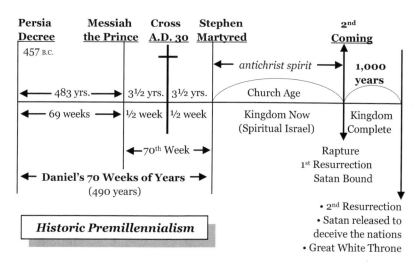

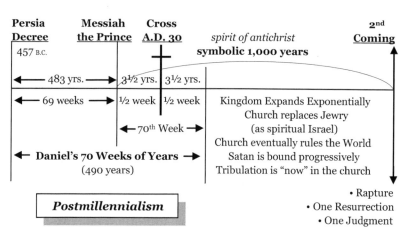

It is necessary to point out one thing about Partial Preterism—it's gaining popularity and teaches that a good portion of end-time prophecies are "non-literal." In my opinion, this is a dangerous approach to interpreting prophetic Scriptures, because it diminishes the importance of remaining alert to actual "literal" signs of the last days.

My concern is, will they be ready if they're wrong? How about those they teach? Will they even see the Antichrist coming when he comes, if they don't believe he will ever exist as a person?

Biblical hermeneutics can be applied to examine this "non-literal" approach. In his book, *Interpreting the Scriptures*, Kevin Conner provides a list of five "Methods of Interpretation." The three I mention below seem to apply to the Partial Preterist's way of interpreting end-time prophecies. Here they are (wording adapted and condensed):[589]

- ***The Allegorical Method***. This approach presumes the true meaning lies beneath the plain meaning of Scripture. It's problematic because there are no real guidelines or boundaries and is founded on the assumption that what God said plainly is not really what he meant.

- ***The Mystical Method***. This approach presumes multiple meanings lie beneath the plain meaning of Scripture. It can be misleading because its foundation is that God meant many other things than what he actually said.

- ***The Devotional Method***. This approach searches beyond the plain meaning of Scripture for spiritual meaning. It's dangerous because personal application may ignore the plain literal sense of what God was saying.

---

[589] Kevin J. Conner and Ken Malmin, *Interpreting the Scriptures: A Textbook on How to Interpret the Bible* (Portland, OR: City Bible Publishing, 1983), 13-14.

When interpreting the Bible, especially verses that deal with eschatology, it's safer to use the oldest method of interpretation since the days of Ezra the scribe.[590] This is the method (below) I use, and is the most accurate one to use.

- *The Literal Method*. This approach presumes if the "literal" sense makes plain sense then seek no other sense. It assumes that the plain meaning of Scripture is reliable. It assumes that all who believe will understand the Scriptures. It assumes that the Scriptures communicate what God wants man to know. And it doesn't exclude the figurative, spiritual meaning, application, or depth of meaning. [591]

---

[590] See Nehemiah 8:1-8
[591] Kevin J. Conner and Ken Malmin, *Interpreting the Scriptures: A Textbook on How to Interpret the Bible* (Portland, OR: City Bible Publishing, 1983), 15-16.

Chapter 45

Christian Millennialism

I CAN ONLY IMAGINE how much your head is swimming by now with all these different views on the millennium. It's hard to keep up with, isn't it? It still is for me and I'm a perpetual student of these things. It also would be easy to jump from one view to another in agreement, because they all seem to present some pretty good cases to support their positions.

Many of my brothers and sisters in Christ, who are scholars, serious students of the Word of God, and lovers of Christ, have formulated these views. There are some seriously significant historical and contemporary names, with very impressive credentials, who embrace one of these five views. I applaud everyone who desires and attempts to understand the end times with integrity. I applaud you for taking the time to ponder and consider the case I have made in this book of *my* views on eschatology, because it shows a hunger and passion on your part to want to know what awaits God's people. With all that said, I cast no aspersions on anyone who believes differently than me on this subject, because we're all looking for answers and truth about the hope that lies ahead.

Ever since God called me to preach in 1973, I have remained sobered by the fact that any of us who teach must stand before God to give an account for what we believe and teach others.[592] In the case of eschatology, no one can clearly see every detail about events that have not happened yet. We can only offer our best understanding and grasp of truth with as clear a conscience as possible and, hopefully, without making our views an *immutable*[593] gospel. This is why I fall upon God's grace through Paul's words to the church at Corinth:

> Now we see but a poor reflection as in a mirror; *then* we shall see face to face. Now I know in part; *then* I shall know fully, even as I am fully known.[594]

Given the five views of the millennium in the previous chapter, let me say that my studies have brought me to a *hybrid* interpretation of sorts, where I agree with different aspects of some of those views while attempting to remain balanced. So I wish to present you now with the parts I *do* agree with and arrange them in an order (accompanied by a chart) of how I see it visually.

The view I've arrived at is a sixth view called *Christian Millennialism,* a term originally used by Kevin Conner to describe the distillation of his collective observations. If you're a serious student of end times, you won't find a more thorough treatise on the subject than Kevin's book, *The Christian Millennium.* I highly recommend it. Of all the six views I've examined, I've adopted "Christian Millennialism" as the most balanced view when applying hermeneutics to end-time prophecies. Let's take a look.

The 70th Week of Daniel's 70-Week Prophecy

Christian Millennialism sees Daniel's 70-week prophecy fulfilled and completed at the second coming of Christ. The

---

592 James 3:1
593 Unchangeable
594 1 Corinthians 13:12

first 69½ weeks are fulfilled up to the cross in A.D. 30 when Jesus is cut off in the middle of the 70th week. The last half of the seventieth week is picked up in Revelation chapters 11 through 18, the only other place you'll find "three-and-one-half years" mentioned in end-time prophecies.

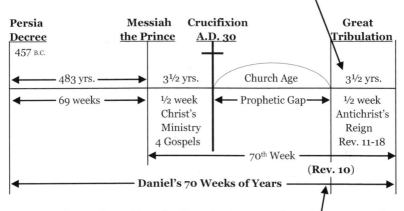

I addressed earlier, in Revelation 10, that John eats the little scroll (Daniel's book). He then begins to prophesy the events of the last three-and-one-half years, leading up to the second coming of Christ.

Unlike future dispensationalists, I believe that every place Revelation mentions a three-and-one-half-year period it isn't a reference to one of two different halves of the seventieth week. I see it as the same three-and-one-half period describing different events and activities happening at the same time. In the "Charts" section in the back of this book, I present a more detailed chart of Daniel's 70-week prophecy.

Jew and Gentile—the two become one

Christian Millennialism does not see the church as parenthetical but *the* plan God had devised before time, in his eternal purposes; that is, to bring every tribe, language and nation into his family as a new creation in Christ.595 The root of Abraham, the patriarchs, the prophets, the covenants, the Law were all part of the "redemptive" plan, and the necessary foundation for the purposes of God to bring both Jew and Gentile together. Gentiles needed the root, the natural olive tree of the chosen people, so that they, who were not a people, could be grafted into the olive tree and become God's people when they received Christ.596

Jesus broke down the middle wall of partition between Jews and Gentiles and removed the animosity through his blood covenant, the New Covenant, which he established and ratified at the cross. His "new" covenant fulfilled and established the Abrahamic Covenant created to bless "all" the families of the Earth.597 Both Jew and Gentile, in Christ, are now a part of the Kingdom of God, a kingdom that is manifested and expressed on Earth, as it is in heaven, through the vehicle of Christ's church. In Christ, there is no Jew, no Gentile—all are one in him.598

With this in mind, Christian Millennialism doesn't profess a nationalist, political, theocratic Jewish millennium. It also doesn't endorse Old Testament practices of animal sacrifices and ritual ceremonies happening in the millennium. According to the book of Hebrews, Jesus made all Old Testament animal sacrifices and rituals obsolete and, therefore, all the Law, the Psalms, and the Prophets were fulfilled in him.599

To go back to animal sacrifice is *covenantal confusion*, because in the millennium, there'll be no sinners who will require animal sacrifices for sin. We don't require animal sacrifices today, because we have Jesus. So why—even if

---

595 2 Corinthians 5:17; Ephesians 2:11-19; Galatians 6:15
596 See 1 Peter 2:9-10 with Romans 11:17-24
597 Genesis 12:2-3
598 Galatians 3:26-28
599 Matthew 5:17; Hebrews 8

there were sinners in the millennium— wouldn't the blood of Jesus be adequate enough to save people's souls then? The New Covenant had replaced all the Old Testament covenants. It is and always will be an everlasting covenant, never needing to be replaced.[600]

The millennial population

As I've shared earlier in this book, I believe only Christians will populate the millennium, due to the overwhelming evidence of Scriptures that show no sinners will survive the second coming of Christ. I understand why some believe there'll be sinners then, because it's difficult to reconcile which nations Satan will deceive at the end of the millennium.[601] I'll address that more in my sequel: *In the Light of Eternity.*

The Christian Millennium will be home to the "redeemed" from all ages under their respective covenants— Hebrew, Jew, and Gentile alike—from all of human history. They'll be rewarded and positioned in Christ's kingdom according to their deeds done in this life, not according to their ethnic roots. There'll be ethnicity, yes, but not the supremacy of one nation over another. All will be one in Christ Jesus, but not all will be rewarded the same. Jesus will love all, but not all will carry the same rank and responsibilities he assigns them.

The rapture and the tribulation

Christian Millennialists do not see evidence in Scripture of a "two-stage" coming of Christ—that is, a "secret" rapture seven years before Jesus returns as physically as when he ascended.[602] Instead, the rapture is seen taking place at the

---

[600] Hebrews 9:11-15
[601] Revelation 20:7-8
[602] Acts 1:10-11

second coming, after the three-and-one-half years is completed. This includes the first resurrection of the righteous dead, followed immediately by the "rapture" of the bride company which had been hidden and preserved in the desert.[603]

The book of Revelation is approached "literally" in the symbolism of events that will take place in the last days. I don't relish such times as these, where the ungodly will be judged. But like the children of Israel in the land of Goshen in Egypt, it's necessary that we'll be in the vicinity of the judgments God pours on the Earth, before and during the Great Tribulation. I wish it didn't have to be that way; it will be a difficult and dark time. That's why my hope lies in the victorious and glorious bride of Christ and the harvest of souls she will gather. Throughout history, the church has experienced numerous degrees of severe persecution and we'll not escape the last one coming, if we're alive at that time.

The Antichrist

Christian Millennialism believes that the "spirit" of the antichrist is already at work in the world, and has been since the church began. It is the spirit that now works in the "children of disobedience"[604] and lies within many symbolic historical figures and their government systems—such as Nimrod, Pharaoh, Nebuchadnezzar, Antiochus Epiphanes, Nero, Herod, Hitler and others. John wrote in his first epistle that this antichrist spirit was already at work in the world back then,[605] and we can still see it at work in the world's systems today. In fact, this spirit is in everyone who doesn't

---

[603] 1 Corinthians 15:51-52; 1 Thessalonians 4:16-17; Revelation 12:6, 14
[604] Ephesians 2:2
[605] 1 John 4:2-3

acknowledge Jesus as Lord and savior, but rejects the fact of his deity.[606]

In the end, there will be a complete embodiment of this antichrist spirit in the man of lawlessness, the beast of Revelation 13. He'll be a world ruler and dictator, according to the Scriptures.

Jesus said many would come in the last days—literal people who will claim to be Christ. Paul warned, in his letter to the Thessalonians, that a "literal" person is coming. So when considering the plain text of the Scriptures, it would be a stretch to believe that the "antichrist" would *not* be a specific person, but only symbolic of governmental systems.

It is the beast, the Antichrist, who will come against God, blaspheme his name and his people, and gather an army against him in the battle of Armageddon. He'll be wise and claim to be *the* messiah. To ignore this and attribute it to the past—as come and gone—is to ignore Paul's warning that before Jesus returns in his second coming, there will come a great falling away of saints and a "man" of lawlessness will arise to deceive the world through false signs and wonders.

When did that happen in history? Who was this man of lawlessness, if he had already come? Yes, Christians have fallen away, and there have been many "wanna-be" Antichrists, but Paul pinpoints the timing of this man at the "end of the age," just before Jesus returns.[607] And Paul goes on to say that this man of lawlessness, the son of perdition, will be overthrown and destroyed by the breath of Christ's mouth and the splendor of his coming. This is confirmed in the exact same description John gives in Revelation 19 of what Jesus will do to the beast and the False Prophet, who have both performed miraculous signs.

---

[606] 1 John 4:3
[607] 2 Thessalonians 2:1-11

For all these reasons given, Christian Millennialists see a "literal" Antichrist-beast—a physical, wicked, human being, who will be thrown alive into the lake of fire.[608]

Satan and the resurrections

Christian Millennialism believes in a "literal" 1,000-year period and places it after the visible, physical return of Christ. When Jesus returns, he'll take Satan, physically bind him with a great chain, lock him up in the Abyss and seal it so that he can't influence or harm anyone for a thousand years.[609]

At the end of the thousand years, the second resurrection takes place. It is the resurrection of the ungodly wicked and nations.[610] Satan will be released from the Abyss to pick up where he left off—deceiving all the resurrected nations he can to join his hatred and hostility against God and his people. Collectively, these nations are called "Gog and Magog" and will gather together for battle against the camp of God's people.[611] These nations will be devoured by a deluge of fire and brought before the Great White Throne for final sentencing and punishment.[612] It's at this time that everyone's eternal destinies are settled by the court of the Ancient of Days.

> As I [Daniel] looked, thrones were set in place, and the **Ancient of Days** took his seat.
>
> His clothing was as white as snow; the hair of his head was white like wool.
>
> His throne was flaming with fire, and its wheels were all ablaze.

---

[608] Revelation 19:17-20
[609] Revelation 20:1-3
[610] Daniel 12:2; John 5:28-29; Revelation 20:5 (the parenthetical sentence)
[611] Revelation 20:7-9
[612] Revelation 20:11-15

> A river of fire was flowing coming out from before him.
> Thousands upon thousands attended him; ten thousand
> times ten thousand stood before him.
> The court was seated, and the books were opened.
>
> —*Daniel 7:9-10*

The chart below is how I see the events unfold. You'll see a more detailed version in the "Charts" section at the back.

Christian Millennialism

Cyrus' Decree	Messiah the Prince	Cross A.D. 30		Bride	Second Coming	White Throne
457 B.C.						

←— 483 yrs. —→ | 3½ yrs | *←— antichrist spirit —→* | Church Age | 3½ yrs. | 1,000 yrs. | Eternity

←— 69 wks. —→ | ½ wk. | Kingdom of God | ½ wk. | Christian
4 Gospels | Jew/Gentile—One New Man | Antichrist | Millennium
(Prophetic Gap) | Rev. 11-18
(Rev. 10)

←——————— 70th Week ———————→

←——————— Daniel's 70 Weeks of Years ———————→
(490 years)

Rapture
1st Resurrection
Satan Bound

• 2nd Resurrection
• Satan released to
  deceive the nations
• Great White Throne

In the light of eternity

I have mentioned my sequel to this book several times now. *In The Light of Eternity* will address a number of things that Revelation doesn't reveal about what our lives will look like during the 1,000-year reign of Christ. It's one of the most exciting studies I've ever embarked on and have taught it in many churches over the years. It'll be the crown to the story of Revelation and God's eternal plan for our lives. It will also provide a greater hope for the times you and I might go through before Christ returns.

It was for this hope that many have gone before us, looking for a country of their own. Not a country in this life, but a better country, a heavenly one,[613] with a city that God has prepared for those who love him.

> He has made everything beautiful in its time. He has also set **eternity** in the hearts of men; yet they cannot fathom what God has done from beginning to end.
>
> *—Ecclesiastes 3:11*

---

[613] Hebrews 11:13-16

Chapter 46

A Closing Word

I AM A FALLIBLE human being, limited in my scope and understanding of the height, width, depth, and breadth of God's infinite wisdom and knowledge. I'll never fully grasp the vastness of his treasures that await us in heaven and in the age to come. I can only press on in my learning.

For this reason, I recommend that you lay the teachings I've presented to you before the Lord and ask the Holy Spirit to shed light on what's good and what's not. Only he can reveal and teach you truth; we have an anointing from him to do so, according to John.[614]

Next I ask that, if you come to embrace these teachings, then hold them loosely. God may want to reveal more to you or tweak a little of what you believe. I always want to remain open to the Holy Spirit's leading, and have no desire to be dogmatic about these things.

I believe in holding fast to obvious truths, but those things that are still obscure and require cold, hard reality to confirm—those are God's to take and discard where I'm wrong. I refuse to lose sleep over things that are subjective and require continued revelation to build upon the foundation laid. When it comes to convictions of eschatology, I have no dog in the fight of arguing over

---

[614] 1 John 2:20, 27

*non*essentials, though I may strongly challenge the methods of interpretation used.

Being a good steward of God's Word requires honesty and integrity. We need to share our insights with a clear conscience and an open hand, ready to make adjustments whenever time uncovers additional truth. That's my commitment to those I teach on this subject.

Maybe, possibly, hopefully and *could be* are all viable answers in this department. So at the end of the day, it will still come down to our best understanding.

I also want to remind us all that when it comes to future prophecies, not even John and Daniel understood all they wrote down for us in the future. To quote again what Kevin Conner said in the Foreword: "Only history proves prophecy."

Occupy till he comes

This subtitle statement is the King James Version of Luke 19:13. It is in the context of a parable Jesus gave about ten servants who were given responsibilities by their nobleman before he left for a distant country and told them to "occupy till I come."

The nobleman would return one day as king to examine these servants and see what they did with his investments. Two of them doubled what was given them while the third one hid his money and returned it without increase.

Of course the nobleman, now a king, was pleased with the first two, but upset with the last servant who made no effort. He had told his three servants, "Do business (occupy) with what I've given you until I return."

The moral application to this story is that you and I have been given the gift of salvation, spiritual gifts and talents, and multiple opportunities through life to reproduce and increase what the Lord has invested in us. While he's away, we must not hide these investments because we believe our King might return at "any moment." Instead, we must keep on with living out our lives and be about our Father's business until Christ returns.

When I was a young and immature Christian, I dissuaded others from going to college, or going after a career and other such nonsense because I mistakenly thought Jesus was coming at any moment. So why bother?

That was before history (40 years later) that the "any moment" didn't come about like I was certain it would at that time.

Because we don't know and can't claim certainty until *history proves prophecy*, we must live life as though he could come today, while living it as though he may not—i.e., continuing to be faithful stewards and increase what he's given us to multiply until he returns to reward our efforts. Keep one eye on the sky, ready to meet him, and the other on the plow, looking straight ahead. That's how I live.

Stay humble—watch out for Bride pride

As for the concept of the bride of Christ, I ask that you be careful with this teaching and don't turn it into a cloak or excuse for "elitism" or "legalism" upon your life and others. The day you think you qualify enough for the bride is the day you begin to trust in what you think *you're* doing to make that happen. The focus then is placed on "self and works," rather than a *relationship* with Jesus.

Just because I know about the concept of the bride of Christ—that is, if it's correctly interpreted—doesn't make me ready to meet him. As I look at my life today, I know there are so many areas I have yet to surrender to Jesus; many of which I'm unaware of. For one, I know I have pride in my life in ways I haven't even discovered, at least not until the Holy Spirit reveals it to me.

If I put my trust in a list of things that I believe would qualify me, then I'll begin to measure everyone else by those same standards of which I could be way off the mark. I'm unable to judge myself and my motives, let alone the hearts and motives of others. Such a mindset would take me down the path of "Bride Pride," and I assure you, that's not healthy.

If this is a serious piece of truth in the end-time puzzle— and I believe it is—then, yes, serving God should be taken seriously, but more importantly, "loving" God is the operative word.

To qualify for the bride of Christ requires only one true, authentic thing, and that's loving him with all your heart, soul, mind and body. It's a biblical way of saying, "Be all in!"

How "being all in" looks to you, as you walk that out, is between you and God. Don't start adding self-imposed rules or laws you think will help you make it when the Bridegroom comes. There's enough in the Bible to show you how to love God intimately and passionately. Obedience to the Holy Spirit's promptings, for one, will be a very good indicator of the depth and width your love has for him.

At the risk of sounding like I'm contradicting myself, I advise you to walk in the peace of being Christ's bride *today*. That way you're not focusing on your deficiency, but rather *his* sufficiency. If you keep your mind on things above—God himself—and not on things of this earth—where you fall short—then you don't have to wait to see if you qualify.

You must realize that you're already "betrothed"[615] to him *today*, with the seal of the Holy Spirit[616] upon you as the down payment or dowry for your life together. So enjoy him as his bride right now, *today*. Live in total awareness of his

---

[615] 2 Corinthians 11:2—"I am jealous for you with godly jealousy. For I have **betrothed** you to one husband, that I may present you as a chaste virgin to Christ." (New King James Version)
[616] Ephesians 1:13-14

love and grace, anticipating the joy you'll experience on that day when he comes for you. Don't focus on what you aren't; focus on who he is. Keep your eyes on him, abide in his vine, cling to him, love him with all your heart and you'll be ready with enough oil in your lamp to meet him.

Discipleship—increasing the King's investment

Because I want so badly for Christians to experience this kind of love and intimacy with Christ, I've designed a way to equip God's people to discover this through discipleship.

In 2011, God showed me that a return to discipleship will come to the church and he gave me a system to contribute as a resource for that movement. It is a system that develops a lifestyle of discipleship and is called *The Discipleship Group, 26 Weeks with God through Partnership*. Testimonies from those who have participated in a discipleship group claim it has exponentially accelerated their love and knowledge of God.

As of this writing, the first three of six books are done. Each book is a journey of 26 weeks with *six* sections of weekly assignments that you experience with two or three others. Each week layers upon the previous weeks, and each book layers upon the previous books, until you have gone through all six books. That comes to three years of training— the same amount of time Jesus invested in training his disciples.

If you'd like to learn how to experience discipleship and disciple others, then here is a simple, yet profound way to grow in your Christian walk. It can help in laying a strong foundation for becoming an *overcomer* in the last days.

To order your book, email me at: **jay@jayzinn.com**

Or go to: **www.iZeeBooks.com**

Coming in 2015

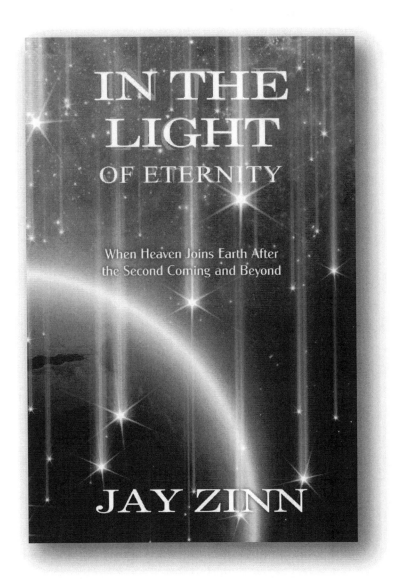

APPENDIX

Acknowledgments

First, I thank God for my wife, Roseann, and the sacrifices she makes to allow me the amount of time I need to hole up in my office and prepare a manuscript for a book. Her grace, encouragement and support have made this book possible.

I'm also thankful for my friend, Cec Murphey, who inspires and encourages me to pursue my dream to write. His mentoring, teaching, and coaching have given me the tools to express my thoughts and ideas on paper.

My friend, Sloan Milliken, a literary major who has helped me hone my writing skills.

I am thankful for my "anonymous" line editor, who spent countless hours polishing my book for print. She's meticulous and I appreciate her expertise.

Then there's my graphic artist, Megan Byrd, who continues to knock out amazing cover designs. I am always happy with her images, which skillfully reflects the content of my books.

Finally, I must list the great men who have contributed on many levels to my journey studying eschatology.

First, there's Pastor Jim Quigley. He opened my eyes to the truth that Jesus was coming back. His class on Matthew 24 provoked my salvation decision on January 9, 1972.

My pastor in Anchorage, Dick Benjamin, who first took me through the book of Revelation during Bible School in Anchorage. He introduced to me the concept of the bride of Christ.

My Bible School teacher, Dick Strutz, who first taught me how to interpret Daniel's 70-week prophecy. That foundation continues to unlock the events of Revelation.

Pastor W.H. Offiler (who taught Dick Benjamin) became a teacher to me through his incredible eschatological insights that he left behind in his books. I never had the privilege of meeting him, but I'm the product of his passion and conviction to understand end-time truths.

Offiler's protégé, Pastor W.W. Patterson, explained the truths he discovered in the book of Revelation. Through his notes and the personal sessions I had with him, he provided greater clarity and understanding of Revelation and Daniel.

Finally, I am grateful to my teacher, Kevin J. Conner, who has written the most incredible in-depth books on end times and hermeneutics I've ever read. His writings and seminars have provided me with the tools to correctly handle God's Word and interpret the Scriptures. Brother Conner became my friend and mentor through his letters, books, phone calls and private one-on-one sessions. He brought me even deeper into the vast truths in Daniel and Revelation. In my opinion, he's among one of the greatest teachers of truth I know. To him I owe so much.

Author's Bio

I became a Christian on January 9, 1972 while serving in the Air Force in Florida. During a month-long mission trip to Nicaragua, a calling began to stir in my heart, and was later confirmed by a spiritual encounter I had with God in prayer.

Not long after, orders came to me for a new assignment to an Air Force base in Anchorage, Alaska, and brought me into a thriving church in the fall of 1973. It was called Abbott Loop Christian Center, pastored by Dick Benjamin. My calling was confirmed in that church, through prophetic ministry. After three years of equipping and training, Dick and his church ordained me, and then sent my wife, Roseann, and me with a team of five people to plant our first church in Fort Walton Beach, Florida. I've planted two others since then.

After 40 years of pastoral and teaching ministry, I now serve the church as "Jay Zinn Ministries, Inc." During my journey pastoring my churches, I acquired my Doctorate of Ministry and a Ph.D. in Theology through Logos Christian College and Graduate School in Jacksonville, Florida.

In the last decade I became one of the founding members of Vanguard Network International, an accountability group of apostolic and prophetic ministers and churches. I serve on the team as an apostle and mentor to other pastors and churches. I also travel each year to minister nationally and internationally as a conference speaker.

On a personal note, I've been a published artist with Penny Lane Publishing and have my own studio and website gallery called, Jay Zinn Art (www.jayzinnart.com). I'm also the author of the novel, *The Unveiling*, published in 1997. Lord willing, the second, revised edition will be published in 2017.

As for my family, I have been married to my bride and life partner, Roseann, since 1974. We have two adult children, and a granddaughter.

To ask questions or leave comments about how this book has encouraged you, contact me at:

jay@jayinn.com

My original and published art may be found at:

www.jayzinnart.com

My other published works, will be released in 2015 through my publishing company, iZee Books at:

www.iZeeBooks.com

My mailing address is:

Dr. Jay Zinn
P.O. Box 306
Davidson, NC 28036

To learn more about the seminars I schedule
on the book of Revelation,
check out my availability or itinerary at
my Jay Zinn Ministries website:

www.jzministries.org

Hermeneutics Must Apply

ESCHATOLOGY IS a jigsaw puzzle that can only be put together a piece at a time. This is a project that requires the right tools to know where to place each piece. The application of these tools is called "hermeneutics," which is *the art and science of interpretation.*

Kevin Conner and his protégé, Ken Malmin, have written an outstanding textbook on these principles.[617] I've been to Kevin's seminars twice and have also taught a condensed version of his book in weekend seminars. He's also written a book about the principles used to interpret the book of Revelation.[618]

Another great textbook on Hermeneutics is written by J. Edwin Hartill called, *Principles of Biblical Hermeneutics.*[619]

Everything you've read in my book has had to go through the rigors and scrutiny of these principles. You simply cannot interpret end-time prophecies without it. Not if you want checks and balances to come alongside subjective revelation and inspiration.

So here are the tools or principles necessary for interpreting eschatology, and a brief description of what each one does:

---

[617] Kevin J. Conner and Ken Malmin, *Interpreting the Scriptures: A Textbook on How to Interpret the Bible* (Portland, OR: City Bible Publishing, 1983).

[618] Kevin J. Conner, *Principles of Interpreting the Book of Revelation* (Blackburn, Victoria: Acacia Press Pty. Ltd., 1995).

[619] J. Edwin Hartill, *Principles of Biblical Hermeneutics* (Grand Rapids, MI: Zondervan Publishing House, 1947).

The Context Principle (the First Principle of Hermeneutics)

This principle avoids the danger of taking an isolated passage or verse to prove a misguided theory or doctrine. It sheds light on near or remote passages relating to the same theme in the context of the whole Bible. It also lets clear statements of Scripture (on the same theme) interpret the obscure.

The First Mention Principle

The first time a *subject* (not just a specific word) is mentioned in Scripture, this principle unlocks the door into a progressive unfolding of truth threading its way throughout the Bible. This comes in handy when you're looking for the origin and nature of a particular topic. For example, Babylon is first noted in Genesis as the first city founded and built by Nimrod.

The Comparative Mention Principle

This is the principle that compares "spiritual things with spiritual." Certain subjects and themes (with more than one verse or passage) can be clarified (or interpreted) by comparing or contrasting points of resemblance or differences. You'll notice that I used this on several occasions in my book, such as comparing the contrasts of Jesus with the Antichrist or the similarities of the two witnesses, Moses and Elijah.

The Progressive Mention Principle

This shows how a theme or subject will progressively unfold with *added details* as it proceeds through the Bible. Those additional details relate to truths that God revealed at the very first mention of the theme or subject.

The Complete Mention Principle

This principle uses *all* Scripture references on any given subject to determine the interpretation. It works in tandem with the First Mention and Progressive Mention Principles.

The Election Principle

This principle illustrates how God sovereignly selects **persons** and **nations** involved in carrying out his eternal purposes. It clarifies passages or verses related to God's process of election, which is based on God's foreknowledge.[620] In the case of eschatology, it's important in discovering the selection process of God through foreknowledge regarding the righteous and the ungodly.

For instance, Judas Iscariot and the Antichrist share the same title. Both are referred to as the "son of perdition."[621] In Greek, *perdition* means *loss* or *ruin*. Judas lost his place among the twelve apostles by betraying Jesus, leading to his ruin and destruction.

By foreknowledge, God knew about Judas' greed and love of money. If the Antichrist is a fallen apostle like Judas, then God has foreknowledge of his character, too. Like Judas, I believe the Antichrist will lose his place among the twelve last-day apostles, and face ruin and ultimate destruction.

The Covenant Principle

The Bible is a book of nine covenants. This principle helps interpret Scriptures with *covenantal language*. To uncover the literal, clear, and basic meaning of any Scripture requires an understanding of "which covenant" is being referred to. It also helps to know which elements of the older covenants have or have not been *filtered* through the cross, which establishes the last and current covenant—the New Covenant.

In my opinion, the Covenant Principle is neglected when it comes to studying eschatology. You cannot use this tool and come to the conclusion that the Mosaic Covenant could actually be reinstated in the millennium. That's why I referred to such an interpretation as *covenantal confusion*. All covenants, after the Edenic Covenant, are steps in the ladder toward the New Covenant.

---

[620] 1 Peter 1:1-2 with Romans 8:28
[621] John 17:12; 2 Thessalonians 2:3; Revelation 17:11—all referring to the Antichrist (Kings James Version).

You never can go back to any of the previous covenants that the New Covenant has made obsolete.

The Ethnic-Division Principle

This principle is used to interpret any verse or passage in light of God's *appointed* ethnic divisions. For example:

Acts 17:26-27

> And He has made from one blood every nation of men to dwell on all the face of the earth, and has (pre)**determined** their **pre-appointed** times and the boundaries of their dwellings.

It doesn't take long to see that the greatest controversy in eschatology surrounds the nation of Israel and all the other nations made up of Gentiles. How (and where) will they find their place in the millennium? In the Old Testament, you can find only two major ethnic groups: Israel (Hebrew tribes of Israel) and Gentiles (all non-Israeli peoples and nations). In the Old Testament, God had called Israel to be separate from the world, so a divide definitely existed between God's covenant people and Gentiles. In the New Testament, the cross removed this division. Both ethnic groups are brought together to form a new race—a new creation.

If you do not apply both the *Covenantal Principle* and the *Ethnic-Division Principle* toward interpreting end-times prophecy, you'll wind up with a nationalistic, Jewish millennium with a supreme race over a lesser (i.e., the Jews over Gentiles) and a return to an Old Testament covenant (the Mosaic Covenant), which Christ made obsolete—permanently.

The New Covenant did away with divisions based on ethnicity, superiority or nationality. The Kingdom of God isn't now, nor ever will be again, a Jewish Kingdom (though it does come from Israel's roots going back to Abraham). In God's Kingdom, after the cross, you'll find a new race, a new creation, in which there is neither Jew nor Gentile, slave nor free, male nor female. All will be one in the household of God—the eternal church.[622]

---

[622] Galatians 3:26-29

The Chronometrical Principle

This principle serves to reveal God's measurement of time by divisions and periods, eternally arranged to accomplish his plans and purposes for mankind. These divisions or periods are referred to as "ages" in the Bible. These ages fall into three categories: *Past Ages, the Present Age* and *Future Ages*.

> **Hebrews 1:1-2**—"In many separate revelations—each of which set forth a portion of Truth—and in different ways God spoke of old to [our] forefathers in *and* by the prophets. [But] in the last of these days He has spoken to us in [the person of a] Son, Whom He appointed Heir *and* lawful Owner of all things, also by *and* through Whom He created the worlds *and* the reaches of space *and* the **ages of time**—[that is,] He made, produced, built, operated and arranged them in order."
>
> *The Amplified Bible*

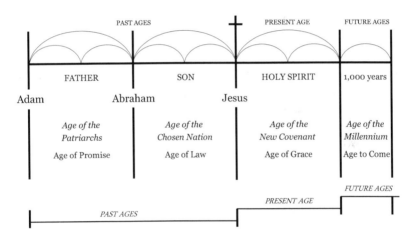

When applied to eschatology, this principle works to minimize any confusion about which particular prophecy is applicable in its appropriate boundaries and setting.

Each of the ages above carries with it a particular covenant or covenants. For example, the Age of the Patriarchs (age of promise) begins with the Adamic Covenant[623] followed 1,500 years later by the Noahic Covenant[624] after the flood recedes.

Next, the Age of the Chosen Nation (age of law) opens up with the Abrahamic Covenant,[625] 2,000 years after Adam and 2,000 years before Christ. Within this Age of the Chosen Nation are the Mosaic Covenant,[626] the Palestinian Covenant (or land covenant),[627] and the Davidic Covenant.[628] All the covenants, particularly the Mosaic, contained laws dealing with the nation of Israel. These laws act as a tutor, so to speak, in order to bring us to Christ.[629]

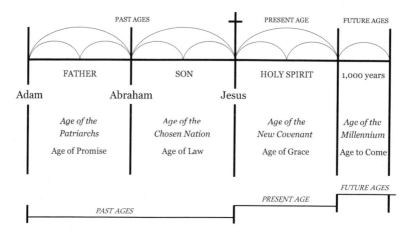

In the Age of the New Covenant (the age of grace), Jesus fulfilled all the covenants in the Old Testament himself through the New Covenant he ratified by his own blood.[630] This covenant is in play today and will remain in play forever through the millennium and beyond into the future ages.

---

[623] Genesis 3:15
[624] Genesis 9:1-17
[625] Genesis 12:1-3; 15:1-19
[626] Exodus 20-40; Leviticus 1-27
[627] Deuteronomy 26-29
[628] 2 Samuel 7
[629] Galatians 3:23-25
[630]Luke 22:20; Acts 20:28; Romans 3:25; Ephesians 1:7; 2:13; Colossians 1:20; Hebrews 9:12, 14, 18; 10:19; 12:24; 13:12; Revelation 5:9

If you look at the bottom of the chart on the previous page, you'll see as each age progresses, you climb higher toward what is better. God never goes back; he moves forward to a better hope, a better sacrifice, a better covenant, better promises, better possessions, a better country, and a better resurrection.

This is why we can anticipate that the Future Age of the Millennium will not return to the Old Testament sacrificial system of animals, as some believe will happen.

A Jewish (Mosaic) millennium isn't *better*; it is inferior to the age of grace that precedes it—the Age of the New Covenant. If we really believe that the New Covenant is postponed until the millennium, then that will be an age of mixing Moses with Jesus. This is the issue Paul disputed constantly with his unredeemed Jewish brethren—i.e., urging his fellow Jews to step up to a *better* covenant than continuing to cling to the Law.

The "age" and the respective "covenant" is key to interpreting end-time prophecies in the Old Testament. For example, you can't put the sacrificial and priestly activity described in Ezekiel 40-48 in the "Age of the Millennium." Because the millennial age is better than any previous one, the Mosaic covenant activities don't belong there. Ezekiel 40-48 may have some spiritual application yet to be discovered as the Holy Spirit sheds more light on those chapters.

The *Chronometrical Principle* is another example of how important it is to apply the tools of hermeneutics to eschatology.

The Breach Gap Principle

When I gave you the prophetic timeline and chart of Daniel's 70-week prophecy, the interpretation I presented in this book showed a "gap" or "breach" between the first one-half week and the last one-half week of the 70th week; i.e., three-and-one-half years of Christ's public ministry for the first half, and three-and-one-half years of the Antichrist's control of the world (see 70-week chart in the back of the book). Many have difficulty reconciling the legitimacy of this break in the timeline; however, it is one of the principles of hermeneutics scholars agree with.

For example, when Jesus taught in the synagogue in Nazareth, he quoted a passage from the prophet Isaiah regarding the fulfillment of his own mission. His last words from the passage ended with, "to proclaim the acceptable year of the Lord's favor."[631] Jesus did not finish the rest of the sentence, which reads, *"and the day of vengeance of our God."*[632] What Jesus was demonstrating, by not quoting the rest of the prophecy, was that the fulfillment of the Word had to stop at that point in time with the Lord's favor.

At his first coming, Jesus came to save lives, not destroy them. However, at the end of the age, he will return to complete the remaining quote of that prophecy, *"the day of vengeance of our God."* The life of Jesus fulfilled Isaiah's prophecy in his first coming, but the rest of it is on hold until he returns with a vengeance upon the ungodly in his second coming. This means there's a "breach" or "gap" in that prophecy's fulfillment—for now.

In the same way, the first 69½ weeks of Daniel's prophecy was fulfilled through the public ministry of Christ to the cross at his first coming. That means the last one-half week (three-and-one-half years) is on hold, until it is unsealed in the last days and carried out to its completion in the second coming. So you see, a "gap" in the prophecy is perfectly legitimate because there is hermeneutic precedence for it in other places in the Bible. I've only shown you one example.

The Law of Double Reference

Not much needs to be said about this principle other than there are characters in the Old Testament whose lives mirror the nature and character traits of *future* persons. By looking at their lives, and the prophecies spoken to and about them (either as a warning or blessing), you'll find a significant reflection of the two and discover truths that can apply to some future individual.

Such examples in eschatology surround Old Testament characters that *foreshadow* the Antichrist and what he will do in the last days. This can be seen in the historical king of Syria, Antiochus Epiphanes in Daniel 11; or the prince of Tyre in Ezekiel

---

[631] Isaiah 61:1-2a with Luke 4:16-21
[632] Isaiah 61:2b with Luke 4:16-21

28:1-10, son of the king of Tyre, who is a clear description of Satan in Ezekiel 28:11-17.

Contrast the character and words of the prince of Tyre (or the son of Satan) in Ezekiel 28:1-10 *with* the character and words of the Antichrist in 2 Thessalonians 2:4, and the beast in Revelation 13:5-6. This is how the *Law of Double Reference* is used to unearth contrasting truths and details of characters in the end times.

The Direct Statement Principle

God means what he says and says what he means. When interpreting any Scripture or passage, always accept the literal meaning of the words of the passage unless there is strong evidence to do otherwise. In other words, *when the literal sense makes sense, seek no other sense.* Of course this includes understanding the original intent and application the writer had in mind in the context of the original language it was written in, the people who were being addressed, and the customary use of the phrase at the time.

There are so many "figures of speech" in the context of eschatology that too many interpreters don't really interpret. Instead they "spiritualize" passages with conjecture and pretext rather than stay within the boundaries of grammatical rules and context. They fail to address first the *literal sense* of the passage or verse and the time or era it speaks to. Once the literal interpretation is discovered, applications can be made—as long as they are consistent with the literal interpretation. Kevin Conner taught me—*one interpretation, many applications.*

In the case of Revelation 20 and the 1,000-year reign, interpreters throw aside the literal sense and turn 1,000 years into an undefined period of time that could mean "forever," then they fit it into whatever timeframe they want. This is very shaky ground to build any teaching on. It shifts like a house built on sand.

The Figure of Speech Group

This is a group of five hermeneutic principles that are *metaphoric* in nature. They are figures of speech in which a word or phrase is regarded as representative or symbolic of an event, person, place, action, or object. It can come in the form of a symbol, type, allegory, or parable. This is demonstrated often in the Old and New Testaments and is especially used in the study of eschatology. Here they are:

1. The Symbolic Principle

Paul alludes to this principle when he coined the phrase: *First the <u>natural,</u> then the <u>spiritual</u>*.[633] Natural things in Scripture can have spiritual meanings through the commonality of their traits. For example, *oil* and *cloud* can spiritually represent the Holy Spirit. The sacrificial *lamb* in the Old Testament is symbolic of Jesus, who John the Baptist referred to as the *Lamb* of God. The color *white* is symbolic in Scripture of *purity*. Because Daniel and Revelation are so filled with images, you must discover the common meaning of the symbol to accurately and literally determine its application in the outcome.

The Antichrist in Revelation 13 is likened to a beast with seven heads and ten horns that resembles a leopard, a bear, and a lion. When artists render a painting of this description, an ugly monster appears. Obviously, the Antichrist won't look this way, but each definition is symbolic of the activity, nature, and character found in this individual. So each symbol requires a literal interpretation of what each will have in common with the Antichrist and his reign on the Earth. First the *interpretation* of the symbol, then the *application* to the Antichrist, whose nature is like a beast in God's eyes. This doesn't describe a "force of evil," it describes the nature, character and role of a lawless man who will rule the world.

2. The Typical Principle

This comes from the word "type" which in the Greek is the word *tupos*. It is an *anticipating* figure, image, or form of something to come in the future. The difference between

---

[633] 1 Corinthians 15:46

a type and a symbol is that a *symbol* is a representation of one thing likened to another.

A *type*, however, is "prophetic" in nature and a *foreshadowing* of something or someone in the future. For example Joseph was a *type* of Christ—both were sold by their brothers for silver.

The materials, structure, design, objects and actions in the Tabernacle of Moses are all *types* of Christ and the church.

Abraham offering up his son, Isaac, as a sacrifice was a *type* of God the Father offering up his Son, Jesus.

Jonah in the belly of a whale for three days and nights was a *type* of Jesus being in the grave for three days and nights and resurrecting.

Types involve symbols, but not all symbols are types. Genuine types are always based on the plain meaning of Scriptures and mostly interpreted by the Scriptures themselves.

The *Direct Statement Principle* goes hand in hand with this principle, as does the *Symbolic Principle*.

Revelation contains the fulfillment of many Old Testament types. For example, in Revelation 2-3, Jesus is seen as the High Priest examining the seven golden lampstands (seven churches).

In Revelation 4-5, Jesus is seen as the Lamb of God before the throne of God in heaven.

In Revelation 6, Jesus is seen as the Rider on the White Horse going forth to conquer men's souls and later seen on a White Horse as the King of Kings, and Lord of Lords.

This principle also applies to Moses and Elijah, the Antichrist, the bride of Christ and more.

3. The Numeric Principle

This principle is an extension of the *Symbolic Principle* in that numbers in the Bible take on symbolic significance.

Numbers are not arbitrary in Scripture, but have been given divine meaning. When numbers are examined in Scripture through the lens of the *Context Mention, First*

Mention, *Progressive Mention* and *Complete Mention Principles*, you find a record emerging with a divine theme. Here are some examples of what numbers represent:

One — Unity
Two — Witness, Division
Three — Godhead, Perfect Testimony
Four — Earth (four corners of the Earth)
Five — Grace, Life, Cross (five wounds in Christ)
Six — Man, Beast, Satan (man created on the sixth day)
Seven — Perfection, Completion, Fulfillment
Eight — New Beginning
Nine — Fruitfulness, Holy Spirit (nine gifts of the Spirit)
Ten — Law, Order, Trials
Eleven — Disorganization
Twelve — Divine Government, Authority
Thirteen — Rebellion

To apply this principle toward interpreting end-time prophecies is significant when considering all the numbers seen in the companion books of Daniel and Revelation. For example, the number **thirteen** finds a common trait throughout Scripture in the context of *rebellion*.

In Genesis, Nimrod (a type of the Antichrist) was the **thirteenth** generation from Adam. He was in rebellion against God and persecuted God's people. It isn't an accident or coincidence that we find the culmination and description of the Antichrist in the **thirteenth** chapter of Revelation. He is in *rebellion* against God and a persecutor of his people—like Nimrod. In Genesis, Nimrod built Babylon and the tower of Babel (confusion). In Revelation, the Antichrist-beast is the one upon whom Babylon, the harlot sits.

4. The Parabolic Principle

A parable is an *earthly* story with a *heavenly* meaning, comparing the natural with the spiritual realm. Jesus used this method of teaching truth to *conceal* truth from the hardened heart, and *reveal* truth to the hungry and open in heart.

It discerns the *moral* found in the story and interprets the symbols within the story. Examples of this can be found in Matthew chapters 13, 18, 20, 22, 25 and in Luke 15. Large portions of Christ's parables deal with end-time images.

Take a look at Matthew 13:24-30, which gives the parable, and Matthew 13:36-43, which gives the interpretation. This is the principle that was used to take the parable in Matthew 25 of the ten virgins (five wise, five foolish) and apply it to the bride of Christ being prepared to go out and meet her Bridegroom.

5. The Allegorical Principle

An *allegory* is a metaphor (figure of speech), which is extended to communicate truth about something under the image of another. It is different than a parable in that allegories use words *figuratively* and parables use words *literally*. There can be many lessons in an allegory while a parable generally has only one lesson. The allegories Jesus used were in phrases like the *salt* of the earth, the *good* shepherd, or the *vine* and the *branches*. The most classic allegory that Paul used was in his letter to the Galatians (4:21-31) regarding the Mosaic Covenant versus the New Covenant. He presented the differences between the two, contending with the legalists, who wanted Jesus, but still wanted to keep Moses, too.

Mosaic Covenant	New Covenant
Mt. Sinai – Hagar	Mt. Zion – Sarah
Slave Woman	Free Woman
Children of Bondage	Children of Freedom
According to Flesh	According to Promise
Old Jerusalem	New Jerusalem
Slavery	Liberty
Law and Works	Grace and Truth
Ishmael Persecutor	Isaac Persecuted
Less Children	More Children

There's a critical component behind this principle, when it comes to interpreting what will happen in the millennium. As mentioned before, certain premillennial views see a reinstated Mosaic economy of animal sacrifices, priests and feasts, and the ritual ceremonies under an alleged New Covenant kingdom inaugurated in the millennium. This view is a fallback to the same problem Paul addressed with the Galatian churches: Jesus + Moses.

In the Christian Millennium, there will only be Jesus, the King and *fulfiller* of the Old Covenant, not Jesus, the *re-institutor* of the Old Covenant.

The Origins of Dispensationalism

THE CATALYST OF the pre-tribulation view was a young Scottish woman named Margaret MacDonald, who had a private revelation in Port Glasgow, Scotland. This took place sometime between February and April in 1830. Her pre-tribulation views were circulated throughout the revival prayer meetings in the western towns of Scotland.

Margaret was a devout, sincere saint who believed God showed her that a select group of Christians would be caught up in the air *before* the days of the Antichrist. This revelation was written down and preserved by an eye-and-ear witness, Robert Norton, M.D. The book he wrote containing this account is titled, *Memoirs of James and George MacDonald of Port Glasgow*.[634] After 1,800 years of a *post-trib/premillennial* view, this was the first time anyone had ever split the second coming into two distinct parts or stages.

John Nelson Darby of the Plymouth Brethren in England visited Margaret's home and adopted this view. He later introduced his expanded teachings on the "secret" rapture in a prophetic conference in 1883 at the Powerscourt House in Ireland.

Another significant figure was a Scottish preacher named, Edward Irving. He also visited Margaret MacDonald and taught this view in a published article in *The Morning*

---

[634] Robert Norton, M.D., *Memoirs of James and George MacDonald of Port Glasgow* (London: John F. Shaw, 1840), 171-176.

Watch in September 1830, espousing the two-stage return of Christ. He had been predisposed toward this view from a book he had translated into English. It's called, *The Coming of the Messiah in Glory and Majesty,* written in 1812 by a Jesuit priest from Chile named Manuel de Lacunza.

The two-stage "any moment" view of the Plymouth Brethren spread to America and other parts of the world in the latter part of the 19th century. John Nelson Darby visited the United States at least five times to promote this teaching.

Pastor James H. Brookes—a prominent dispensational (futurist) premillennialist in St. Louis, Missouri—mentored Cyrus Ingerson (C.I.) Scofield, a rising figure in the late 19th century. Scofield went on to become an ordained Congregationalist minister, a leader in dispensational premillennialism, and a forerunner of Christian fundamentalism in the 20th century.

In 1909, Oxford University Press published Scofield's annotated and widely circulated study Bible with his notes on futurism and dispensationalism. Through the influence of his ever-increasingly popular *Scofield Reference Bible,* fundamentalists made this the most publicized premillennial view out of all the schools of interpretation in the United States. Scofield's notes became a significant source for religious writers like Hal Lindsey (*The Late Great Planet Earth*) and Tim LaHaye (*The Left Behind Series*).

Dave MacPherson, author of *The Incredible Cover-Up* and *The Rapture Plot*[635] contends that his research in the early 1990s revealed that an overwhelming majority of evangelical Bible scholars support a single unified coming of Christ, that is, a *post-trib/premillennial* view. He gives two reasons why Christians are unaware of this fact.

---

[635] Dave MacPherson, *The Rapture Plot* (Simpsonville, SC: Millennium III Publishers, 1994).

First, because post-trib/premillennial scholars haven't been as vocal as the two-stage "any moment" dispensationalists.

Second, because the aggressive dissemination of dispensationalist ideas by the advocates of this doctrine drowns out the other voices.[636]

MacPherson goes on to list some of the most prominent names among *post-trib/premillennial* advocates. They are: F.F. Bruce, John Bunyan, John Calvin, Charles Finney, Adam Clarke, Matthew Henry, John Knox, C.S. Lovett, Martin Luther, Charles Spurgeon, and George Whitefield.[637]

Knowing the source of a doctrine—its roots and origins and how it came to be so popular—is a critical component in determining what and why we believe what we believe. If I were to ask you, "Why are you a Christian?" could you answer adequately? If I were to ask you, "Why are you a Baptist and not another denomination?" could you answer that? Or if I were to ask you "Why are you a Democrat or a Republican or a Libertarian?" would you be able to tell me why?

So I ask the question now, "Why are you an A-millennialist, a Premillennialist, a Postmillennialist, or a Christian Millennialist?" Can you tell me why you embrace one of these views? Can you tell me why you embrace one of the three end-times schools of interpretation: Pre-Tribulation, Mid-Tribulation, or Post-Tribulation?

It is one thing to say we espouse a view because it's popular, it's our tradition, or it's our affiliation with a denomination. It's another to be able to say I believe such-and-such because I did my homework.

---

[636] Dave MacPherson, *The Incredible Cover-Up: Exposing the Origin of Rapture Theories* (Medford, OR: Omega Publications, 1980), 121-123.
[637] Ibid., 123.

I had discovered over the years—in my research—that truth and facts began to challenge my original *pre-trib* views. It's good to be challenged in our beliefs because it requires integrity and an honest evaluation of those beliefs. Are our beliefs grounded in solid research and study, or sitting upon a foundation of the popular, unquestioned opinions and theories of others?

To have strong convictions about something as controversial as eschatology, we must consider this because our beliefs determine our actions and behavior in the long run. And I want to finish my race well.

Bibliography

Conner, Kevin J., and Ken Malmin. *Interpreting the Scriptures: A Textbook on How to Interpret the Bible*. Portland, OR: City Bible Publishing, 1983.

Conner, Kevin J. *Principles of Interpreting the Book of Revelation*. Blackburn, Victoria: Acacia Press Pty. Ltd., 1995.

Conner, Kevin J. *The Book of Revelation: An Exposition*. Vermont, Victoria: K.J.C. Publications, 2001.

Davidiy, Yair. *The Tribes: The Israelite Origins of Western People*. 4th ed. Jerusalem: Russell-Davis Publishers, 2011.

Edersheim, Alfred. *The Temple: Its Ministry and Services*. Grand Rapids, MI: Eerdmans Publishing Company, 1982.

Foxe, John. *Foxe's Christian Martyrs of the World*. Chicago, IL: Moody Press, public domain.

Hartill, J. Edwin. *Principles of Biblical Hermeneutics*. Grand Rapids, MI: Zondervan Publishing House, 1947.

Littman, David. "Islam Grows Stronger at the United Nations." *Middle East Quarterly* 6, no. 3, (September 1999): 59-64. http://www.meforum.org/477/islamism-grows-stronger-at-the-united-nations.

McDowell, Josh, and Sean McDowell. *More Than a Carpenter*. Carol Stream, IL: Tyndale House Publishers, 2005.

MacPherson, Dave. *The Incredible Cover-Up: Exposing the Origin of Rapture Theories*. Medford, OR: Omega Publications, 1980.

MacPherson, Dave. *The Rapture Plot*. Simpsonville, SC: Millennium III Publishers, 1994.

Norton, Robert, M.D. *Memoirs of James and George MacDonald of Port Glasgow.* London: John F. Shaw, 1840.

Pipes, Daniel. "Distinguishing between Islam and Islamism." Middle East Forum, June 30, 1998. http://www.danielpipes.org/954/distinguishing-between-islam-and-islamism.

Vine, W.E. *Vine's Expository Dictionary of Old and New Testament Words.* Nashville, TN: Thomas Nelson Publishers, 1985.

Other Recommended Resources for Study:

Braswell, George W., Jr. *What You Need to Know About Islam and Muslims.* Nashville, TN: Broadman & Holman Publishers, 2000.

Conner, Kevin J. *The Tabernacle of Moses: The Riches of Redemption's Story as Revealed in the Tabernacle.* Blackburn, Victoria: Acacia Press, 1975.

Conner, Kevin J., and Ken Malmin. *The Covenants: The Key to God's Relationship with Mankind.* Portland, OR: Conner/Malmin Publications, 1976.

Conner, Kevin J. *Interpreting the Symbols and Types.* Blackburn, Victoria: Acacia Press, 1980.

Conner, Kevin J. *The Feasts of Israel.* Portland, OR: Bible Press, 1980.

Conner, Kevin J. *The Seventy Weeks Prophecy: An Exposition of Daniel 9.* Blackburn, Victoria: Acacia Press, 1983.

Conner, Kevin J. *The Temple of Solomon: The Glory of God as Displayed Through the Temple.* Blackburn, Victoria: Conner Publications, 1988.

Conner, Kevin J. *The Christian Millennium: Studies in Eschatological Millennial Views.* Vermont, Victoria: K.J.C. Publications, 2000.

Conner, Kevin J. *The Book of Daniel: An Exposition.* Vermont, Victoria: K.J.C. Publications, 2004.

DeHaan, M.R. *The Tabernacle: The House of Blood*. Grand Rapids, MI: Zondervan Publishing House, 1955.

Eberle, Harold R., and Martin Trench. *Victorious Eschatology: A Partial Preterist View*. 2nd ed. Yakima, WA: Worldcast Publishing, 2008.

Offiler, W.H. *God and His Bible: The Harmonies of Divine Revelation*. Seattle, WA: Bethel Temple, Inc., 1946.

Patterson, W.W. *Bible Treasures from the Book of Daniel and The Book of Revelation*. Federal Way, WA: self-published, 1973.

Patterson, W.W. *The Tabernacle*. Federal Way, WA: self-published, 1975.

Tenney, Merrill C., ed. *The Zondervan Pictorial Encyclopedia of the Bible*. Grand Rapids, MI: Zondervan Publishing House, 1978.

Vallowe, Ed F. *Biblical Mathematics: Keys to Scripture Numerics*. Columbia, SC: The Olive Press, 1998.

Wight, Fred H. *Manners and Customs of Bible Lands*. Chicago, IL: Moody Press, 1953.

Zinn, Jay M. *The Unveiling*. Mukilteo, WA: WinePress Publishing, 1997.

CHARTS

% of population
Muslim

90-100
80-90
65-80
50-65
30-50
15-30
7-15
1-7

http://upload.wikimedia.org/wikipedia/commons/b/ba/Islam_percent_population_in_each_nation_World_Map_Muslim_data_by_Pew_Research.svg

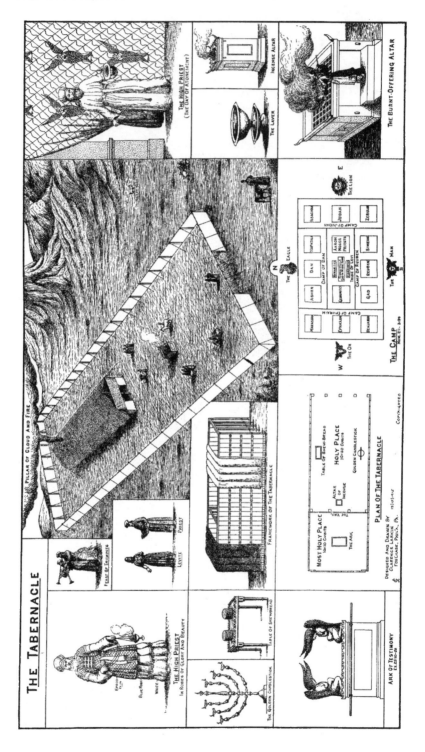

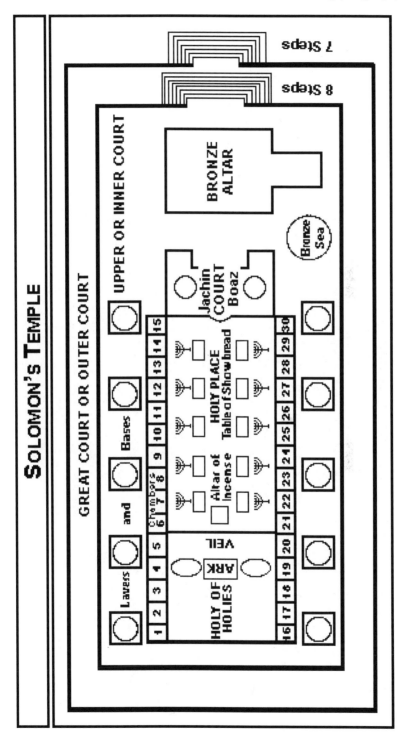

SOLOMON'S TEMPLE

GREAT COURT OR OUTER COURT

UPPER OR INNER COURT

7 Steps

8 Steps

BRONZE ALTAR

Bronze Sea

Jachin
COURT
Boaz

Lavers   and   Chambers   Bases

HOLY PLACE
Table of Showbread

Altar of Incense

VEIL

ARK

HOLY OF HOLIES

1 2 3 4 5 | 6 7 8 9 10 11 12 13 14 15
16 17 18 19 20 21 22 23 24 25 26 27 28 29 30

Pre-tribulation View

This teaches that seven years *before* the visible return of Christ, living Christians are caught up (or raptured) to meet Christ in the air *before* the days of the Antichrist. The dead in Christ will resurrect, also, to meet him in the air first. Those living who reject Christ are left behind to experience worldwide hardships of famine, war, pain, and suffering, brought on by the seven seals, seven trumpets, and seven bowls of wrath in the book of Revelation. They can still be saved, but are left behind to go through the tribulation period. After seven years are complete, Jesus returns with his saints and sets up a millennial kingdom on Earth.

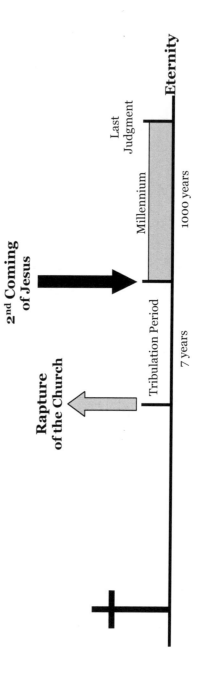

Mid-tribulation View

This teaches that the rapture of the church will occur in the *middle* of the seven years of the tribulation period. Instead of a rapture happening at the beginning of the seven years, Christians will go three-and-one-half years into the seven years of tribulation before the rapture takes place, and before the severest outpouring of God's wrath upon the Earth. It is the least-embraced theory of the three. It also happens before the millennial reign of Christ.

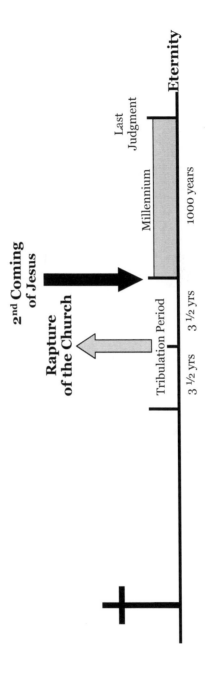

Post-tribulation View

This is the third and longest-held view in church history, and teaches that the rapture takes place at the *end* of the great tribulation. Believers will go through the great tribulation period, many will be martyred by the Antichrist, and those who are alive and remain will be raptured following the resurrection of the dead in Christ at the second coming. Jesus then sets up his millennial reign.

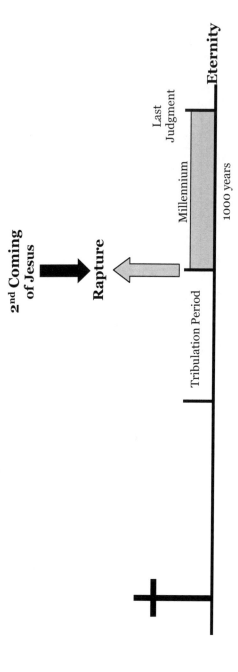

Chart of the Seven Churches
Revelation 2–3

The letters to the seven churches in chapter **2** through **3** have a *literal interpretation* that addresses the spiritual state of each church of that time. From these letters, we can receive the *application* of principles and warnings today of what Christ approves and disapproves. Some schools of interpretation see an additional *prophetic application* coming from the names, similarities, and characteristics of each church, describing a particular *era* of church history.

30 A.D.

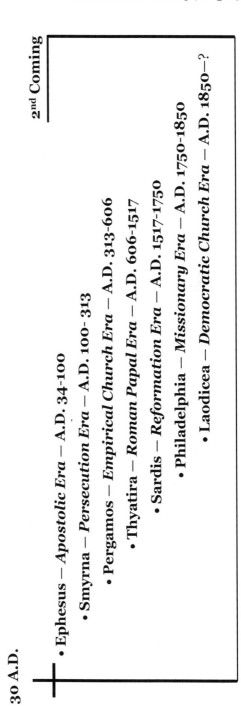

- **Ephesus – *Apostolic Era* – A.D. 34-100**
- **Smyrna – *Persecution Era* – A.D. 100-313**
- **Pergamos – *Empirical Church Era* – A.D. 313-606**
- **Thyatira – *Roman Papal Era* – A.D. 606-1517**
- **Sardis – *Reformation Era* – A.D. 1517-1750**
- **Philadelphia – *Missionary Era* – A.D. 1750-1850**
- **Laodicea – *Democratic Church Era* – A.D. 1850–?**

2nd Coming

Chart of the Seven Seals
Revelation 4–6

In Revelation chapter **4** and **5**, John is taken before the throne of God to witness the activity of the Father, Son, and Holy Spirit, as well as the worship of the heavenly host around the throne. Only the Lamb of God, the Lion of the Tribe of Judah is worthy to take the scroll and open the seven seals. In Revelation **6**, the ***seven seals*** are opened. I see the first five seals opened at the beginning of the Church Age and that Jesus is the rider on the White Horse going forth to conquer people's hearts with the gospel message.

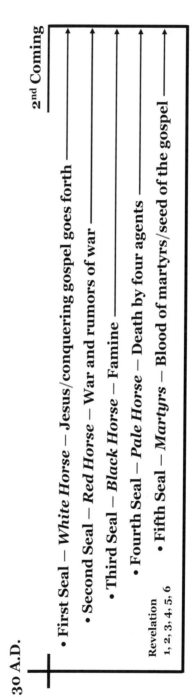

30 A.D.

2ⁿᵈ **Coming**

- First Seal – *White Horse* – Jesus/conquering gospel goes forth
- Second Seal – *Red Horse* – War and rumors of war
- Third Seal – *Black Horse* – Famine
- Fourth Seal – *Pale Horse* – Death by four agents
- Fifth Seal – *Martyrs* – Blood of martyrs/seed of the gospel

Revelation 1, 2, 3, 4, 5, 6

Note: *The opening of a seal is not just a single event, once a seal is opened it remains open and intensifies up to the end of the age.*

Chart of the Seven Trumpets
Revelation 8–9

Revelation chapter **6** ends with the *sixth* seal, which I believe will be opened near the end of the age. It is the first major sign in the Revelation that will be visible to the entire world. Following is the (parenthetical) chapter **7**, then chapter **8** through **9** reveals the "Day of Atonement" and the sounding of the ***seven trumpets***, all prior to the last 3 ½ years until Christ returns.

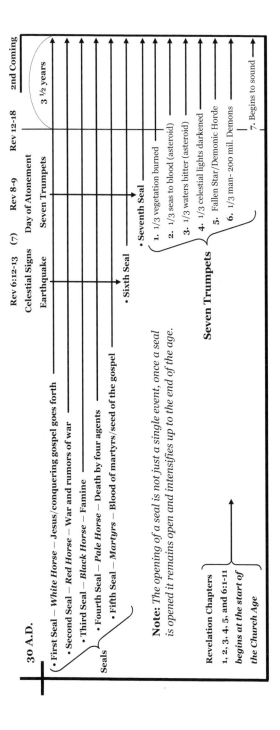

30 A.D.

- First Seal — *White Horse* — Jesus/conquering gospel goes forth
- Second Seal — *Red Horse* — War and rumors of war
- Third Seal — *Black Horse* — Famine
- Fourth Seal — *Pale Horse* — Death by four agents
- Fifth Seal — *Martyrs* — Blood of martyrs/seed of the gospel

Seals

Note: *The opening of a seal is not just a single event, once a seal is opened it remains open and intensifies up to the end of the age.*

Revelation Chapters 1, 2, 3, 4, 5, and 6:1-11 *begins at the start of the Church Age*

Rev 6:12-13 (7) Rev 8-9 Rev 12-18 2nd Coming

Celestial Signs — Day of Atonement

Earthquake — Seven Trumpets

3 ½ years

- Sixth Seal
- Seventh Seal

Seven Trumpets

1. 1/3 vegetation burned
2. 1/3 seas to blood (asteroid)
3. 1/3 waters bitter (asteroid)
4. 1/3 celestial lights darkened
5. Fallen Star/Demonic Horde
6. 1/3 man- 200 mil. Demons
7. Begins to sound

Chart of the Seven Bowls
Revelation 15-16

Revelation chapter **15** opens with seven angels holding the seven last plagues in *seven bowls*. They are poured out in chapter **16** at the very end of the 3 ½ years.

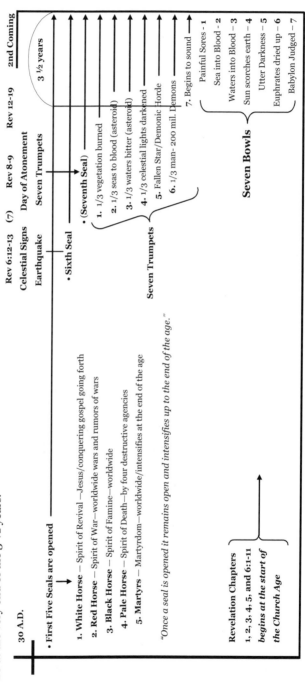

Seven Bowls

Painful Sores - 1
Sea into Blood - 2
Waters into Blood – 3
Sun scorches earth – 4
Utter Darkness – 5
Euphrates dried up – 6
Babylon Judged – 7

7. Begins to sound

Seven Bowls

1. 1/3 vegetation burned
2. 1/3 seas to blood (asteroid)
3. 1/3 waters bitter (asteroid)
4. 1/3 celestial lights darkened
5. Fallen Star/Demonic Horde
6. 1/3 man- 200 mil. Demons

Seven Trumpets

(Seventh Seal)

• Sixth Seal

3 ½ years

2nd Coming

Rev 12-19

Rev 8-9
Day of Atonement
Seven Trumpets

Rev 6:12-13   (7)

Celestial Signs
Earthquake

30 A.D.

• First Five Seals are opened

1. **White Horse** — Spirit of Revival —Jesus/conquering gospel going forth
2. **Red Horse** — Spirit of War—worldwide wars and rumors of wars
3. **Black Horse** — Spirit of Famine—worldwide
4. **Pale Horse** — Spirit of Death—by four destructive agencies
5. **Martyrs** — Martyrdom—worldwide/intensifies at the end of the age

"Once a seal is opened it remains open and intensifies up to the end of the age."

Revelation Chapters
1, 2, 3, 4, 5, and 6:1-11
begins at the start of
the Church Age

THE SEVENTY WEEK PROPHECY

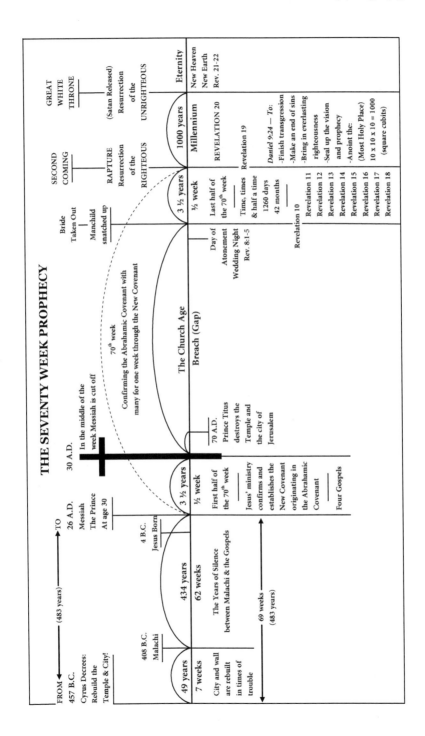

REVELATION 21-22 —New Heavens, New Earth, New Jerusalem

Chart of the Revelation

7 SEALS

1. White Horse (Spirit of Revival – Jesus/conquering gospel) – Rev. 6:2
2. Red Horse (Spirit of War – worldwide) – Rev. 6:3-4
3. Black Horse (Spirit of Famine – worldwide) – Rev. 6:5-6
4. Pale Horse (Spirit of Death/Hell – 4 destructive agents) – Rev. 6:7-8
5. Martyrdom (5 = # of suffering) – Rev. 6:9-11
6. Celestial Signs – (Sun [black], Moon [blood], Stars [falling] – initial quake and great quake culminating at 2nd Coming) – Rev. 6:12-17
7. Silence in Heaven (Day of Atonement – Perfected Bride/Wedding/Marriage consummated/God's seven-trumpet judgments on earth) – Rev. 8:1-5

Parenthetical events: no wind/fresh air (four winds) – Rev. 7:1; Sealing of 144,000 (Womb of the Bride) – Rev. 7:2-8 Tribulation saints (harvest of the Bride) – Rev. 7:9-11

1. Hail, fire, mingled with blood upon earth (1/3rd of trees and vegetation burned) – Rev. 8:7
2. Great burning mountain cast into the sea (1/3rd becomes blood, kills 1/3rd of sea creatures, destroys 1/3rd of ships) – Rev. 8:8-9
3. Great burning star (Wormwood) falls from heaven upon 1/3rd of rivers and springs (1/3rd becomes bitter and kills people) – Rev. 8:10-11
4. Sun, Moon and Stars smitten (1/3rd of day and night [4 hours each] complete darkness) – Rev. 8:12

7 TRUMPETS

5. Falling Star/Locust Demons (fallen apostle [Antichrist] given key to unloose demons to hurt unsealed people 5 months) – Rev. 9:1-12

(This is the first woe) – Rev. 9:5-12 (Note: smoke of pit is religious confusion – great apostasy takes place/see 2 Thess. 2:3; 1 Tim. 4:1)

6. Four angels (fallen-bound) loosed from Euphrates River/200-million demon army released (slays 1/3rd of population) – 9:13-21 (The second woe) – Rev. 9:21; 11:14

Parenthetical vision—a prelude to the seventh trumpet beginning to sound: Angel (Jesus) with little scroll open (Daniel – now unsealed (Daniel 12:4) – Rev. 10:1-4

- John is given the scroll to eat and then prophesies the details of the last 3½ years of the 70th week in Daniel's prophecy (Dan. 9:24-27; 12:4-10) – Rev. 10:8-11

7. Finished "Mystery" – Trumpet begins to sound (Bride gives birth/Manchild is snatched up/Bride taken to Desert) – Rev. 10:7; 12:1-16; 14:1-5

- Parenthetical vision: The Church is measured/the outer court [saints] are given over to the Gentiles to be martyred by the ungodly – Rev. 11:1-2

- Two Witnesses: Moses (the Law-giver) and Elijah (the Prophet) – begin ministry of judgment and testimony/Jewish Revival/comfort to martyrs – Rev. 11:3-13

- Satan is cast out of heaven (The third woe) – Rev. 12:7-12); Bride is removed for preservation to the desert – Rev. 12:6, 14

- First beast [Antichrist] reigns and makes war on Christians and Jews and overcomes them – 13:1-9

- Second beast [False Prophet] initiates idol worship and mark of the beast (666) – 13:11-18; enforced by Harlot Church – 17:1-6 (aids in the genocide)

- Revelation 14 – Manchild company of 144,000 follows the Lamb (Isaiah 9:6-Everlasting Father) – Two Harvests: Grain Harvest/Winepress Harvest

- Revelation 15 (seven angels w/plagues); Revelation 16 – seven bowls (vials) are poured out at the end of the age to judge those who received the mark

1. on the earth – malignant sores, ulcers, boils – Rev. 16:2
2. on the sea – oceans turn into blood/destroys all life and ships – Rev. 16:3
3. on the rivers and springs – turns to blood for the bloodthirsty – Rev. 16:4-7
4. on the sun – intense heat scorches earth and people – Rev. 16:8-9
5. on the throne (Jerusalem) of the beast (antichrist's kingdom filled with darkness–like Egypt Ex. 10:21-28) – Rev. 16:1-11
6. on the Euphrates River – dried up/3 demonic spirits/gather kings of the earth for battle of Armageddon – Rev. 16:12-15
7. on the air – voices, thunders, lightning/great earthquake–flattens all islands and mountains/80-120 lb. hailstones kill ungodly – Rev. 16:16-21

- Revelation 17 (Religious Babylon w/the beast & 10 kings who destroy her) – Revelation 18 (Commercial/Political Babylon judged by GOD)

7 BOWLS [VIALS]

2nd Coming
(Revelation 19)

The Christian Millennial Kingdom
Paradise with the Tree of Life
Saints reign for 1,000 years with Christ

1000 years
Revelation 20

Revelation Index of Chapters

Revelation Index of the Chapters — *cont'd.*

20265795R00235

Made in the USA
San Bernardino, CA
03 April 2015